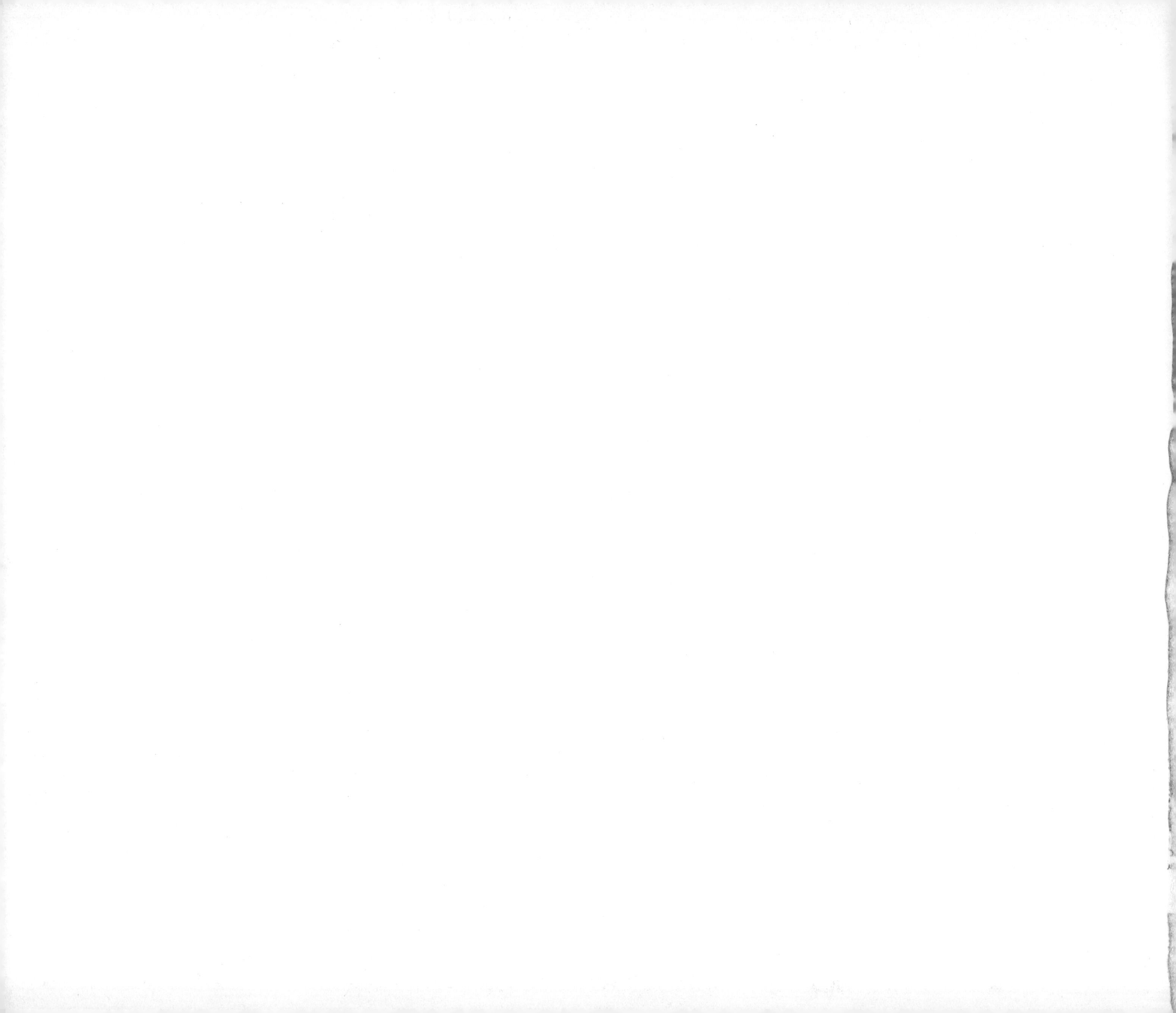

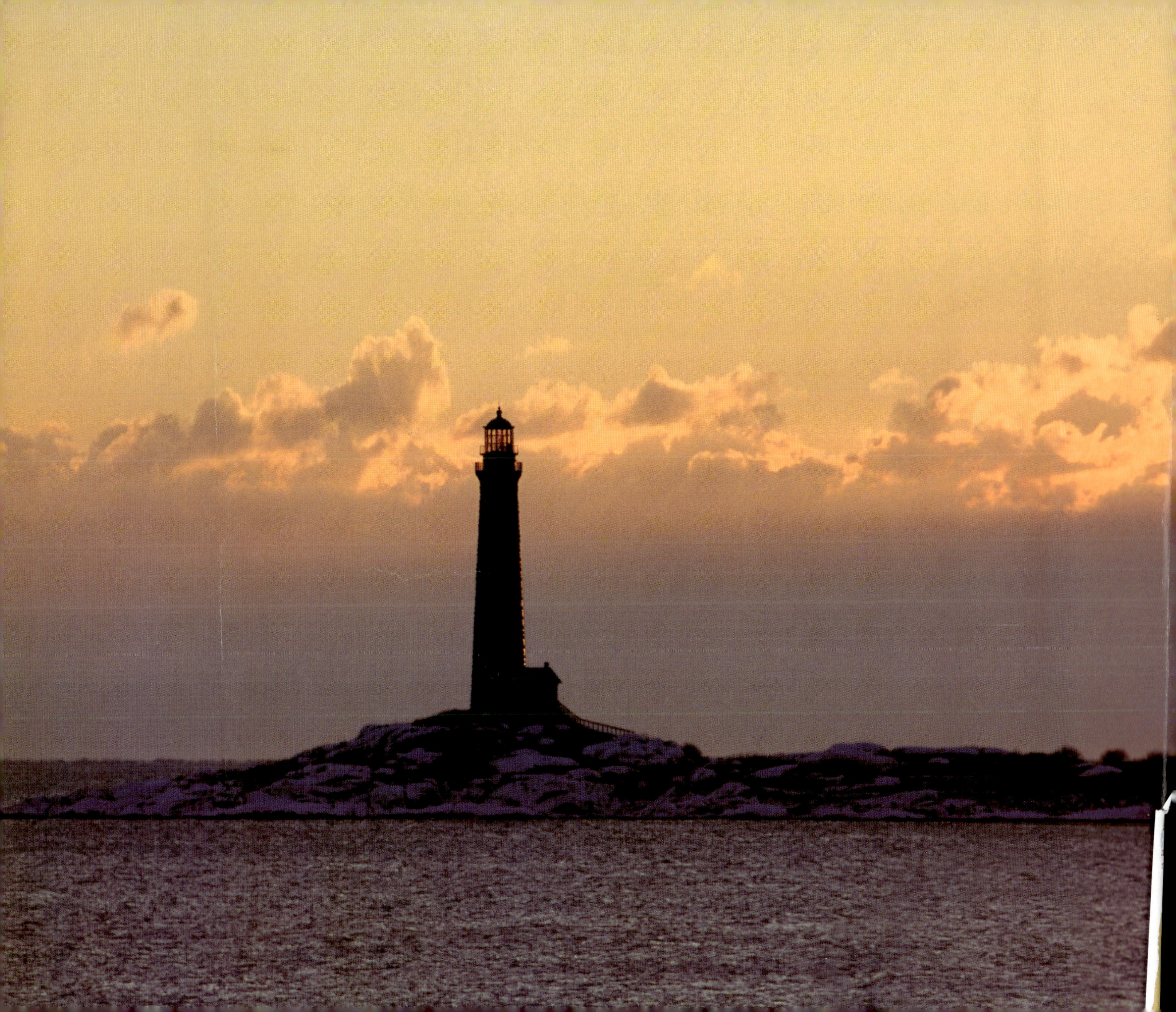

# CAPE ANN

Folly Cove
Halibut Point
Lane's Cove
Plum Cove
Ipswich Bay
Sandy Bay
Essex Bay
Wingaersheek Beach
Hodgkin's Cove
Lanesville
Bay View
Pigeon Cove
Annisquam
Rockport Harbor
Granite Pier
Bearskin Neck
Dogtown Common
West Gloucester
Essex
Whale Cove
Gloucester
Rockport
Loblolly Cove
Long Beach
Thacher Island
Milk Island
Good Harbor Beach
Stage Fort Park
Manchester By-the-Sea
Ravenswood Park
Gloucester Harbor
Bass Rocks
Magnolia
Mussel Point
Singing Beach
Brace Cove
Eastern Point
Magnolia Harbor
133
22
128
127
127A

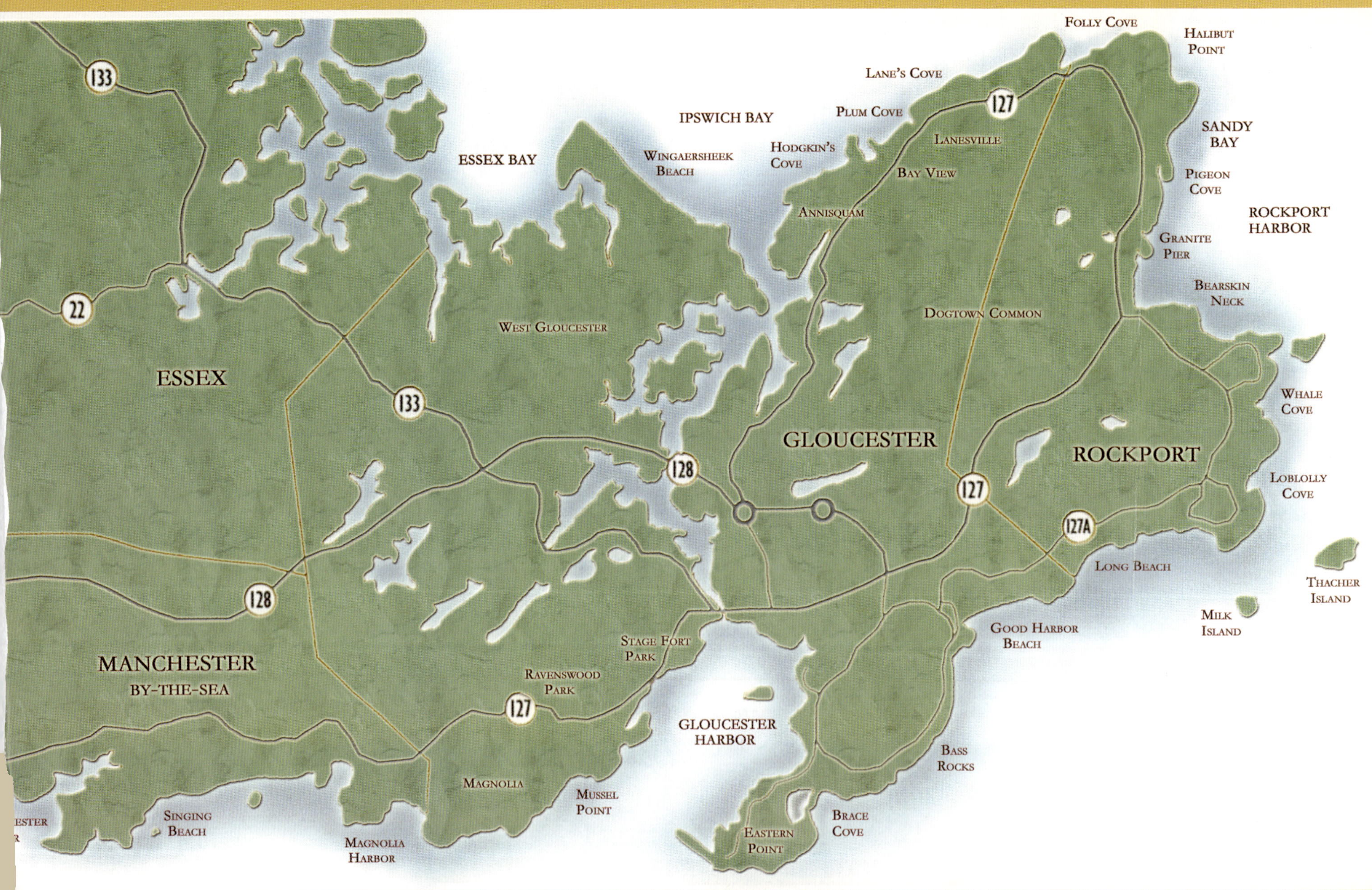

# Cape Ann

Photographs by
Andrew Borsari

Commonwealth Editions
Beverly, Massachusetts

To my publisher, Webster Bull, and the staff at Commonwealth Editions; to Ellie Kaminsky at Borsari Gallery; to Russ Scahill and Heather Wallace for their creative assistance; and to my wife, Elvira, whose loyalty and tireless perseverence made all possible.

This book is dedicated to Henry Campanini, my friend and early mentor.



ISBN-13: 978-1-889833-87-3
ISBN-10: 1-889833-87-8

**Library of Congress Cataloging-in-Publication Data**
Borsari, Andrew
Cape Ann / photographs by Andrew Borsari.
p. cm.
ISBN 1-889833-87-8
1. Ann, Cape (Mass.)--Pictorial works. 2. Ann, Cape (Mass.)--History, Local--Pictorial works.
3. Manchester (Mass.)--Pictorial works. 4. Gloucester (Mass.)--Pictorial works. 5. Rockport (Mass.)--Pictorial works.
6. Essex (Mass. : Town)--Pictorial works. I. Title

F72.E7B59 2005
974.4′5--dc22

Commonwealth Editions, 266 Cabot Street, Beverly, Massachusetts 01915
www.commonwealtheditions.com

Based on a design by Jill Feron/Feron Design

Printed in China

Images from this book are available from the Borsari Gallery, Tuna Wharf, Rockport, Mass. (978-546-9683), or
the Borsari Studio, Ipswich, Mass. (978-356-0042).

For viewing or for further information, visit www.BorsariGallery.com.

Title page image: Thacher Island

*The portrait of Howard Blackburn on page 50 is from the collection of the Cape Ann Historical Association and is reproduced by permission.*

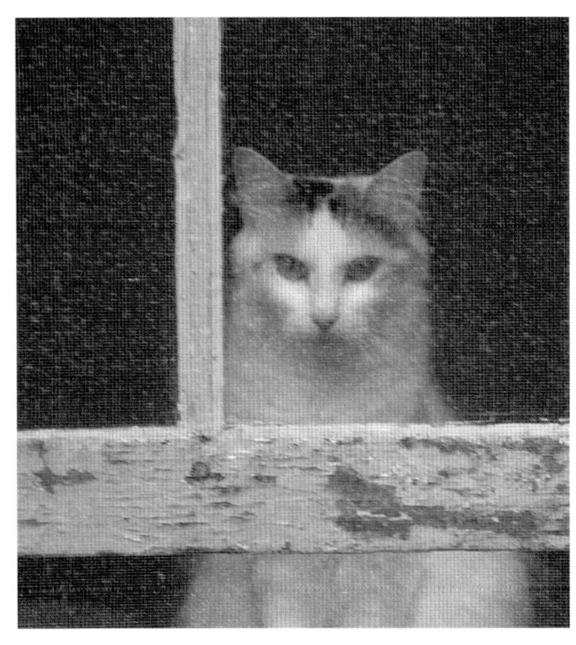

# CONTENTS

# PREFACE

I have had the extreme pleasure of trekking over and photographing both of the great capes of Massachusetts, Cape Cod and Cape Ann. Both are beautiful, but in very different ways. Whereas the subject of this book, Cape Ann, is the lesser known and the smaller, it has a diverse shoreline and a distinct personality. Steeped in history and home to craggy headlands, expansive marshes, and sandy beaches, Cape Ann is arguably one of the most unique capes on the eastern seaboard.

Within a few square miles, Cape Ann encompasses and represents every type of coastline on the east coast with the exception of a mangrove swamp. Its unique geography provides a stretch of shore where marsh and rocky coast collide. Tidal salt marshes are rare to the north, and rocky coasts are seldom found to the south. As varied as their respective coastlines are the towns that make up Cape Ann: Manchester-by-the-Sea, Gloucester (including the proud village enclaves of Annisquam, Lanesville, and Magnolia), Rockport, and Essex.

Cape Ann's deep water and protected harbor laid the foundation for the oldest fishing port in America, Gloucester. The hub of Cape Ann, Gloucester's harbor has two approaches: from the ocean around the rocky tip of Eastern Point, and from Ipswich Bay through the beautiful Annisquam River.

The granite promontory of outer Cape Ann serves as a rugged mantle that endures the constant assault of the North Atlantic. It fiercely preserves the sandy coves and beaches that intermittently adorn the shoreline. Unlike the coastlines to the south that are constantly changing and retreating from the ravages of the sea, Cape Ann's rocky coastline may be called the most primitive because over time it has been altered the least by the erosive forces of the mighty Atlantic.

High up in the hinterland of Cape Ann between Rockport and Gloucester lies Dogtown Common, several thousand acres of deeply wooded conservation land and abandoned granite quarries. Dogtown is shrouded with a strange and mysterious history, and because it is protected land, it lingers quietly in timeless stasis.

The seashore hosts the earth's greatest assembly. Over many years' worth of seasons on Cape Ann, I have followed the light along with the moods of the sea, which range from calm to raging. This stoic cape has inspired me, as it has painters, poets, and writers, from Fitz Hugh Lane to Rudyard Kipling to Joseph Garland. I hope you too will find Cape Ann a special place where the land meets the sea.

*Andrew Borsari*
*Summer 2005*

*Opposite:* Thacher Island Twin Lights, also known as Cape Ann Lights. The Twin Lights are the only surviving multiple lights on the eastern seaboard. When aligned with both towers, a vessel points true north and south.

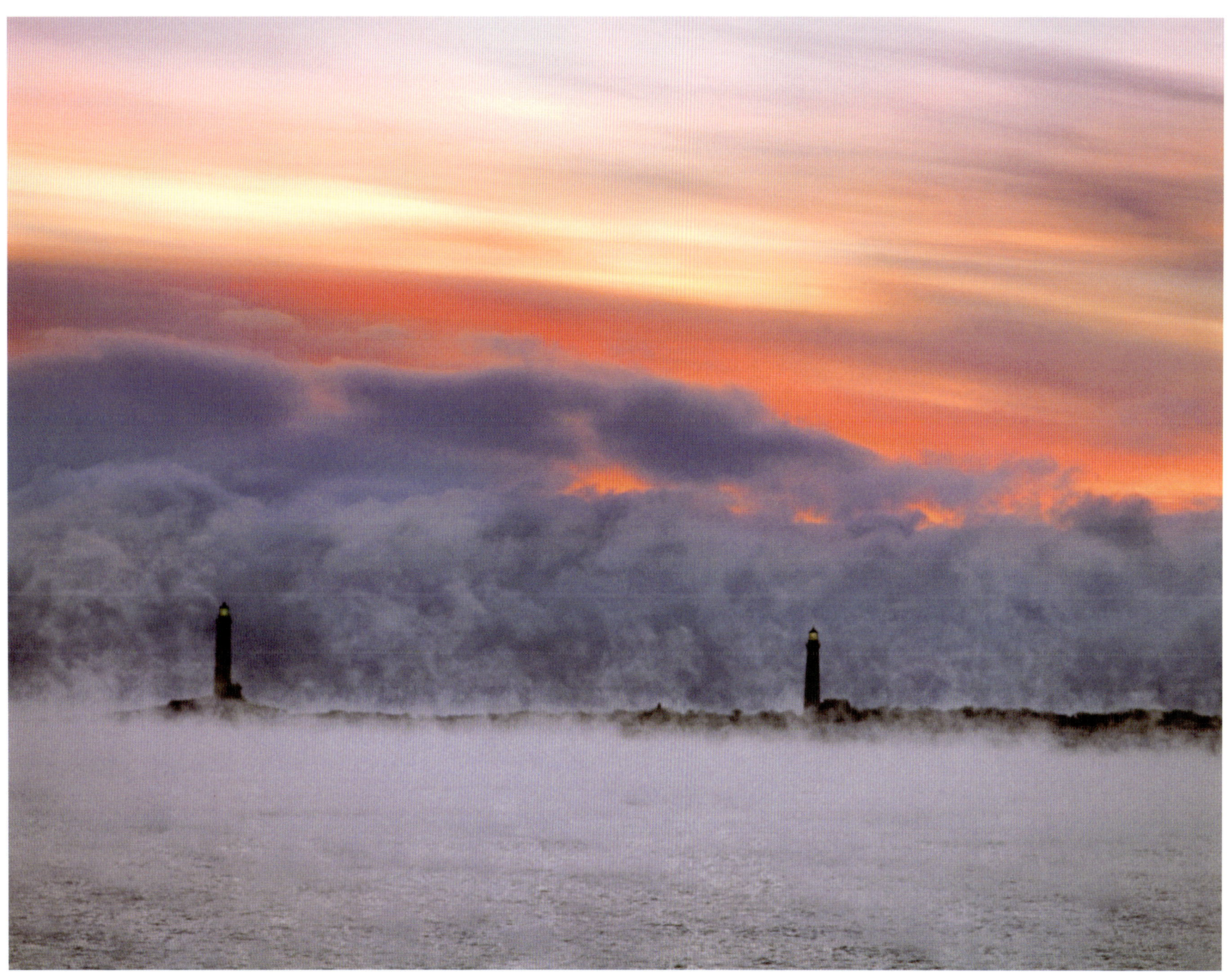

# MANCHESTER-BY-THE-SEA

We know where Cape Ann ends: at the rock-rimmed, surf-swarmed coast. Where does it begin? The Annisquam River makes an island of Gloucester and Rockport, but a cape is more than an island, and tradition, or the chamber of commerce, says that this cape includes Manchester-by-the-Sea and Essex.

A tiny town of nine square miles and little more than five thousand year-round souls, Manchester looms large in the New England imagination. Yes, we here on the North Shore still refer to it as just plain Manchester. The *by-the-sea* business is a recent addition to add aura to a town that needs little.

Manchester looms large with stately mansions and more yachts than any town north of Marblehead. The oldest golf course on the North Shore is here as well, and still one of the most exclusive. Don't you dare call it Essex Country Club, though. That would be so common. It is *the* club of Essex County, at least to its members.

There are many wonderful public spaces here as well, from a solemn colonial graveyard to a beach that sings.

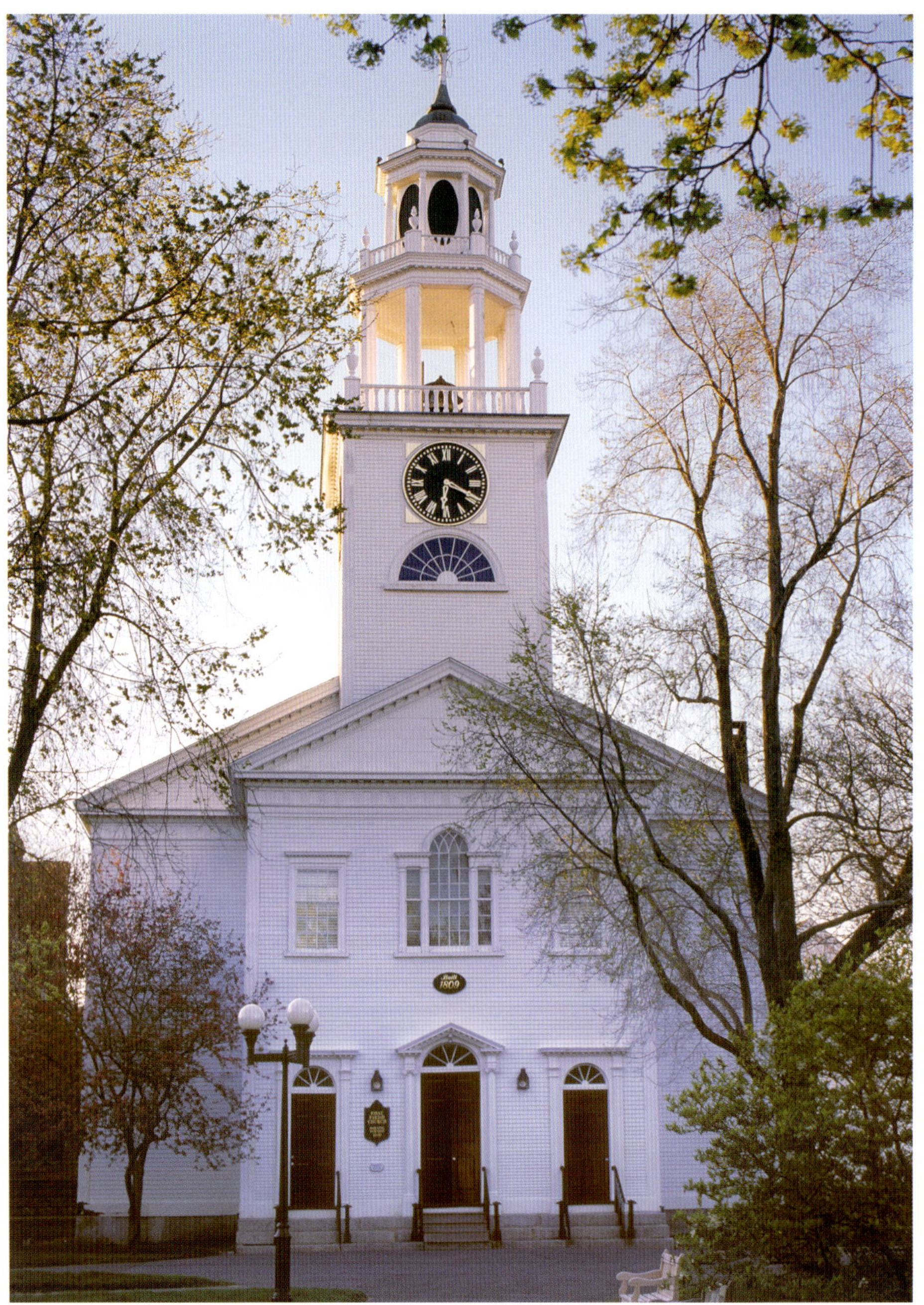

*Above:* First Parish Church Congregational. The meetinghouse, the church's fourth, was built in 1809; the congregation was founded in 1630.
*Opposite:* Manchester Harbor

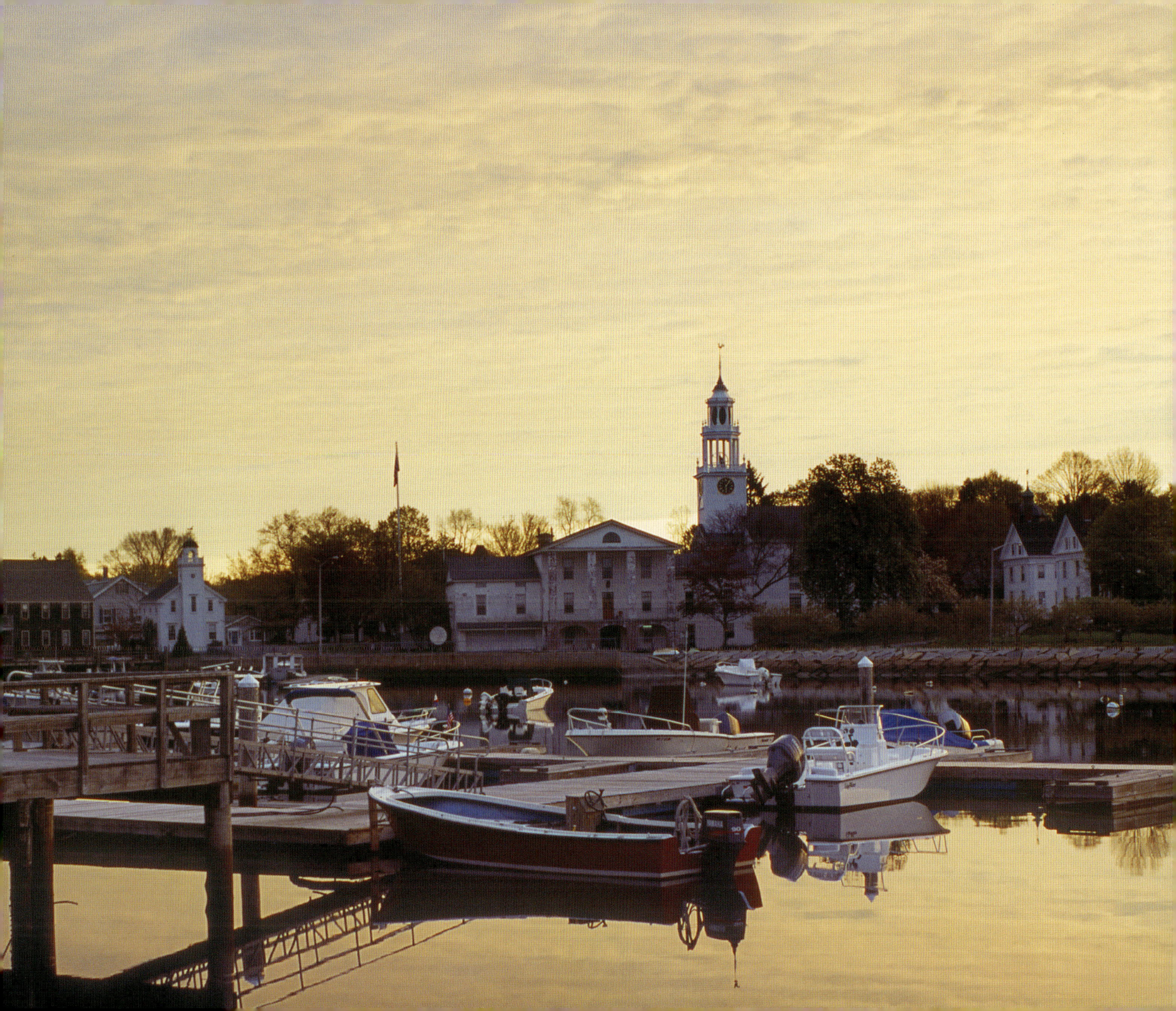

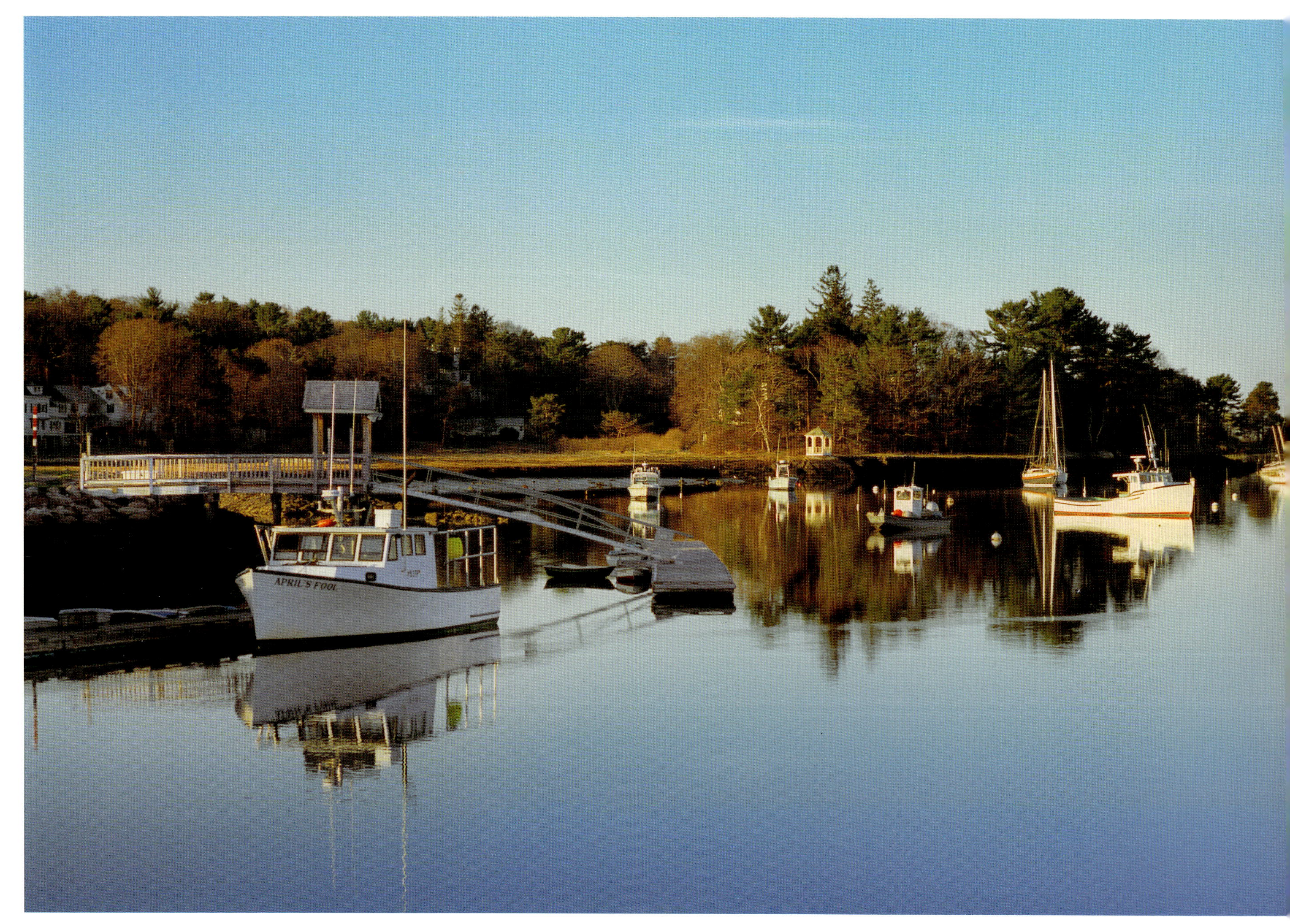


Inner harbor

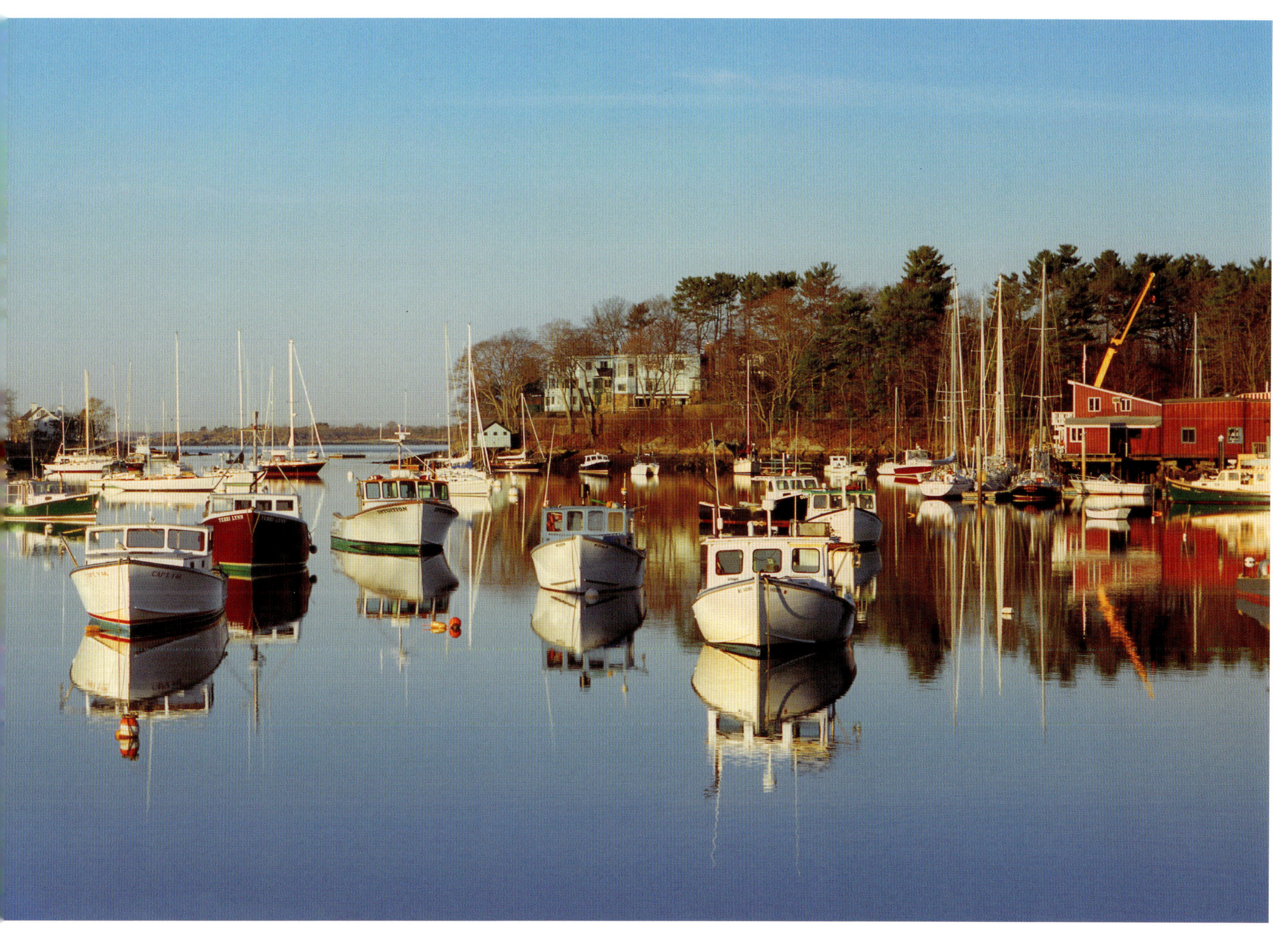

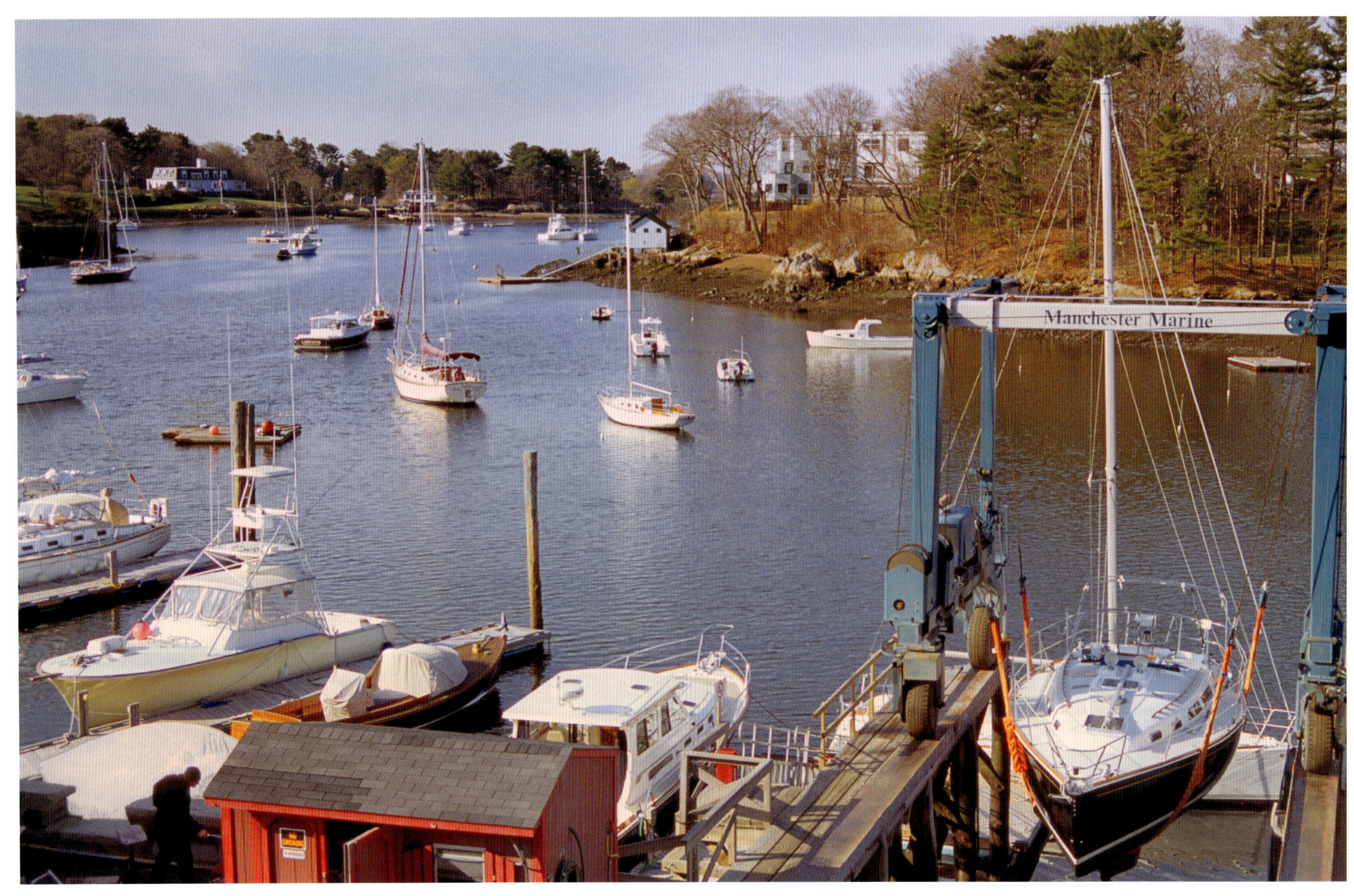


Manchester Marine and Crocker's Boat Yard

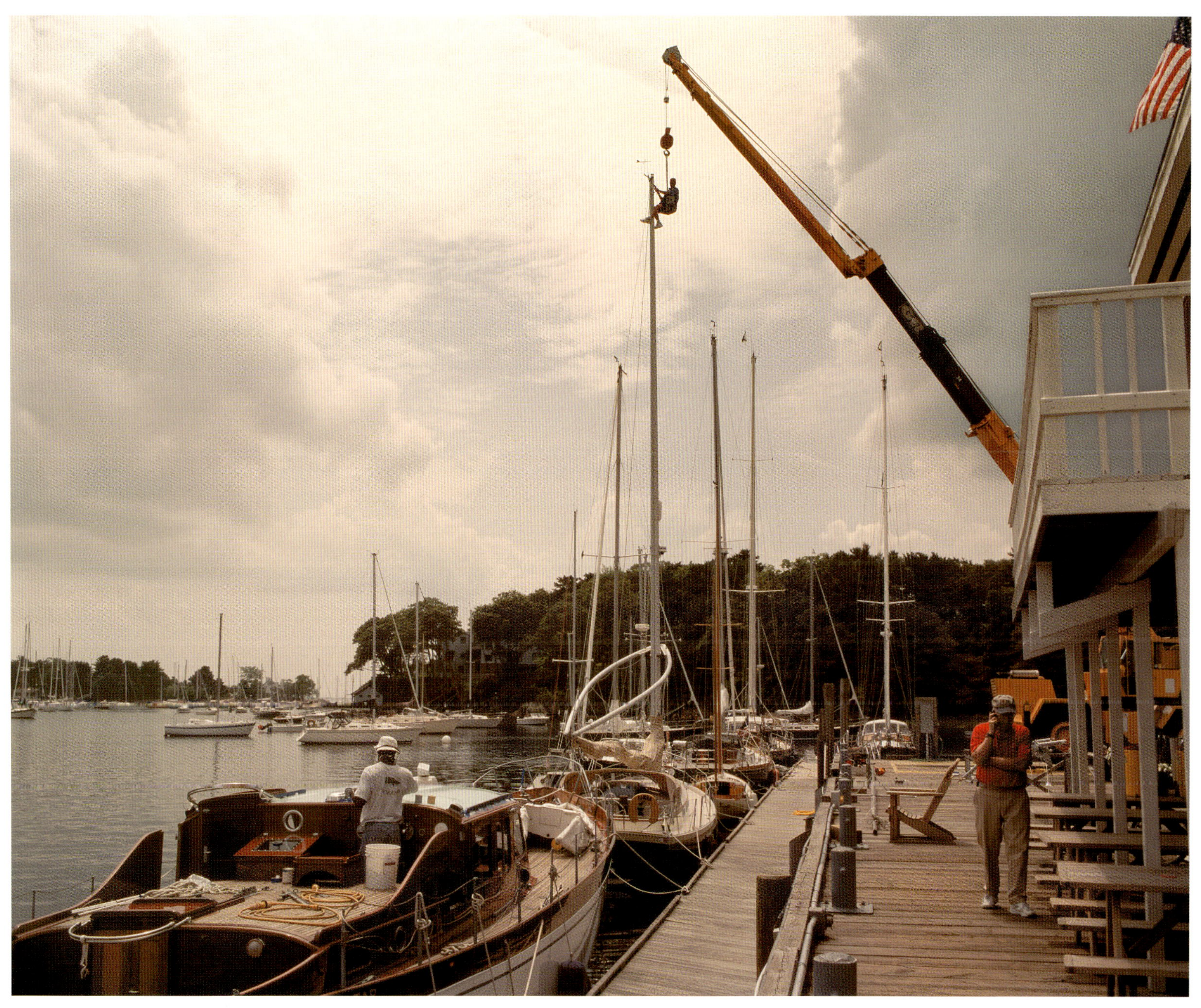

New wind vane on *Simba*

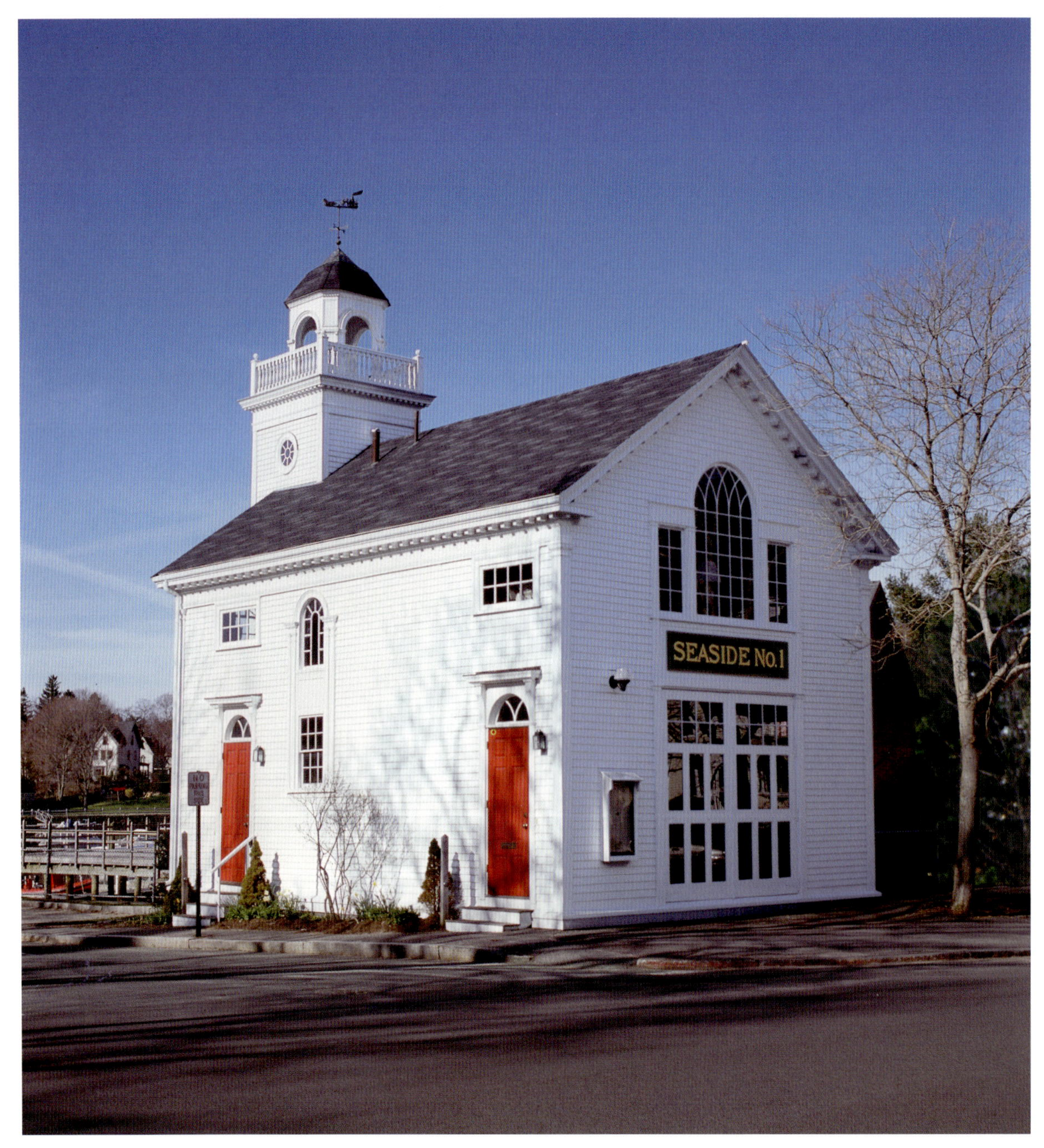


Seaside No. 1, historic firehouse with nineteenth-century horse-drawn pumpers

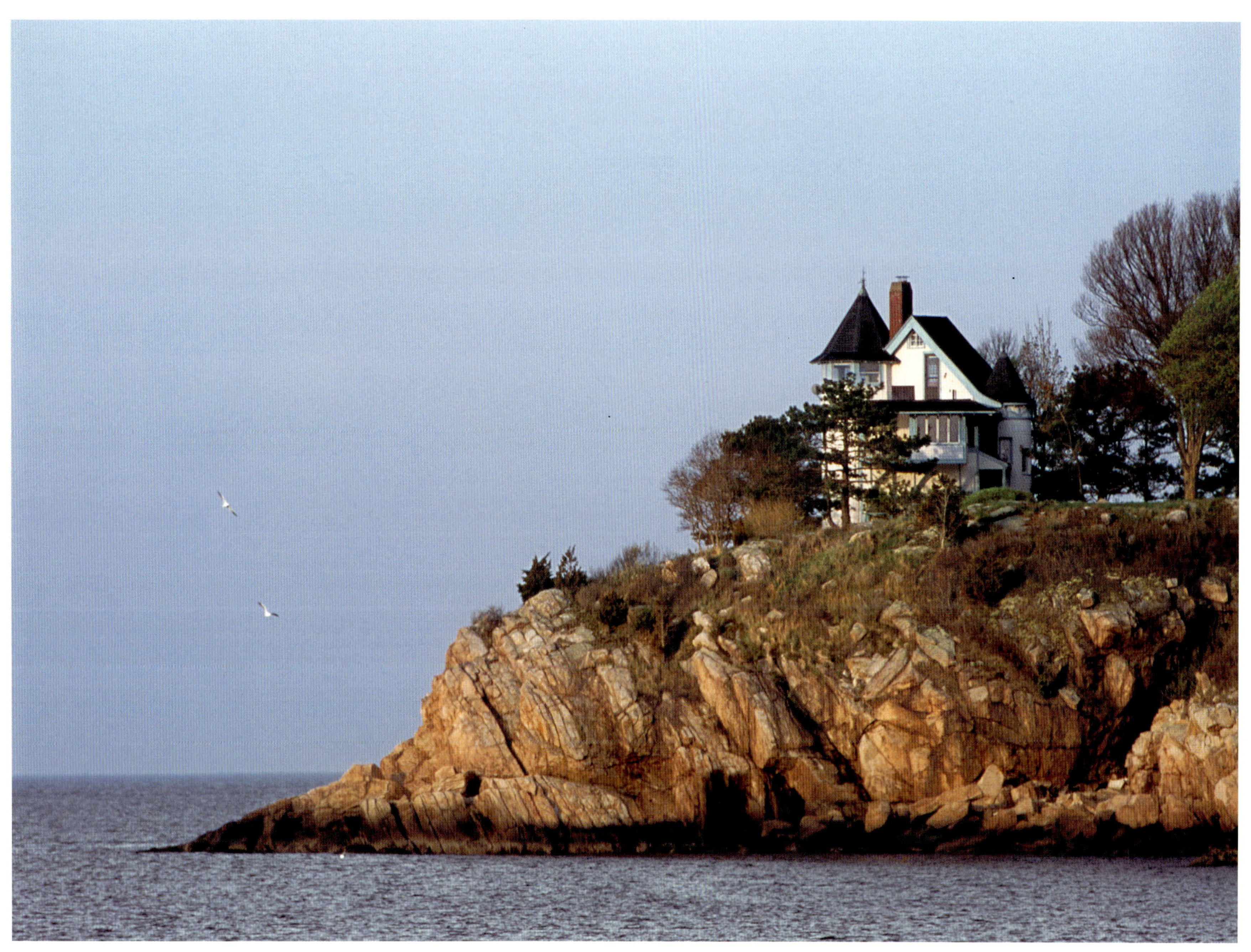

Coolidge Point, the summer home of Thomas Jefferson Coolidge, built in 1902

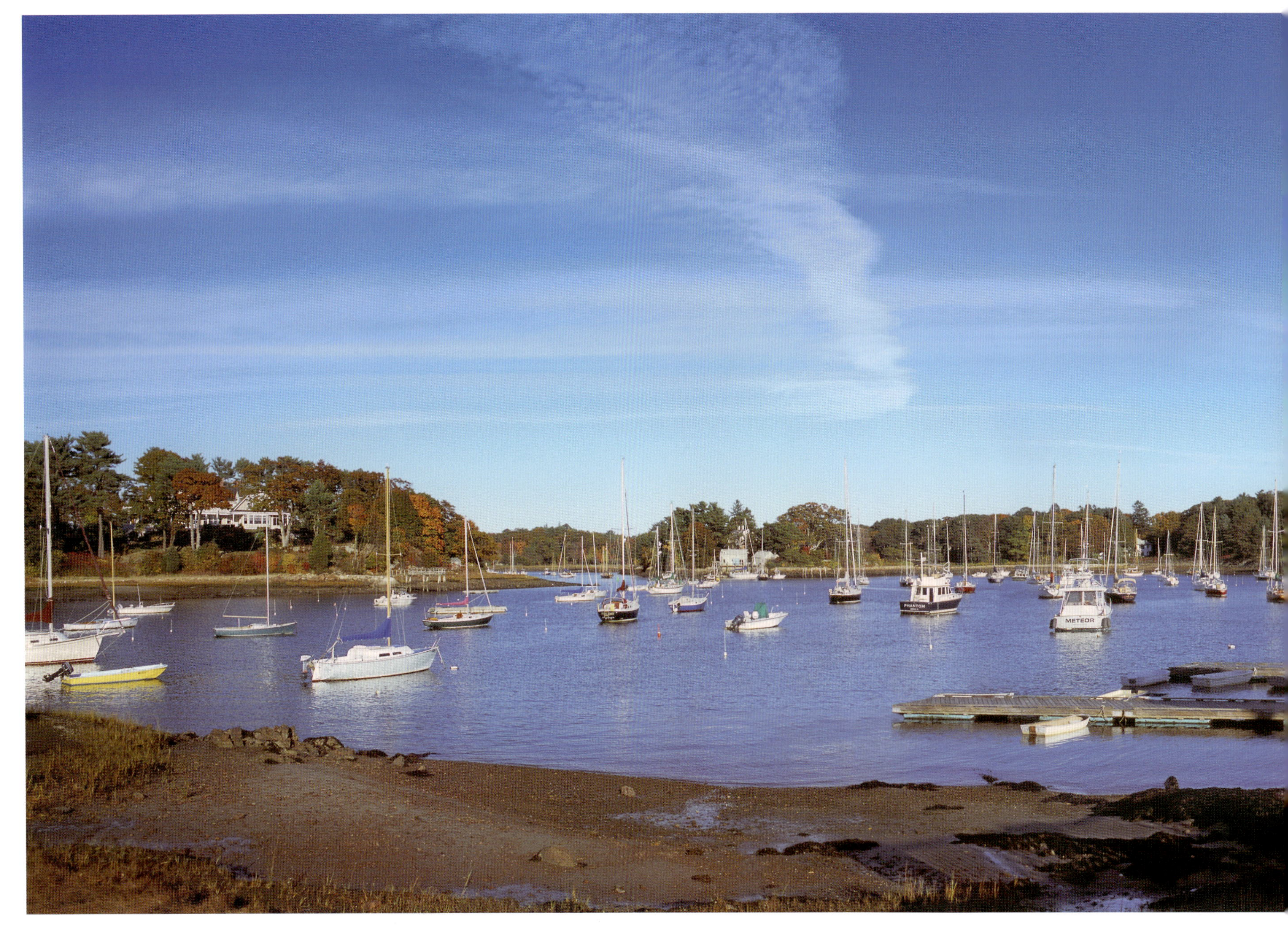


The rotunda at Tuck's Point, Manchester Harbor

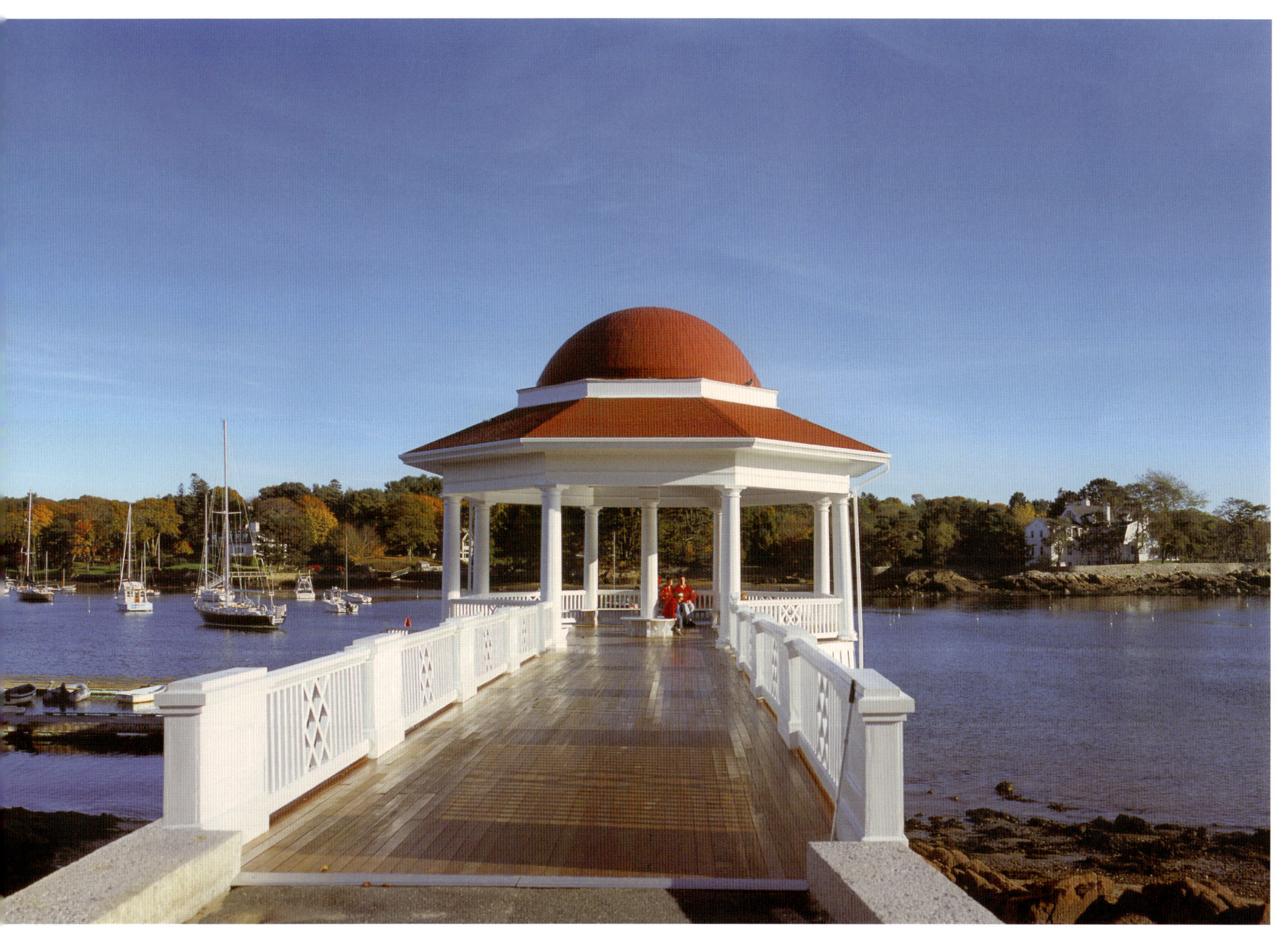

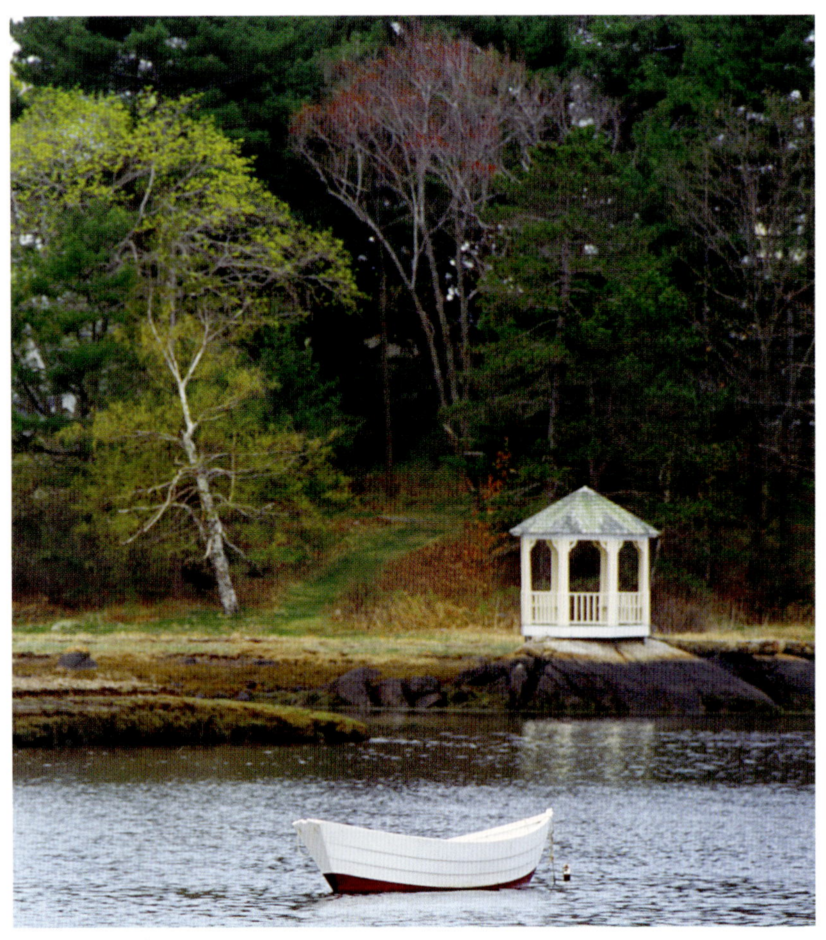

Harbor scene

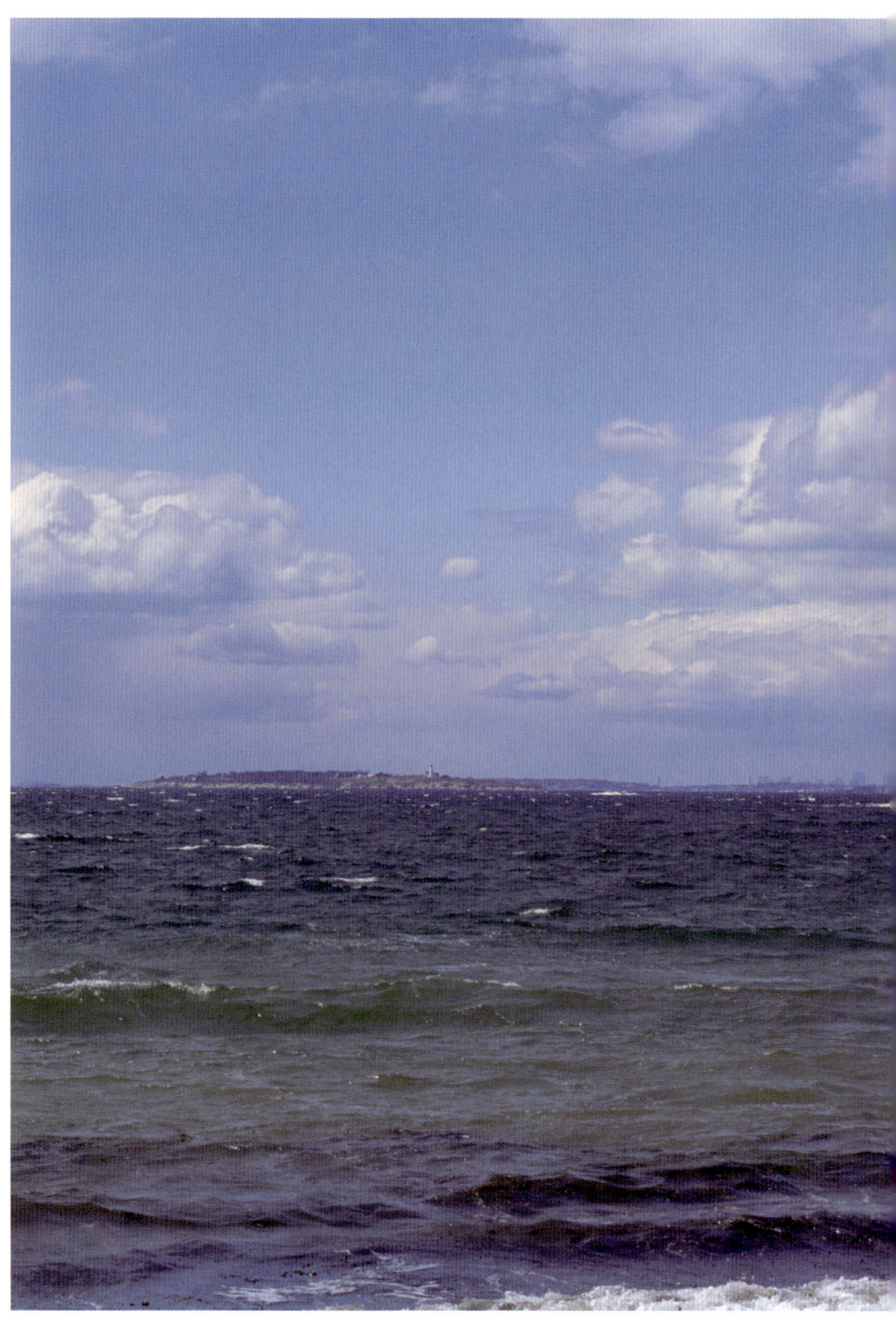

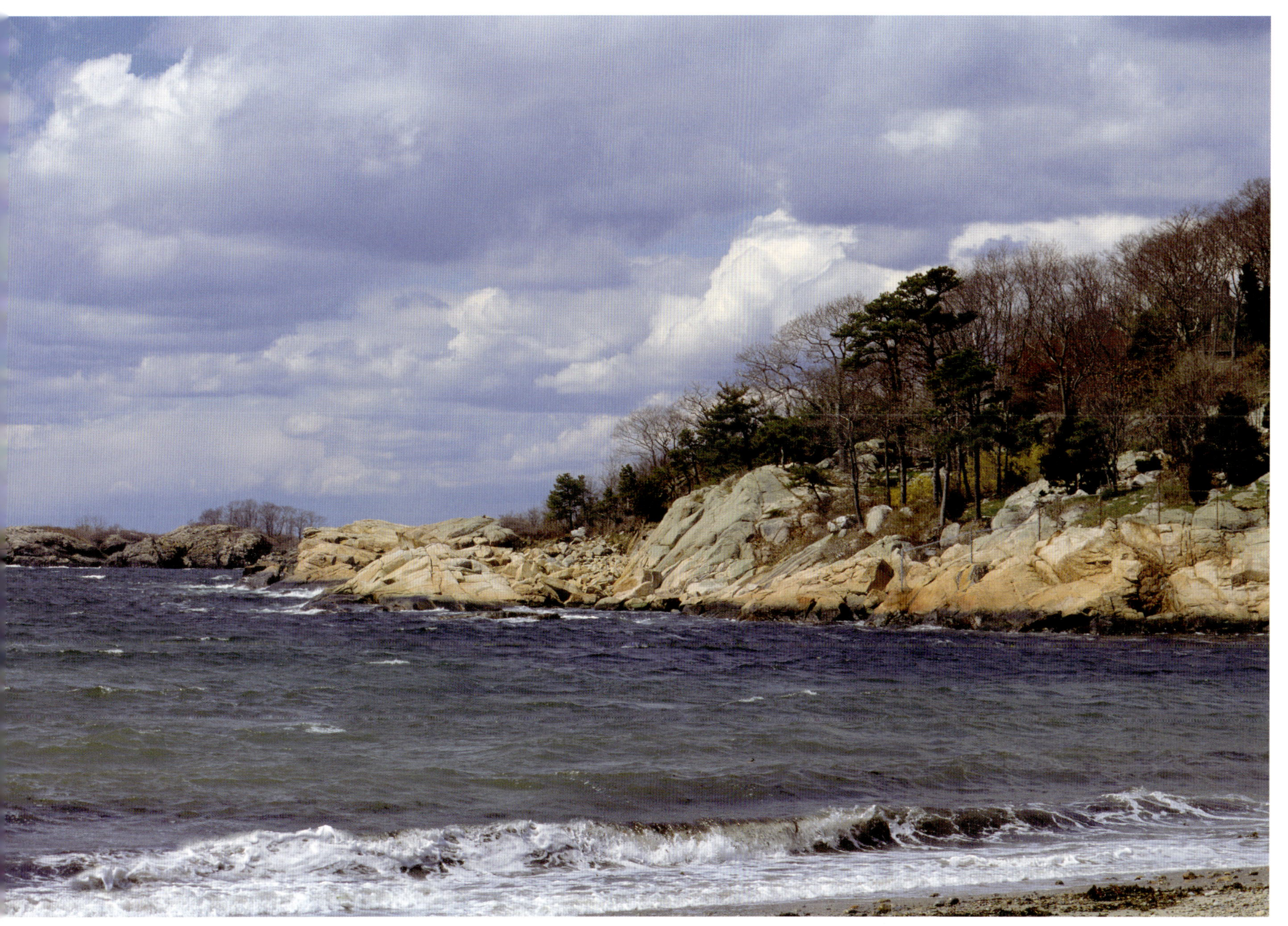

Black Beach, with a view of the Boston skyline

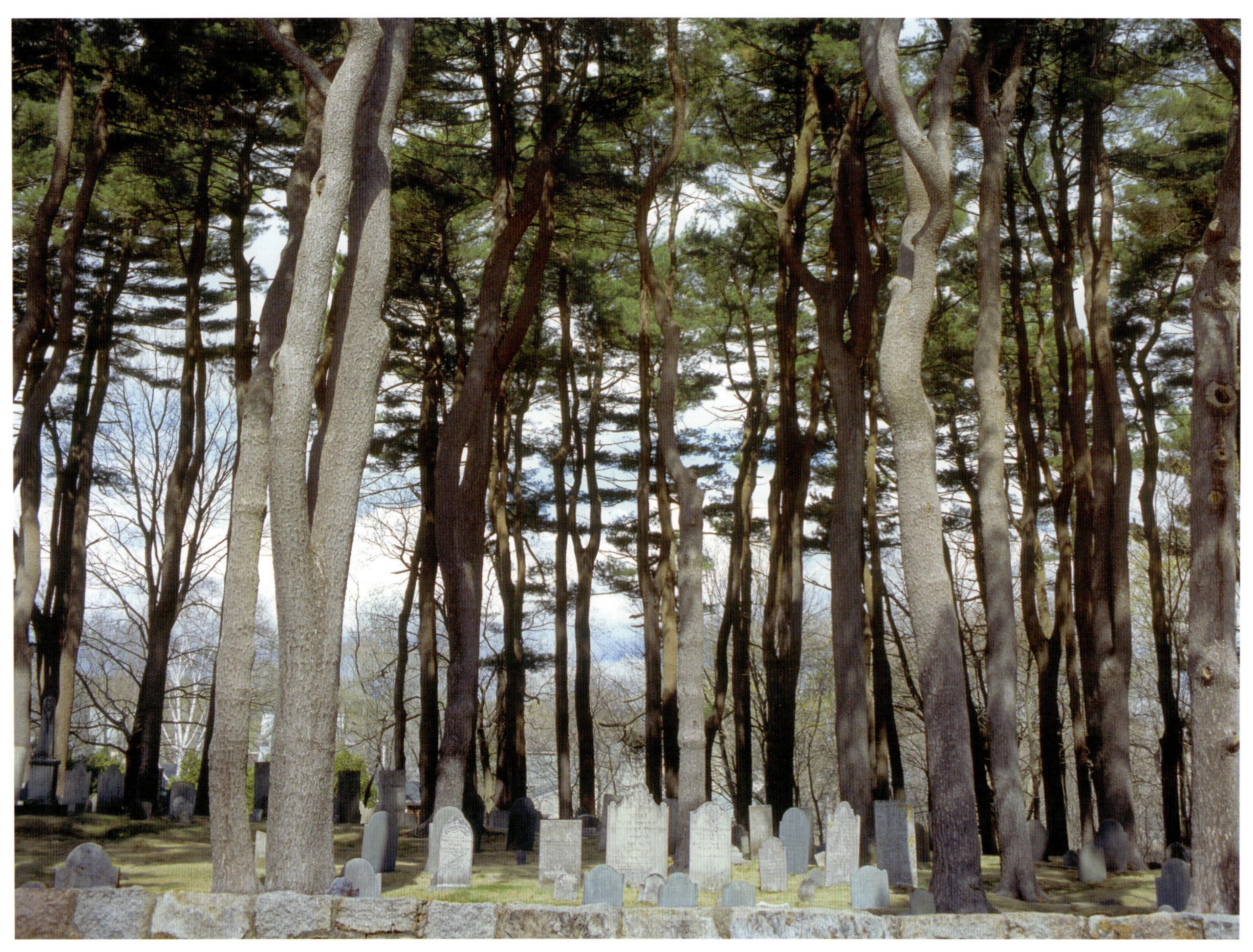

Manchester graveyard,1661, shrouded in tall pines

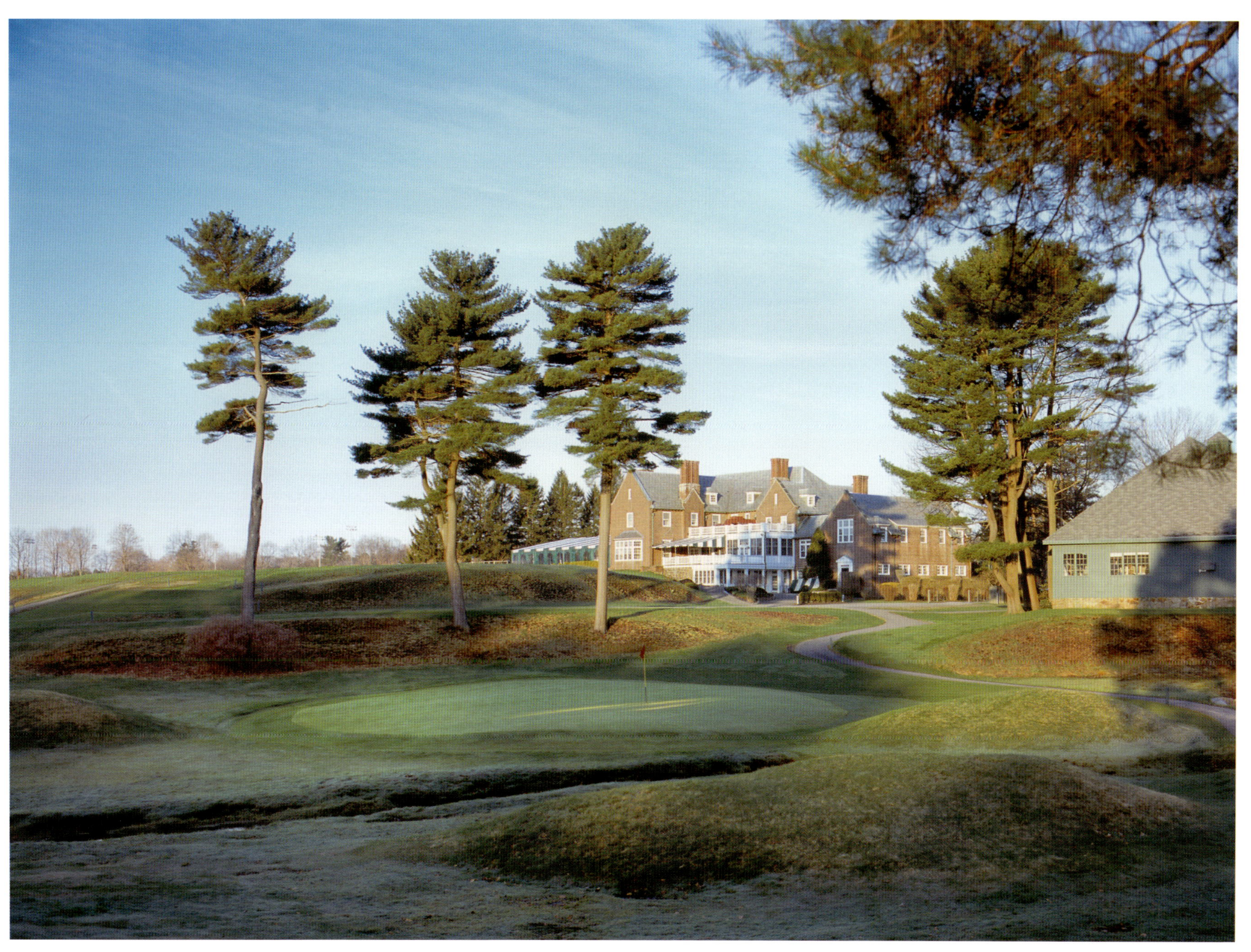

Essex County Club

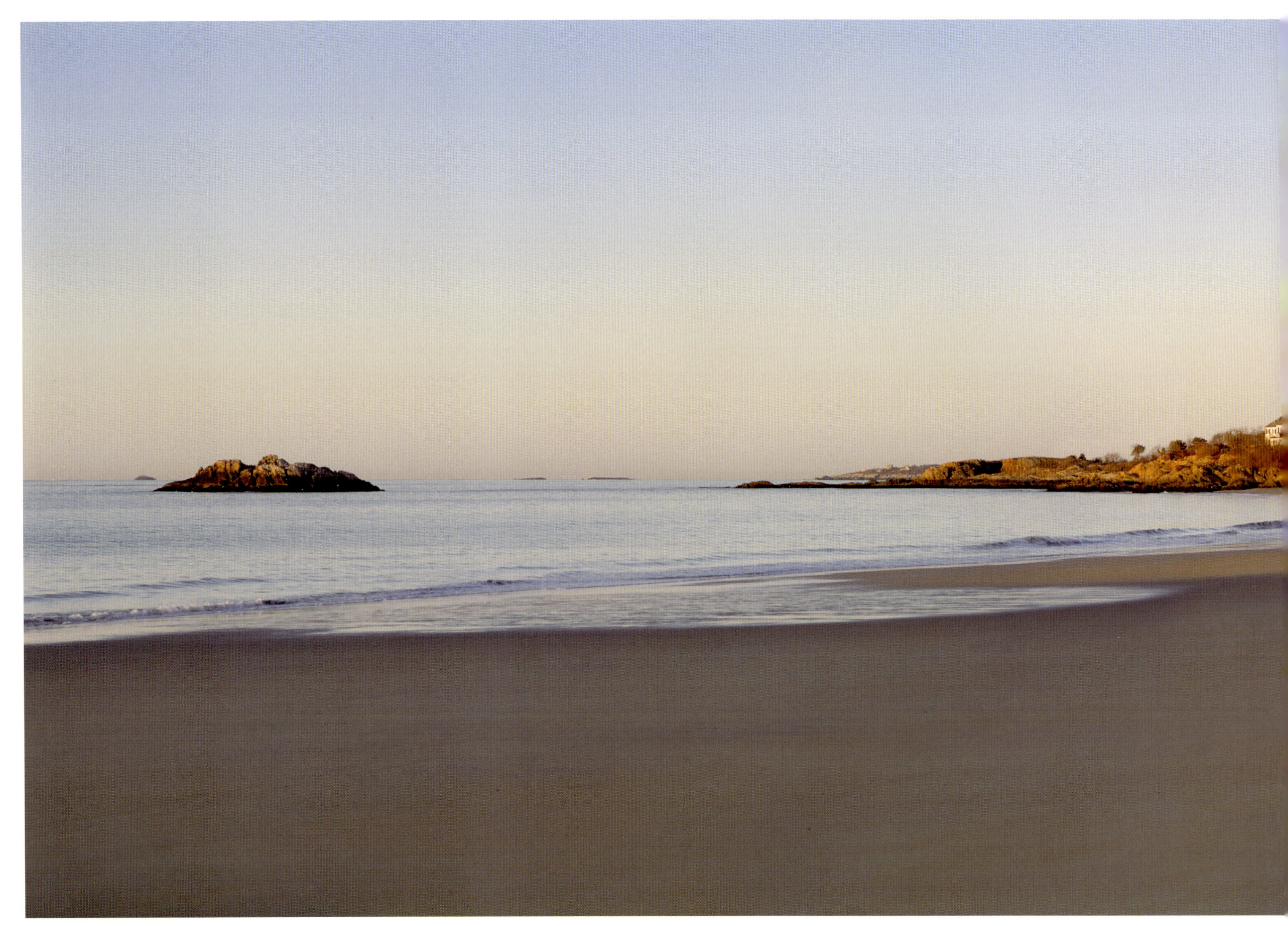

Singing Beach, west view

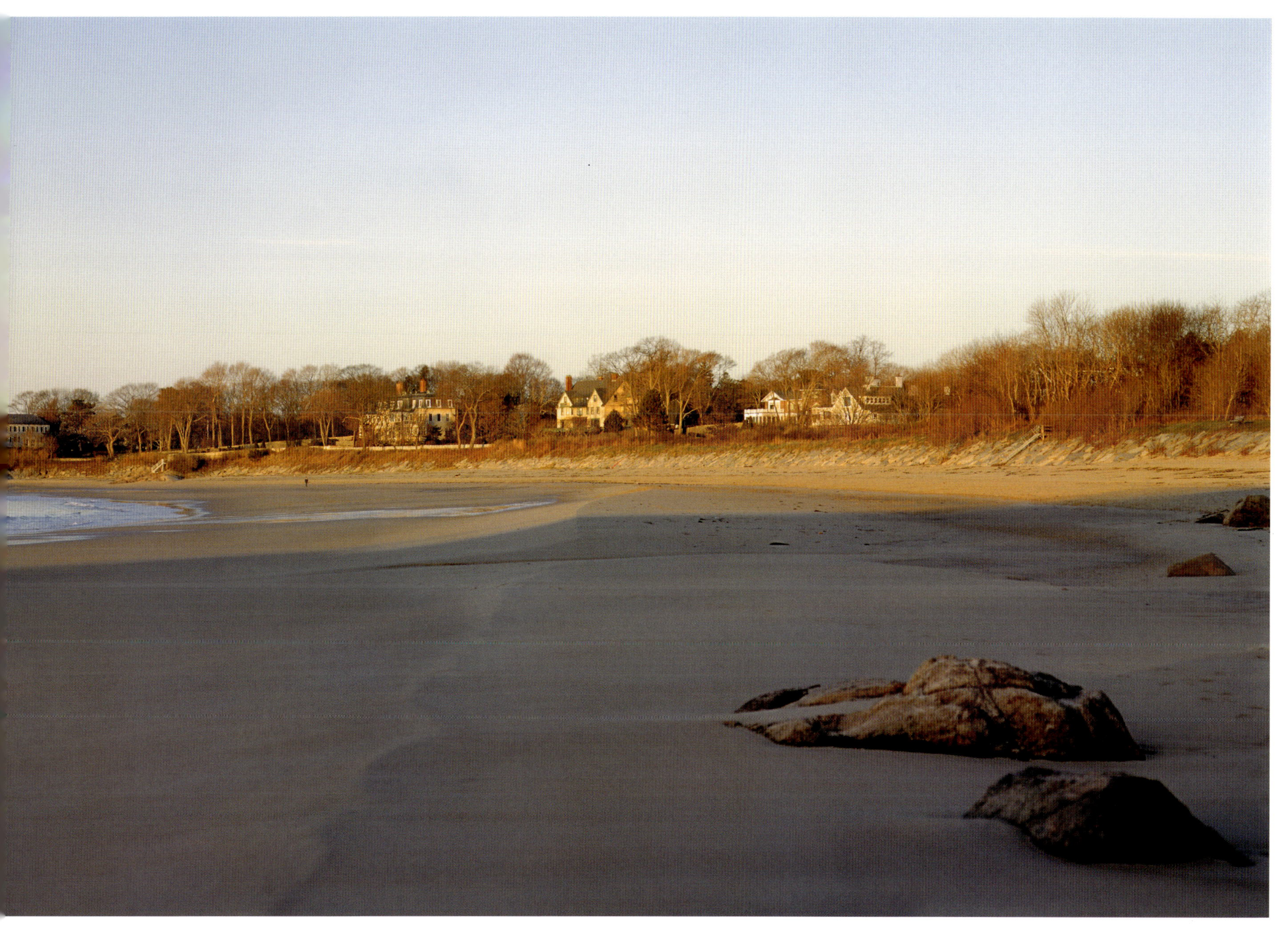

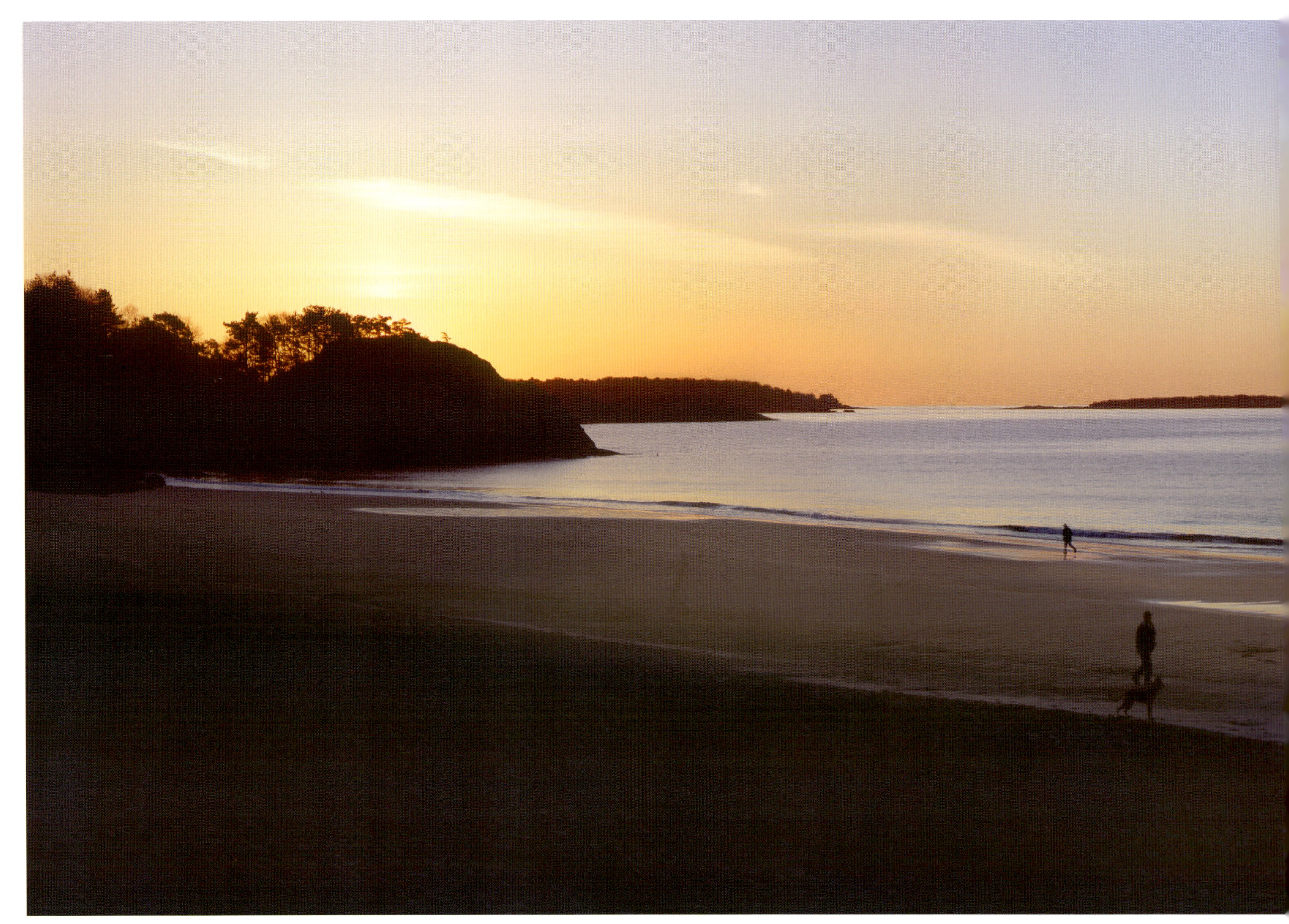

Singing Beach, east view

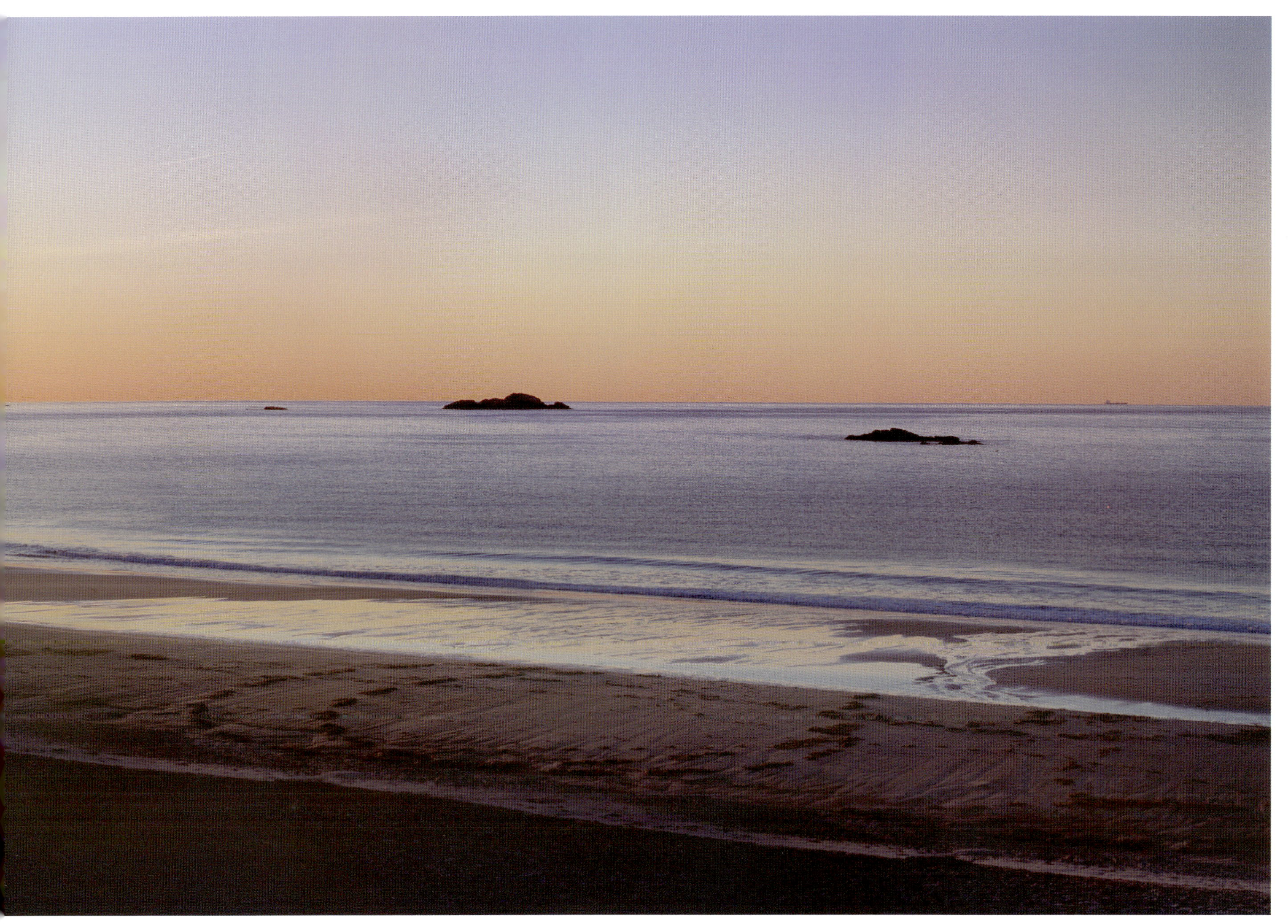

# GLOUCESTER

From Manchester-by-the-Sea, the pilgrim moves up the coast to Gloucester-by-the-Smell. The oldest seaport in America is famous for its fish.

From perilous schooner days of Kipling's *Captains Courageous* to the steel-and-diesel era of *The Perfect Storm,* the town Samuel de Champlain christened Le Beauport ("the beautiful port") has made its living from the sea. Schooners still sail in and out of the harbor, but what's left of the fishing industry here is gritty and industrial.

Still, those who love Gloucester, and they are legion, wouldn't trade it for anything. The nineteenth-century luminist painter Fitz Hugh Lane may have captured the harbor scene most famously, but even a present-day writer like Joe Garland can look back toward the town from Eastern Point and note "the heavenliest light you ever experienced, in its thousand shifting nuances from day to night and night to day."

There's more to Gloucester than harbor, from Magnolia and Good Harbor Beach on the east to Annisquam and Lanesville on the west—with historic, mysterious Dogtown in the middle.

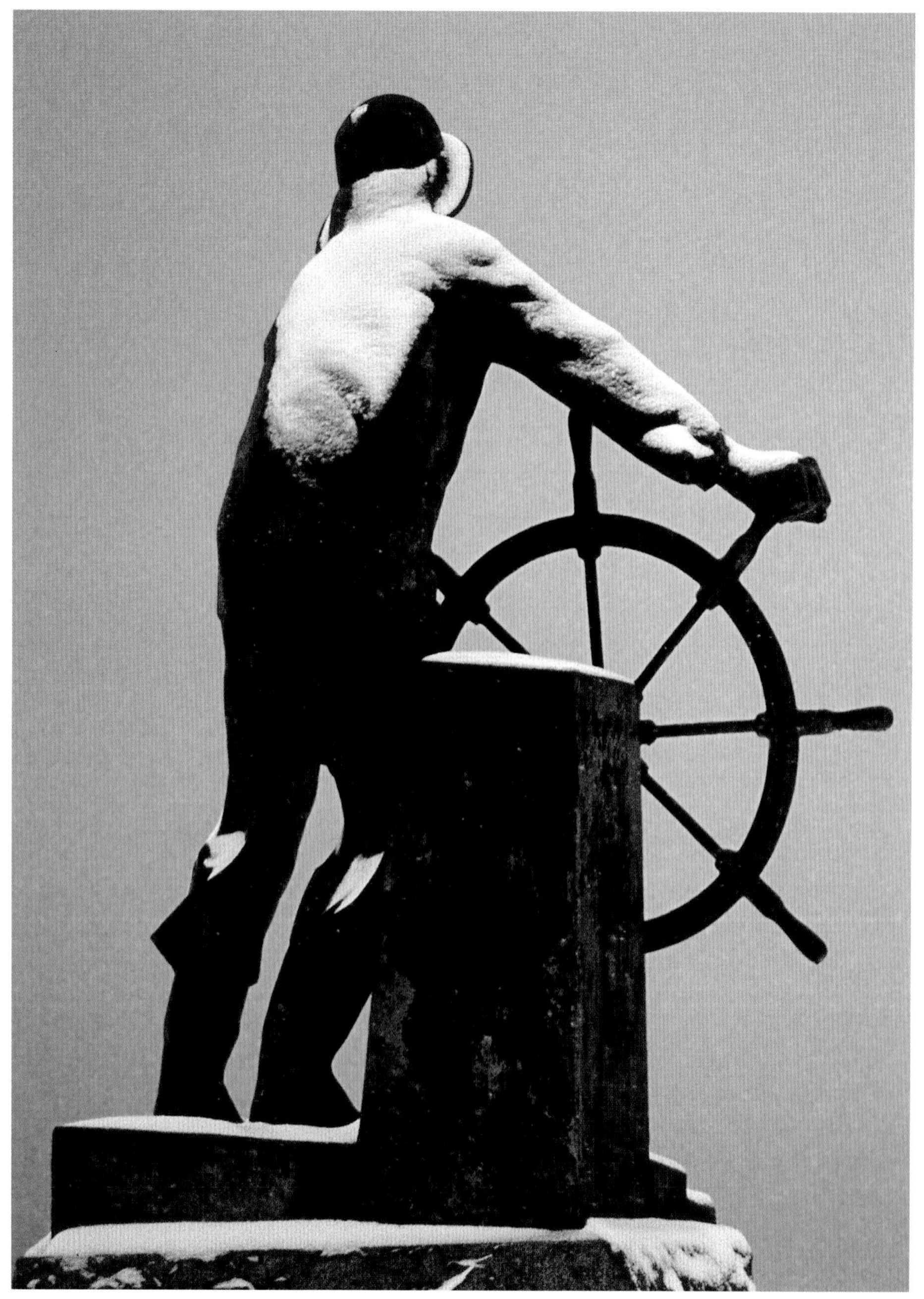

*Above:* The Fisherman's Memorial in winter
*Opposite:* Inner harbor

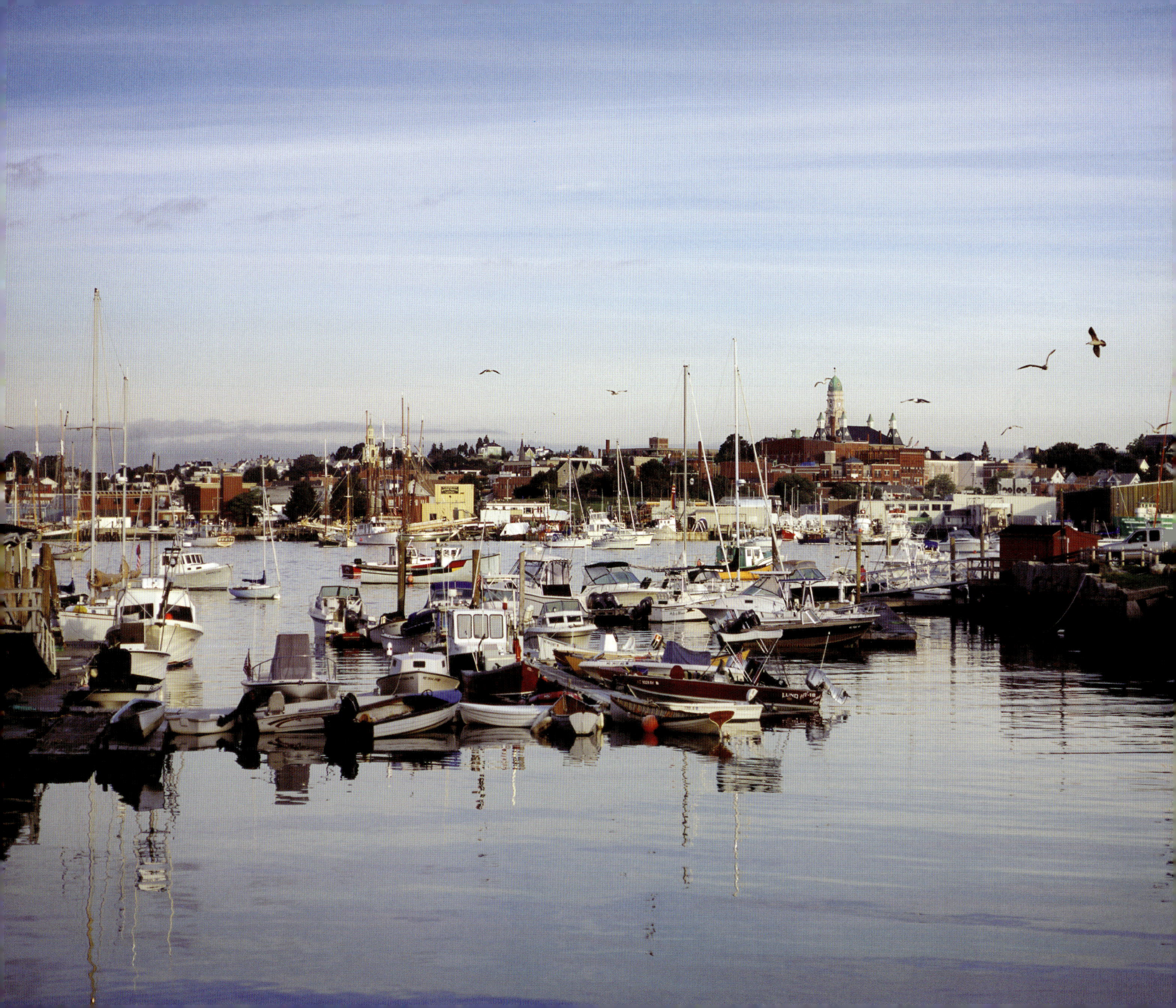

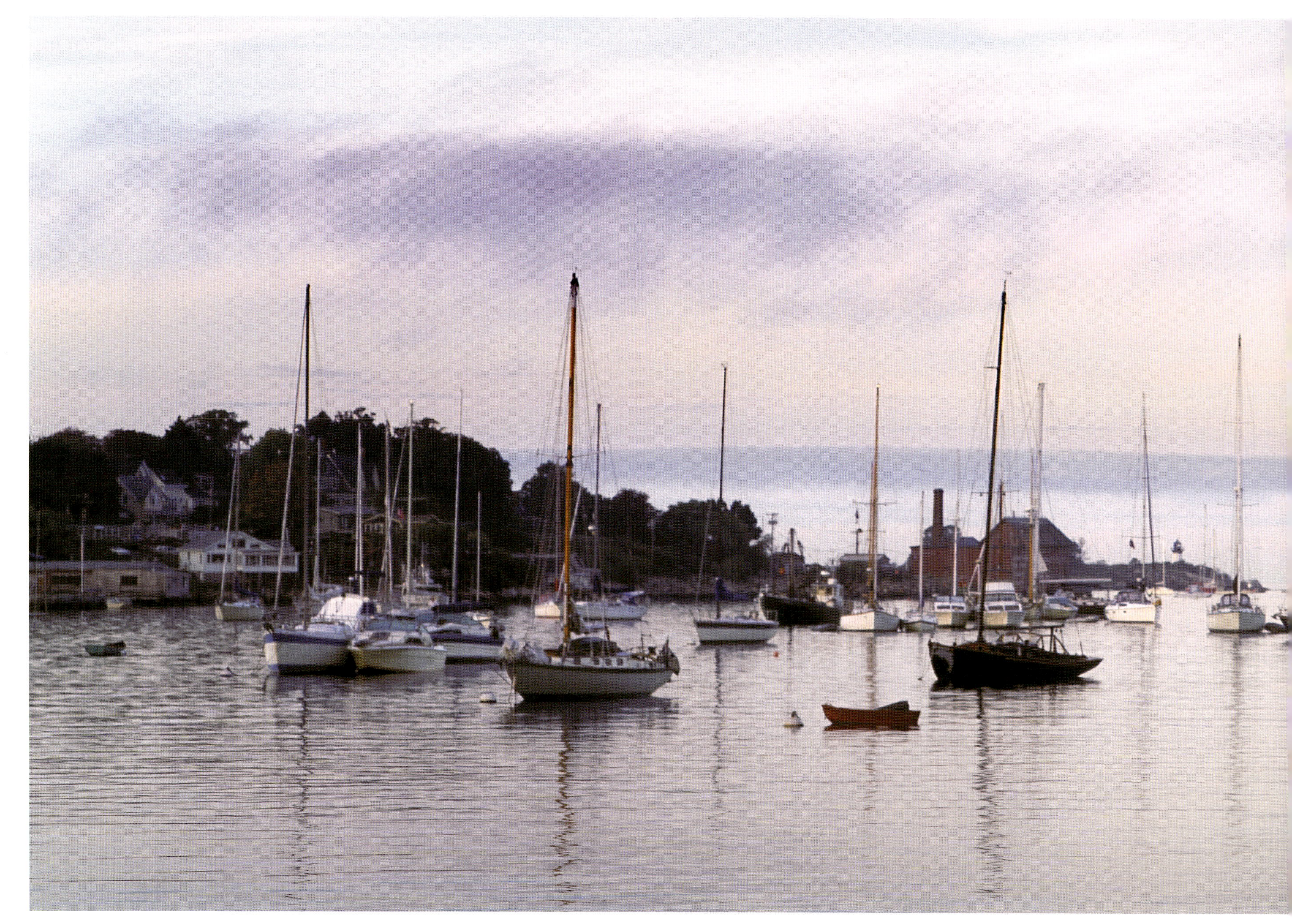

Gloucester Harbor

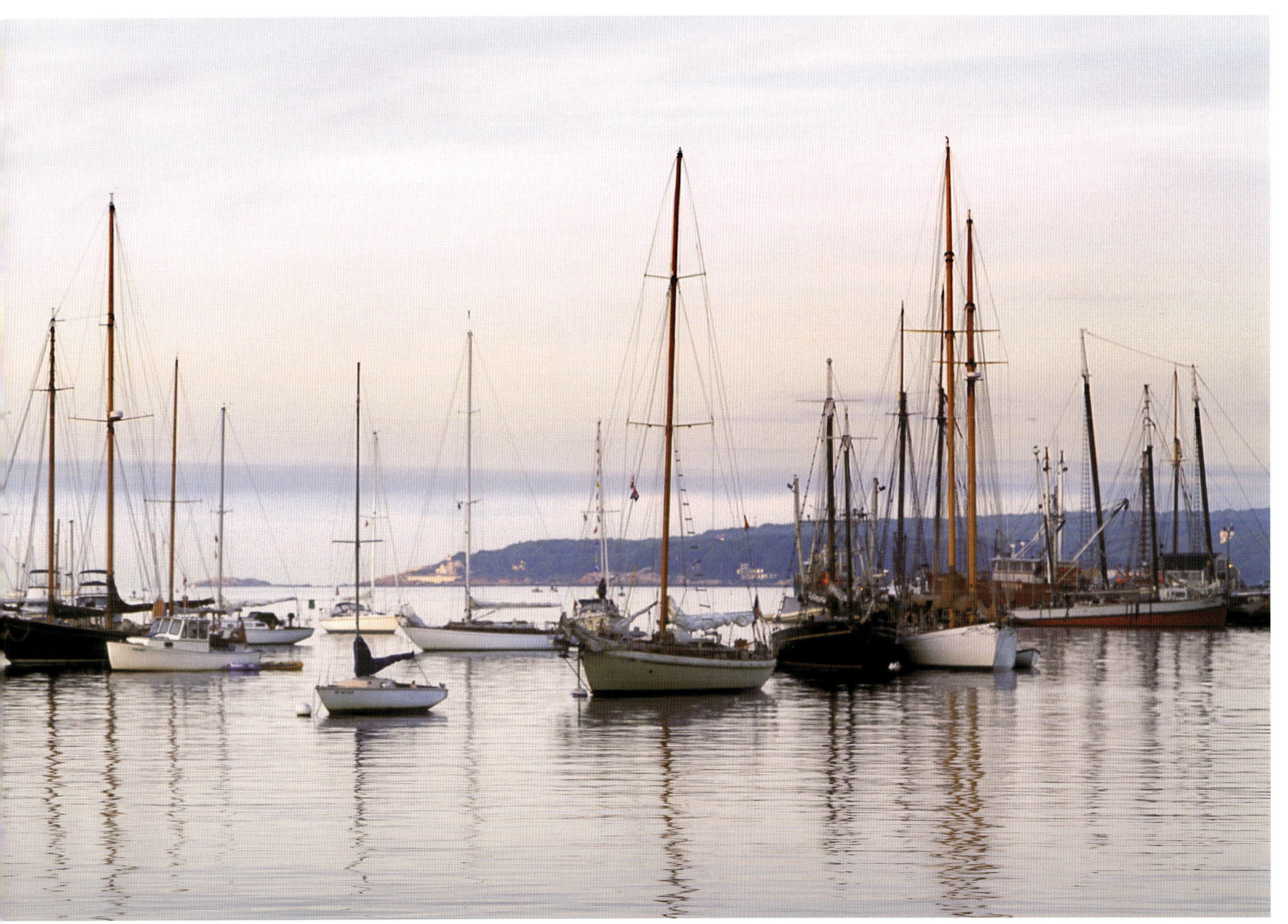

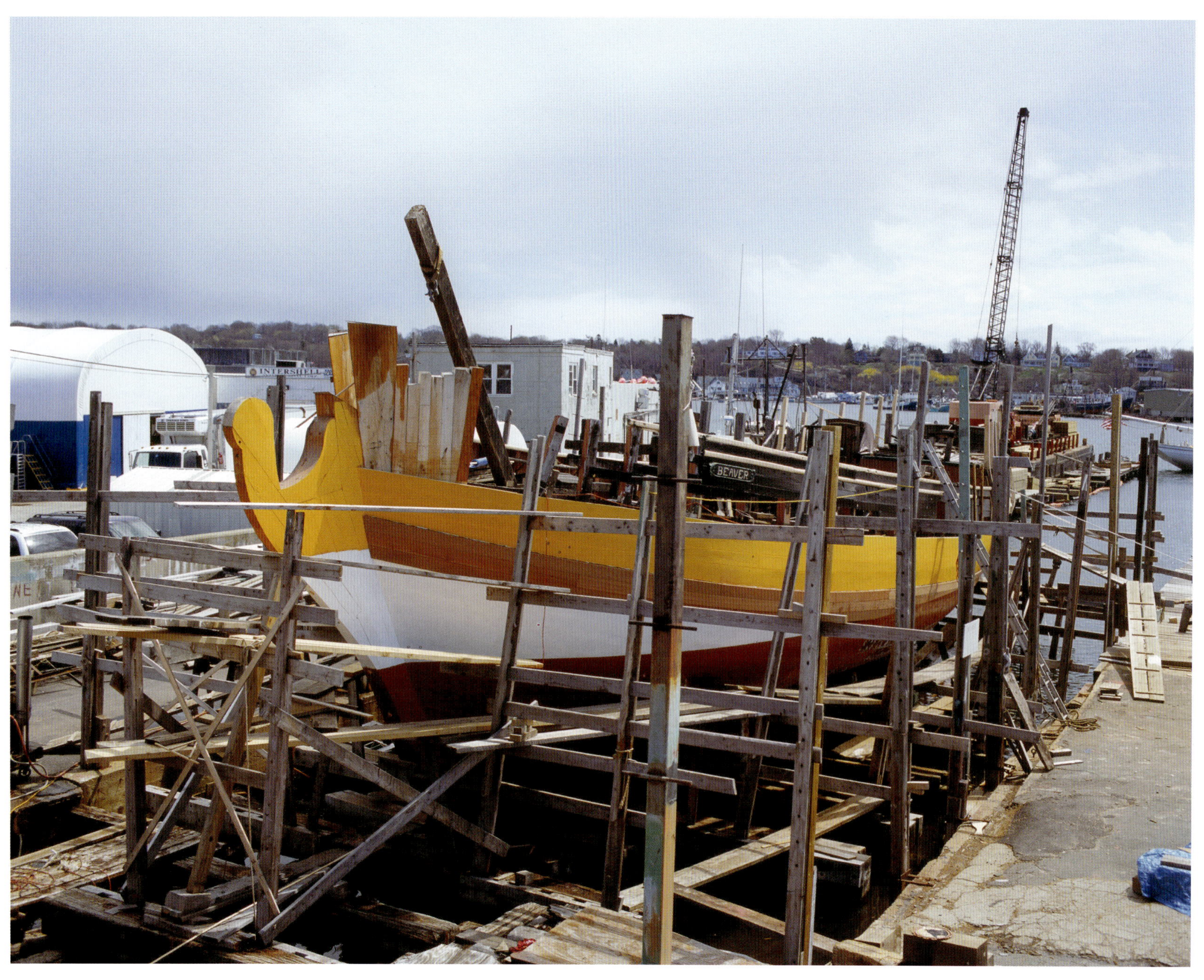


Replanking of the *Beaver II* (replica of the Boston Tea Party ship), Burnham Brothers Marine Railway, Harbor Loop

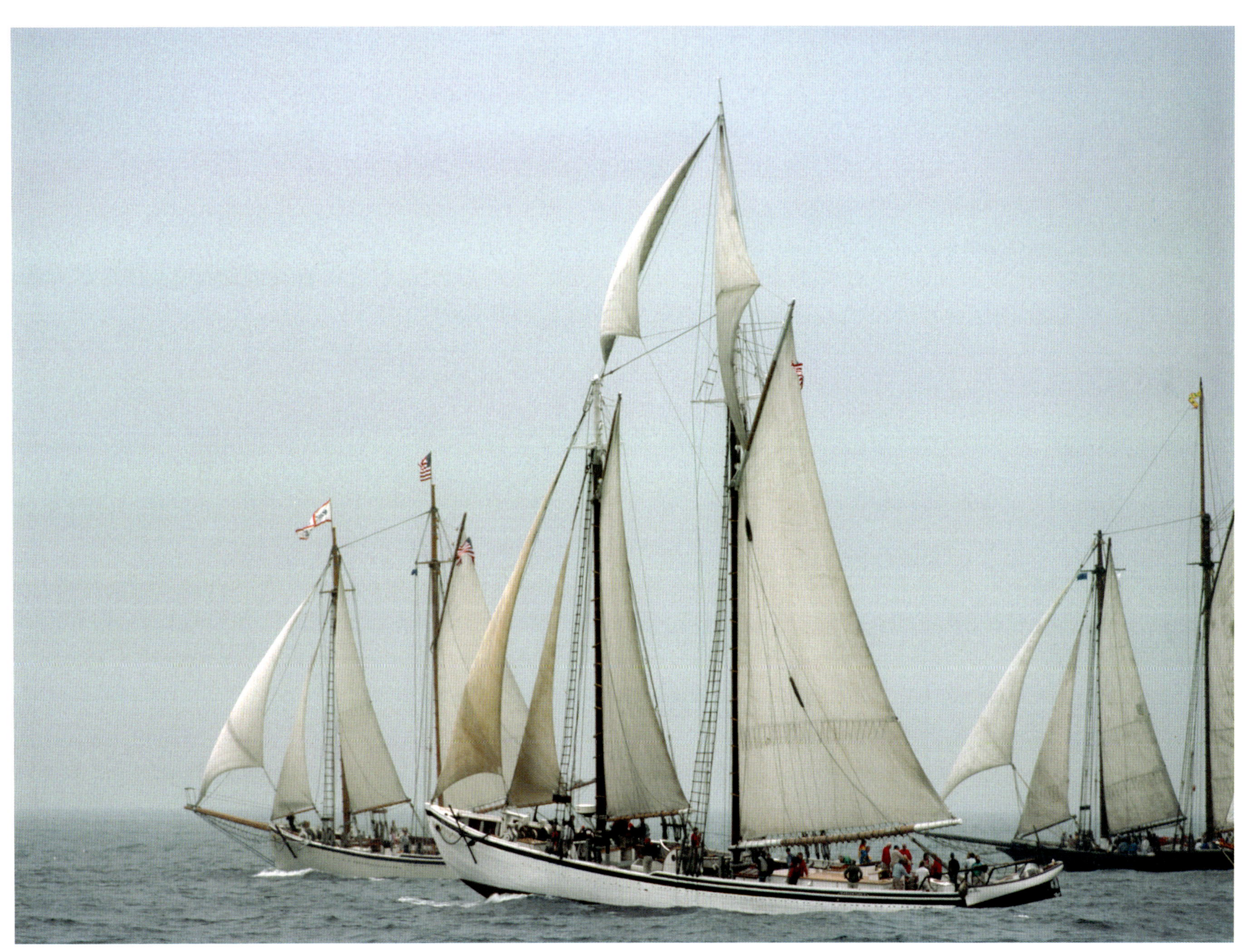

At the Gloucester Schooner Festival: *Adventure, American Eagle,* and *Ernestina*

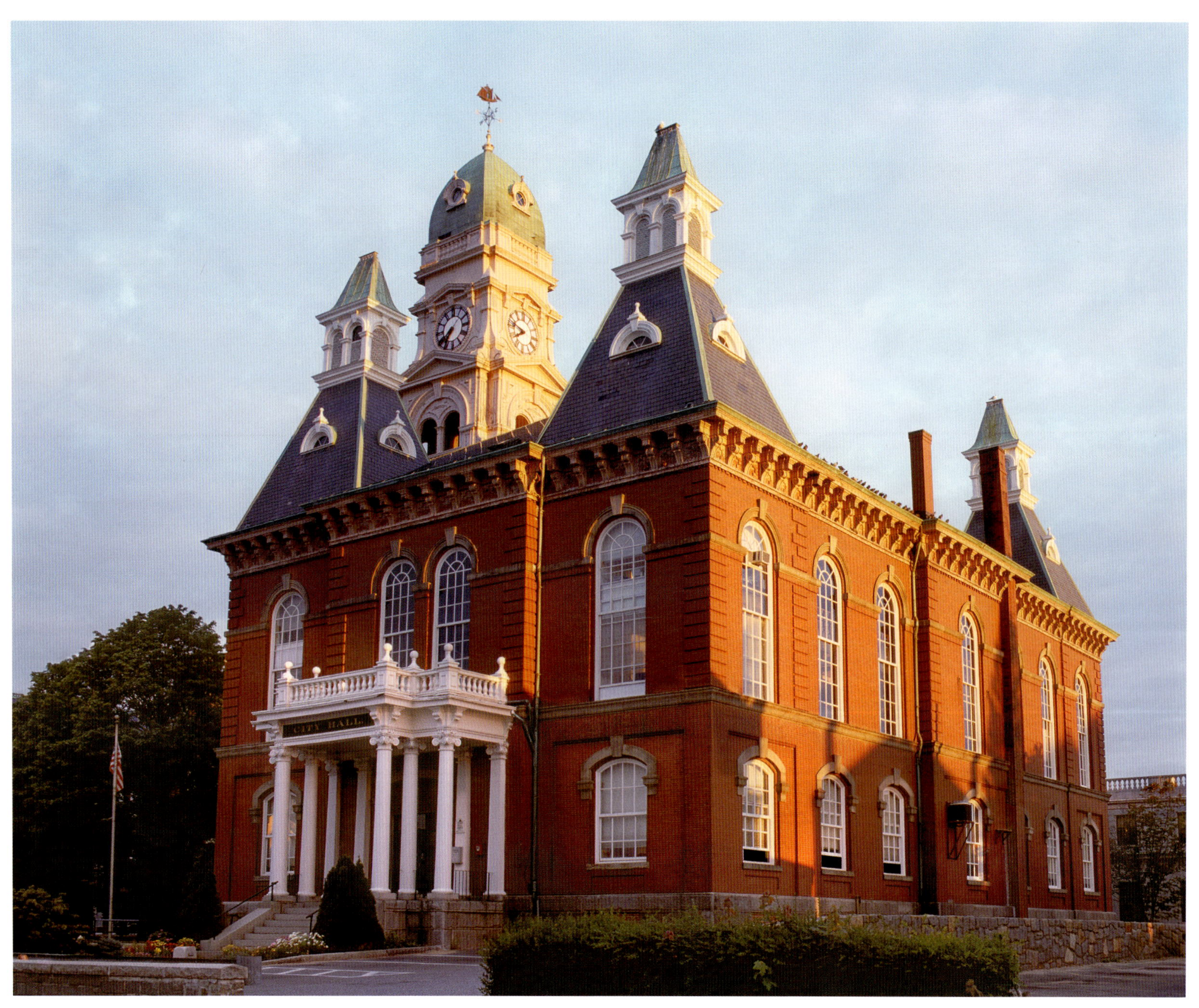


Gloucester City Hall, built 1870–1871, the most prominent landmark on the city's skyline

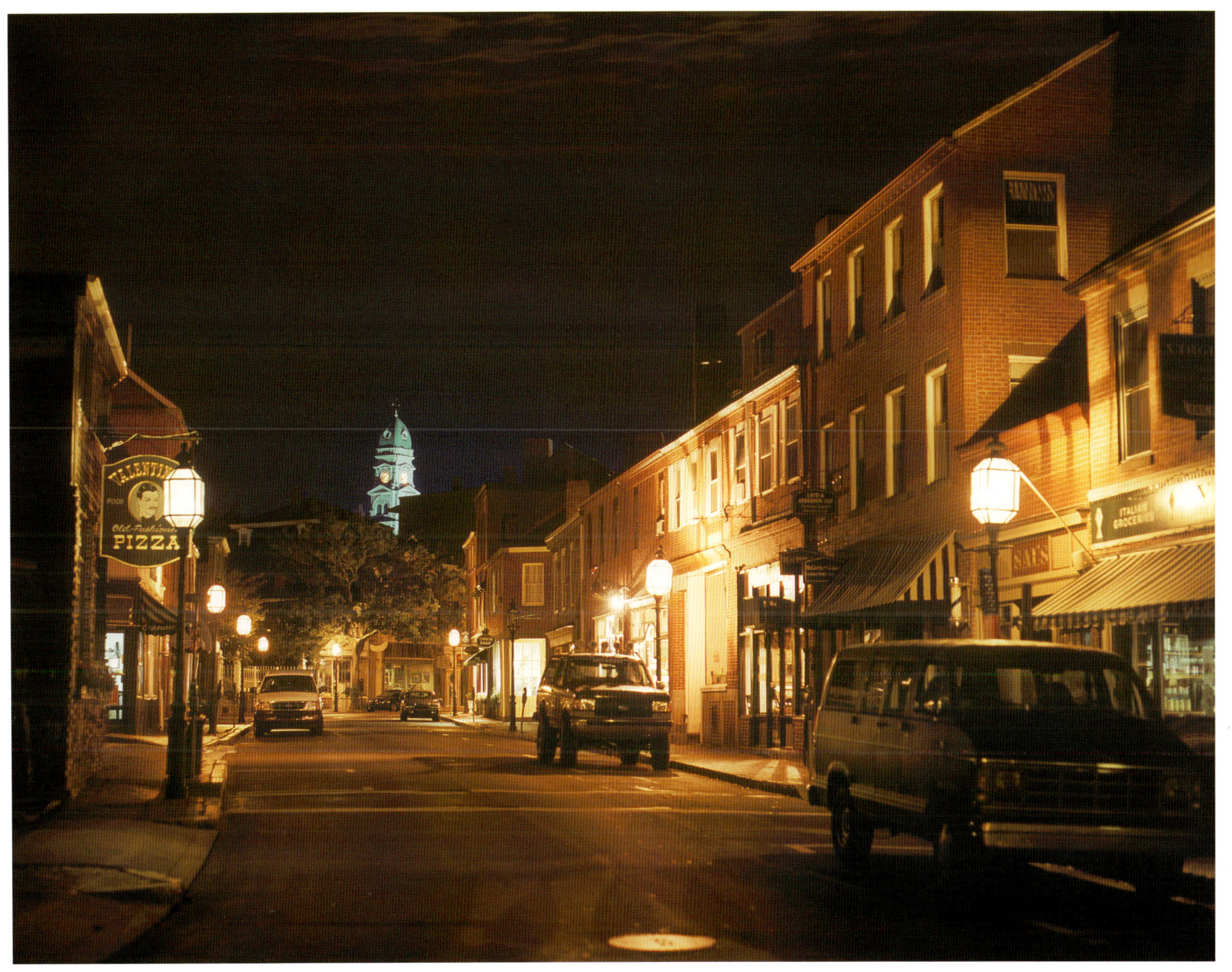


Downtown Gloucester

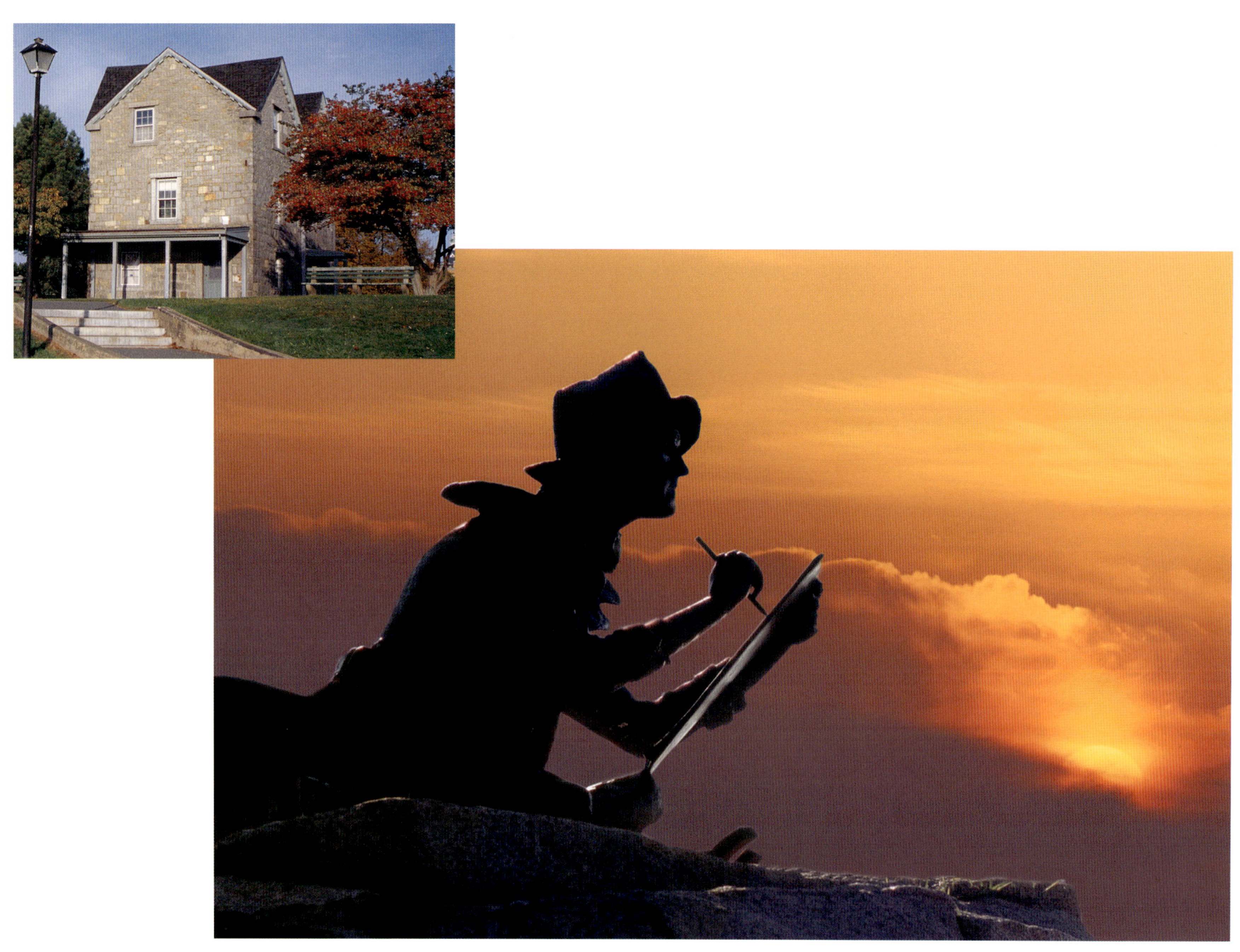

Statue of luminist painter Fitz Hugh Lane (1804–1865), in front of his house at Harbor Loop (inset)

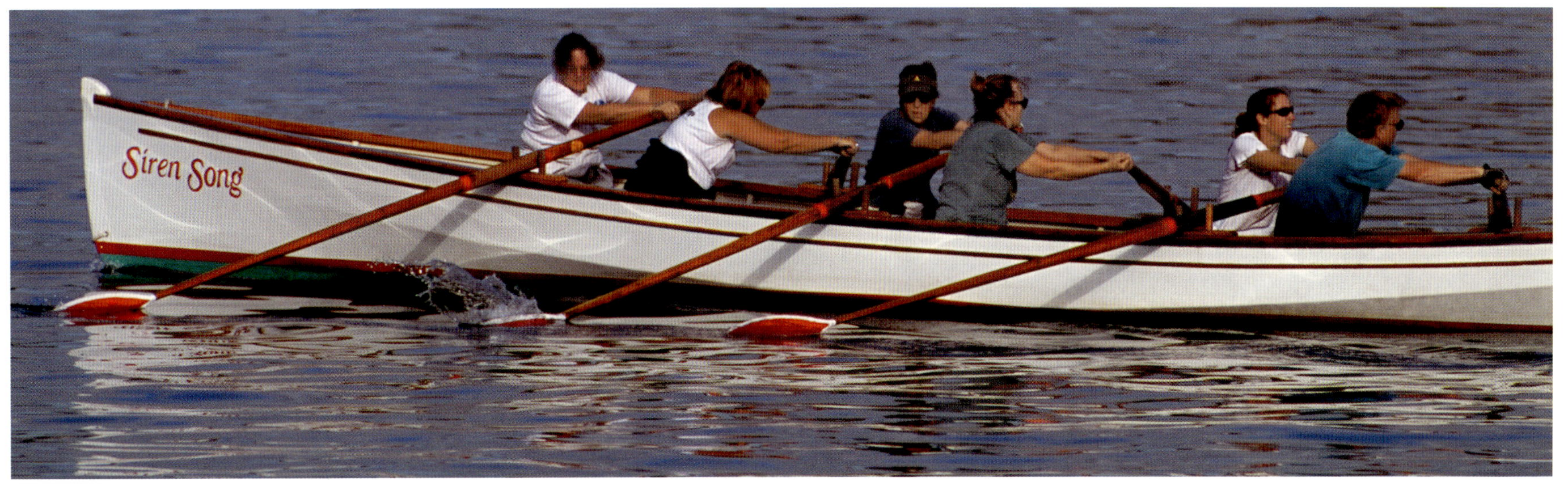


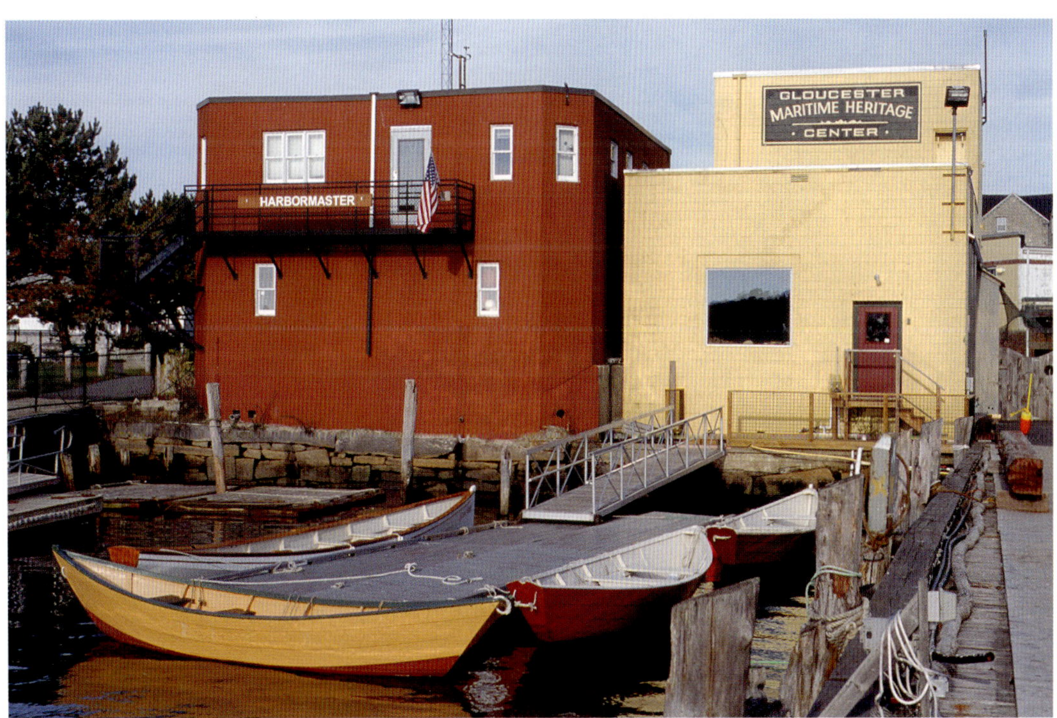


*Top: Siren Song,* a wooden "pilot gig" rowed by members of the Gloucester Gig Rowers Association
*Bottom:* Gloucester Maritime Heritage Center

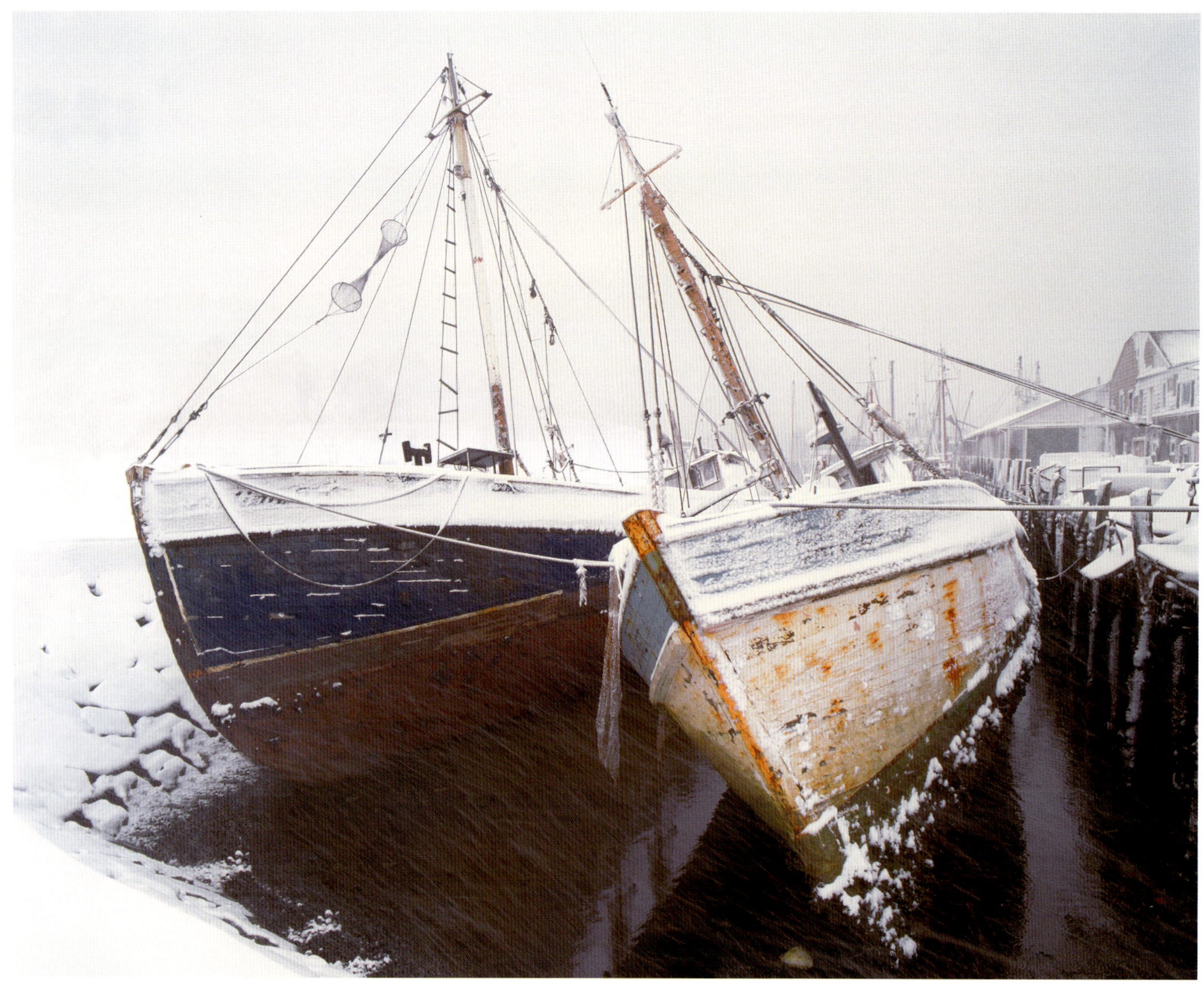

*Nina* and *Gannet,* out of service and waiting to be broken up. With the decline of the fishing industry, these well-known family fishing boats were two among many being bought out by a government program. When I took this photo, a well-weathered fisherman stepped out from a nearby warehouse and approached me. From his gait, I could tell he was used to spending more time on a rolling deck than on land; from his determined step, I could tell I might be in for a confrontation. "You from the goddamn government?" he asked. "No sir, Captain. Been taking pictures of these boats for years—sad to see them go this way." He looked me up and down. His hard, cold stare softening a little, he said, "Well, tell 'em goodbye, kiddo." Then he turned and walked into the white of the snow squall.

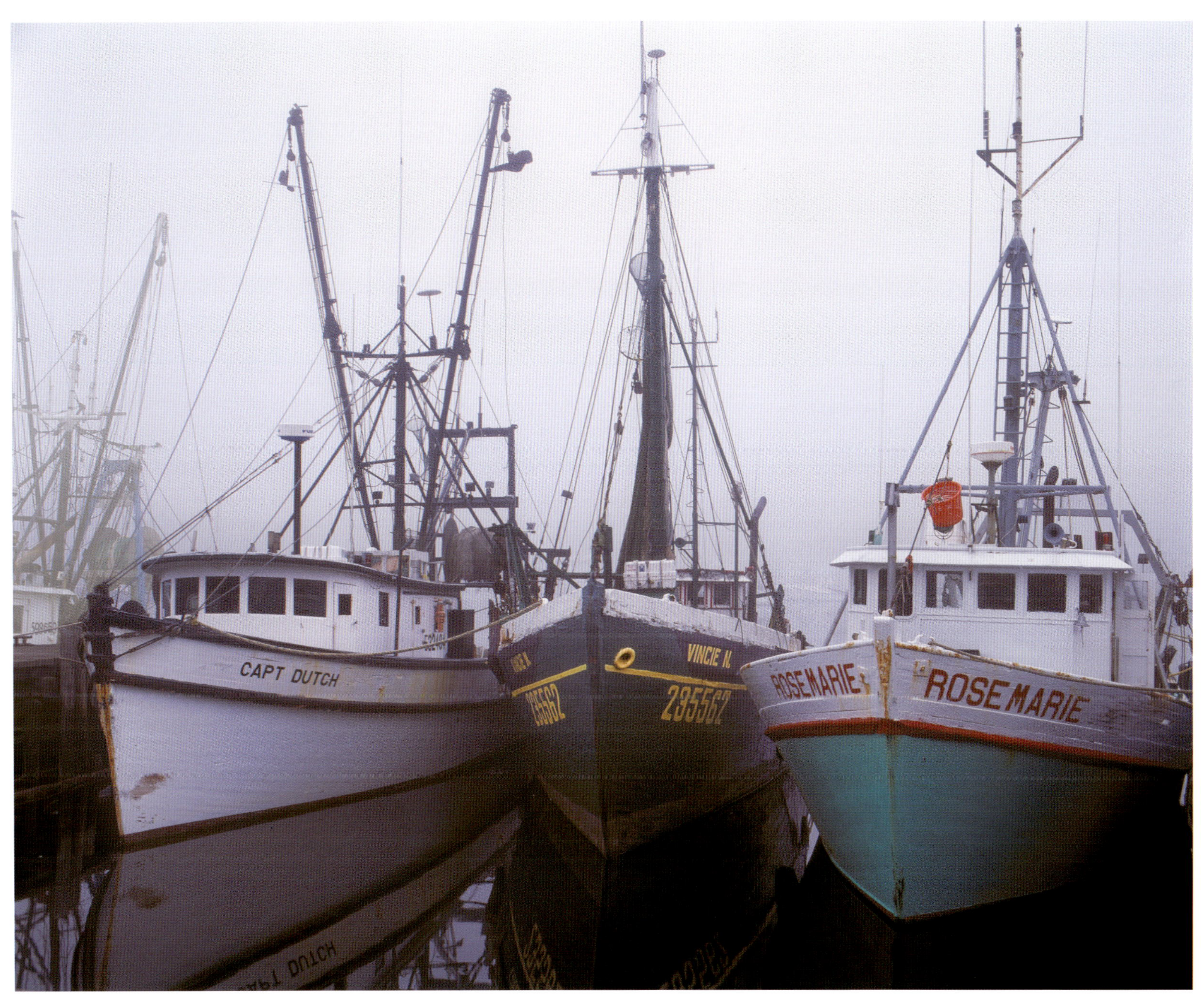


*Capt Dutch*, *Vincie N*, and *Rosemarie*, family-owned wooden fishing boats.
In their wake will come impersonal cold steel corporate boats and the end of an era.

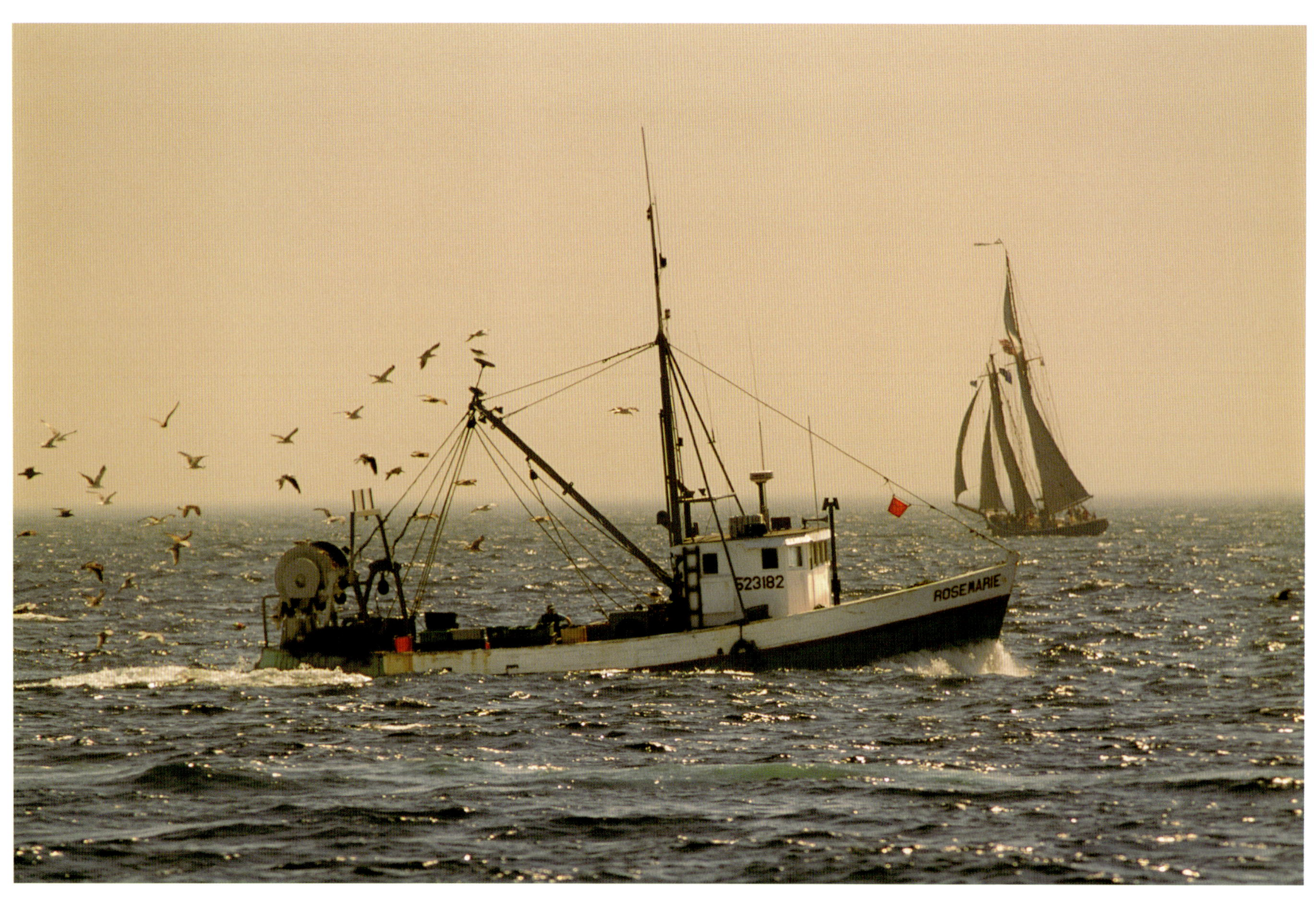


Wooden ships on the water: *Rosemarie* and a schooner

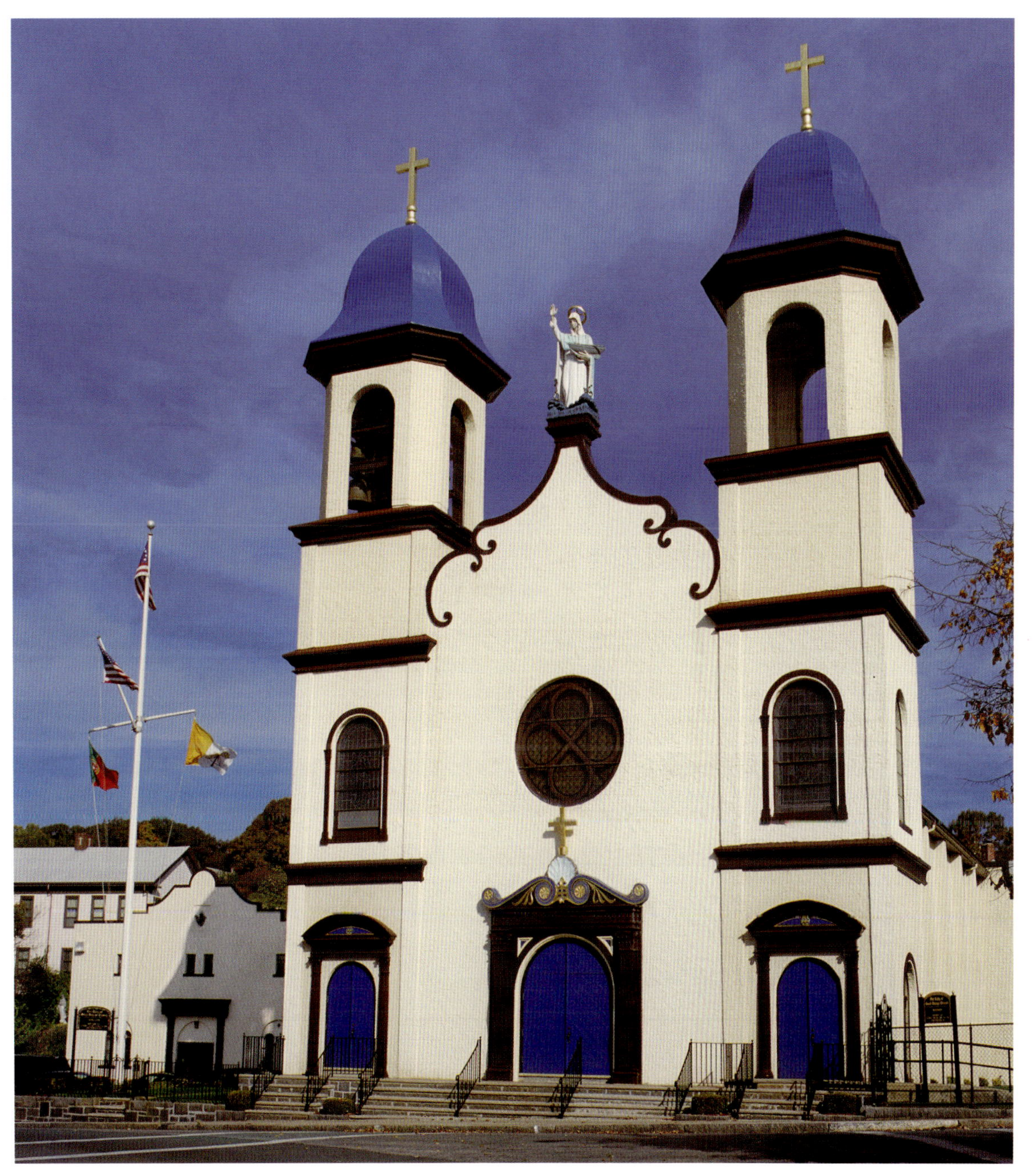

High on a hill overlooking Gloucester Harbor, the Church of Our Lady of Good Voyage was built in 1915 to support the Portuguese fishing fleet. The statue of Mary between the steeples cradles a fishing boat in her arms.

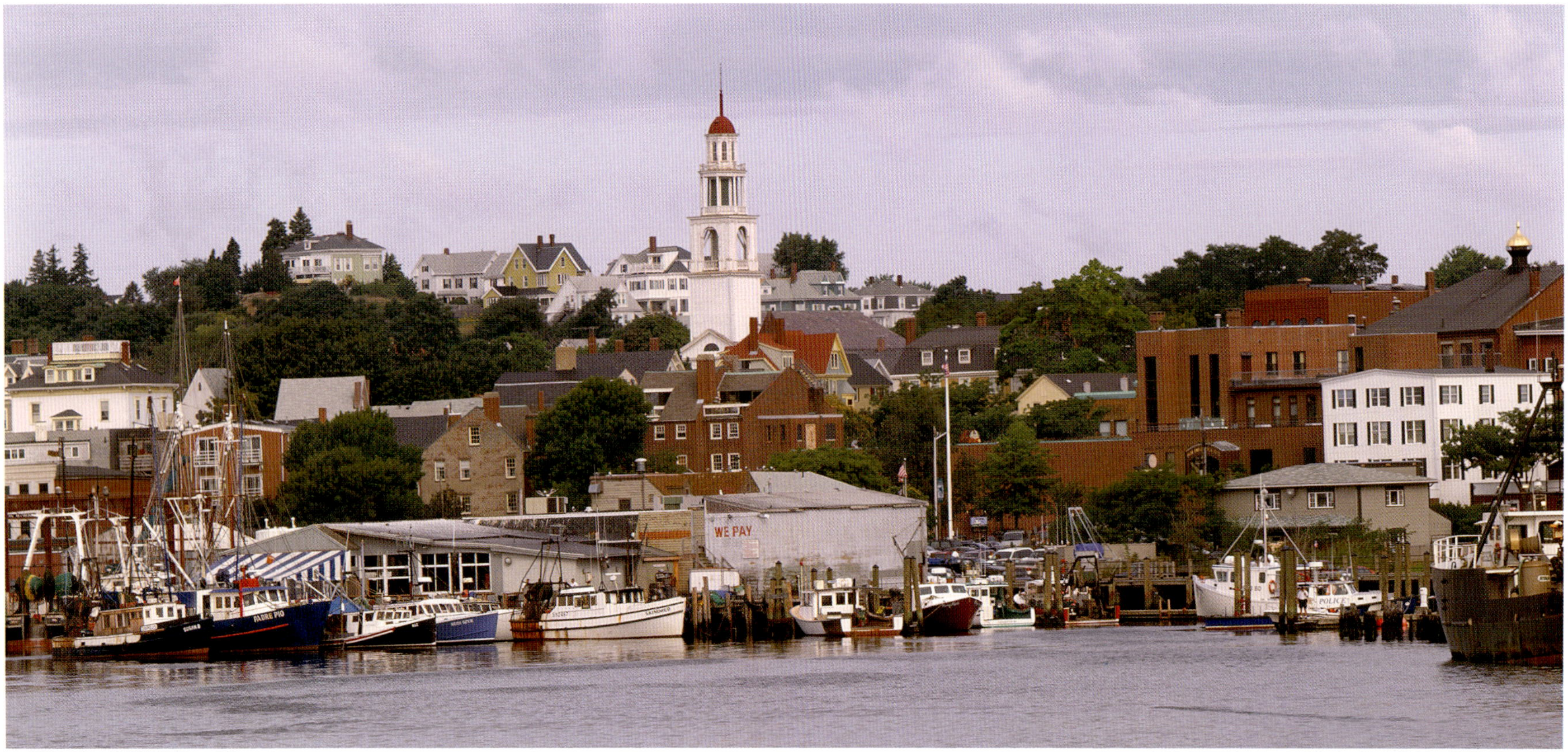

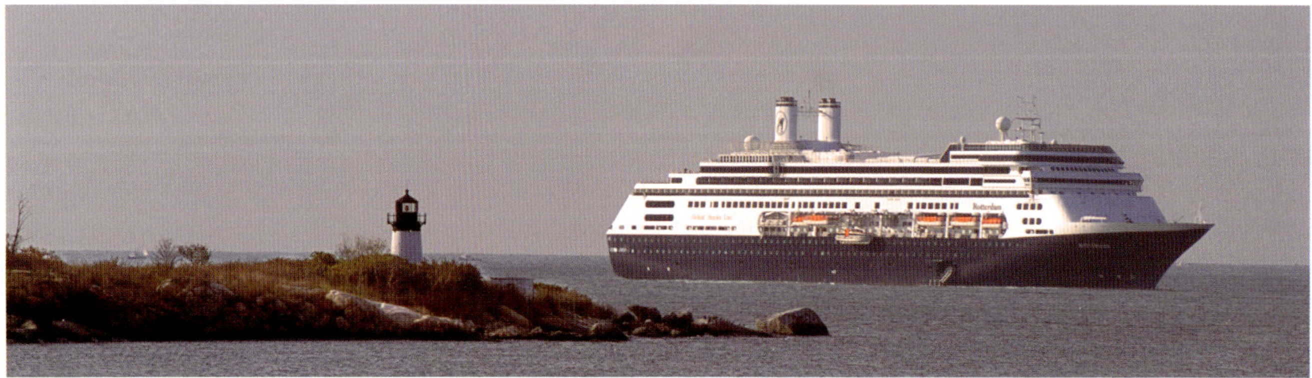

*Top:* Port of Gloucester. Towering above the skyline is the First Universalist Congregational Church, built in 1806.
*Above:* Ten Pound Island, with its light, is dwarfed by the 778-foot *ms Rotterdam* of the Holland America cruise line.
Winslow Homer spent the summer of 1880 on the island and painted approximately fifty watercolors of views in all directions.
*Opposite:* The schooner *Thomas E. Lannon* takes passengers out of Gloucester Harbor daily in season.

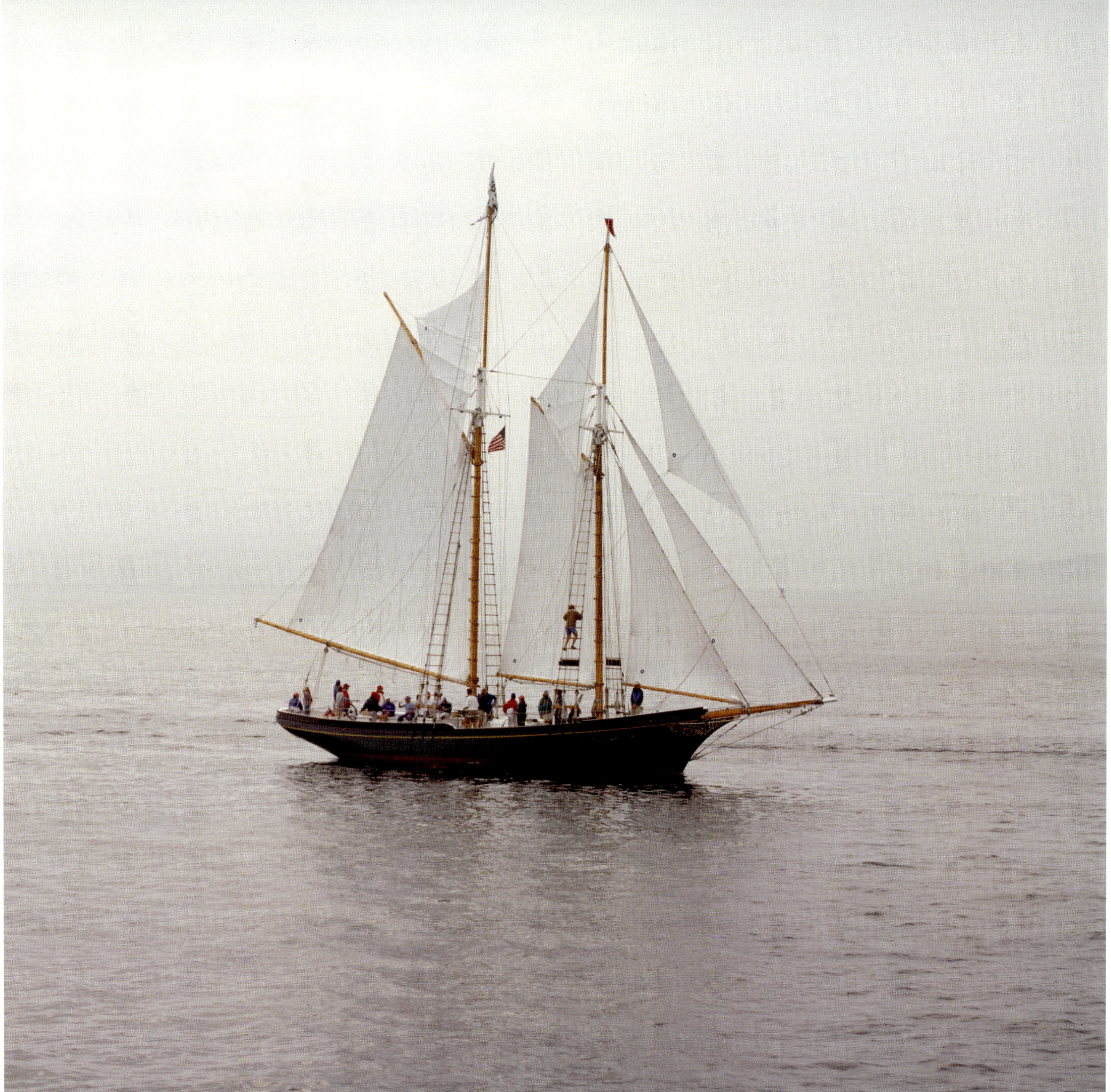

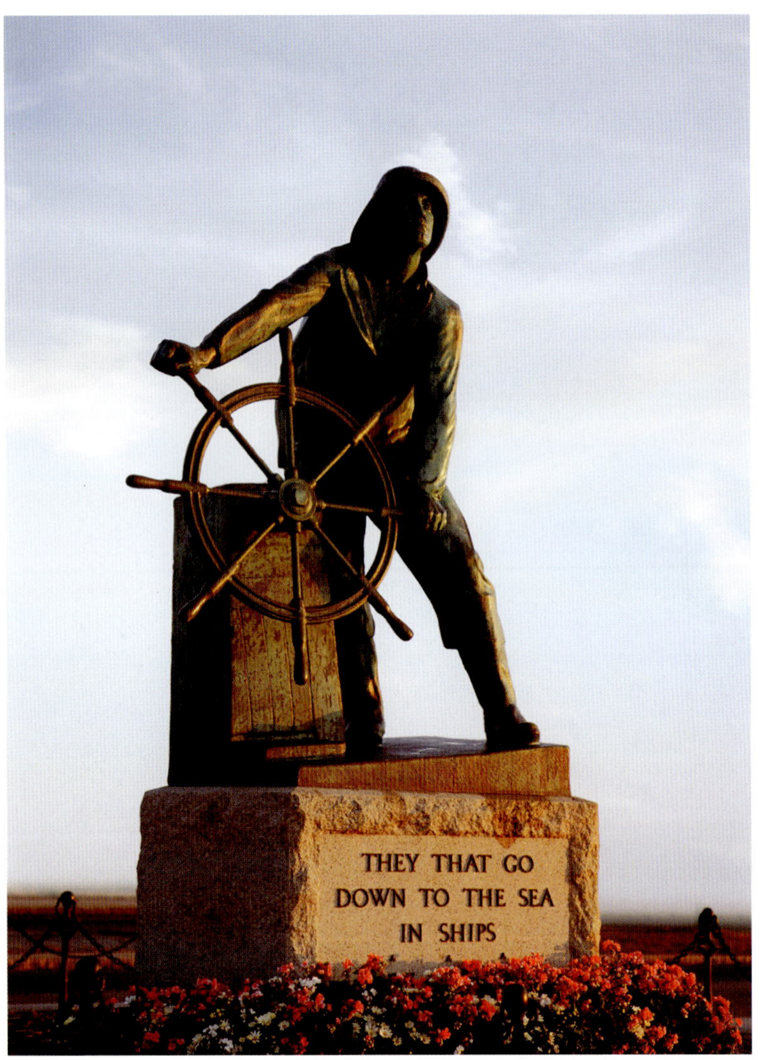


The Fisherman's Memorial, a bronze statue by Leonard Craske also known as the "Man at the Wheel," was installed in 1925, in celebration of Gloucester's 300th anniversary. In 2000 a granite cenotaph (not pictured) was erected nearby, with bronze plaques listing the 5,368 Gloucester fishermen lost at sea between 1625 and 2000.

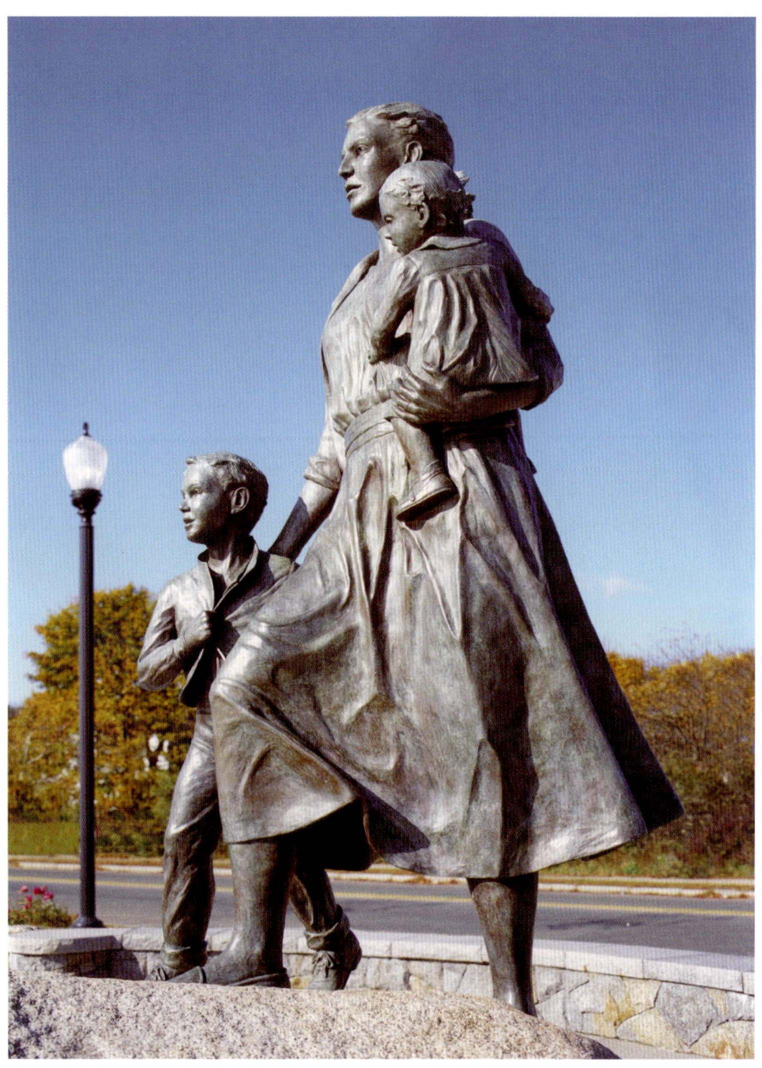

The Gloucester Fishermen's Wives Memorial was erected in 2001. The bronze statue, sponsored by the Gloucester Fishermen's Wives Association, was sculpted by Morgan Faulds Pike.

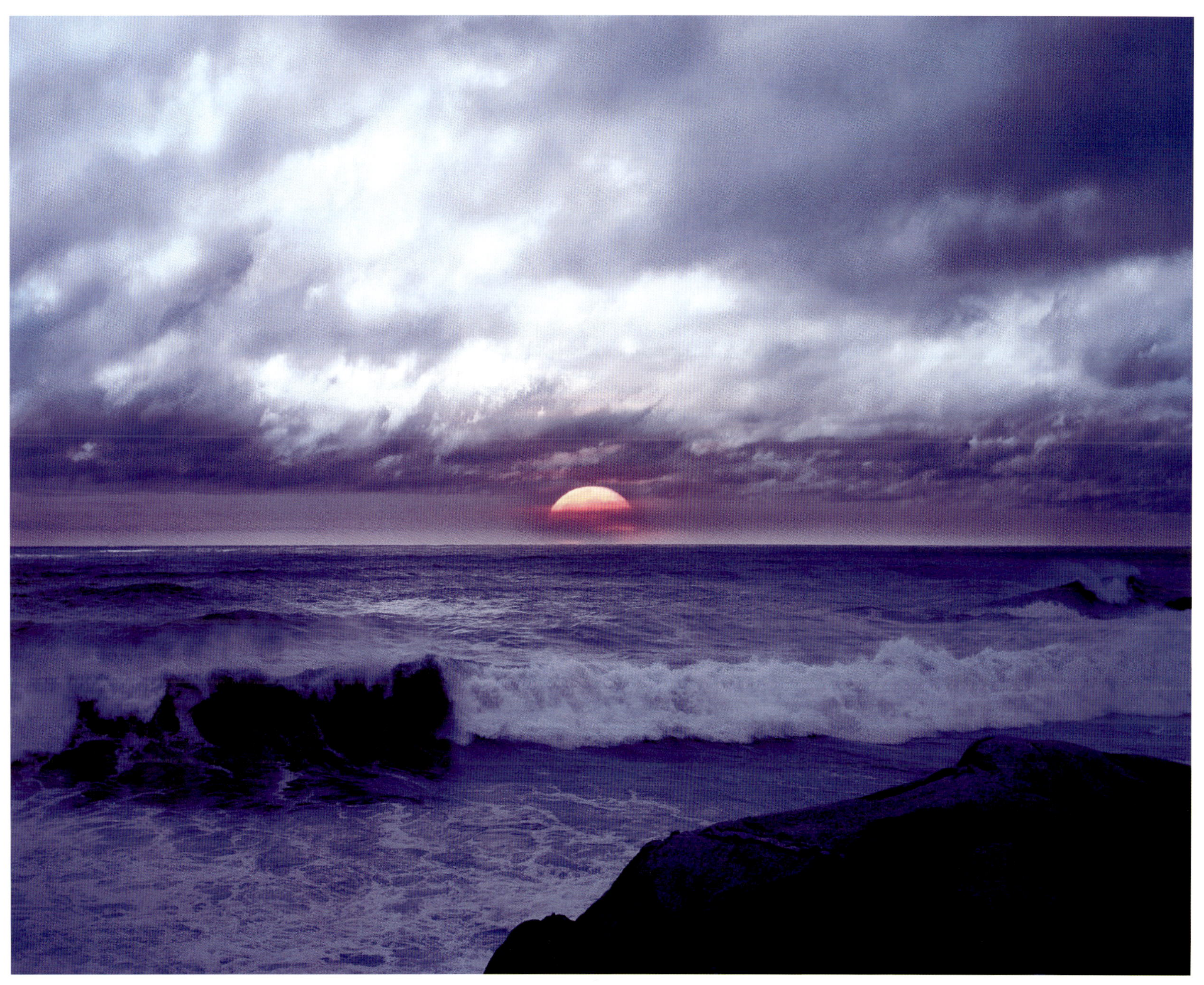

Moonrise over Bass Rocks

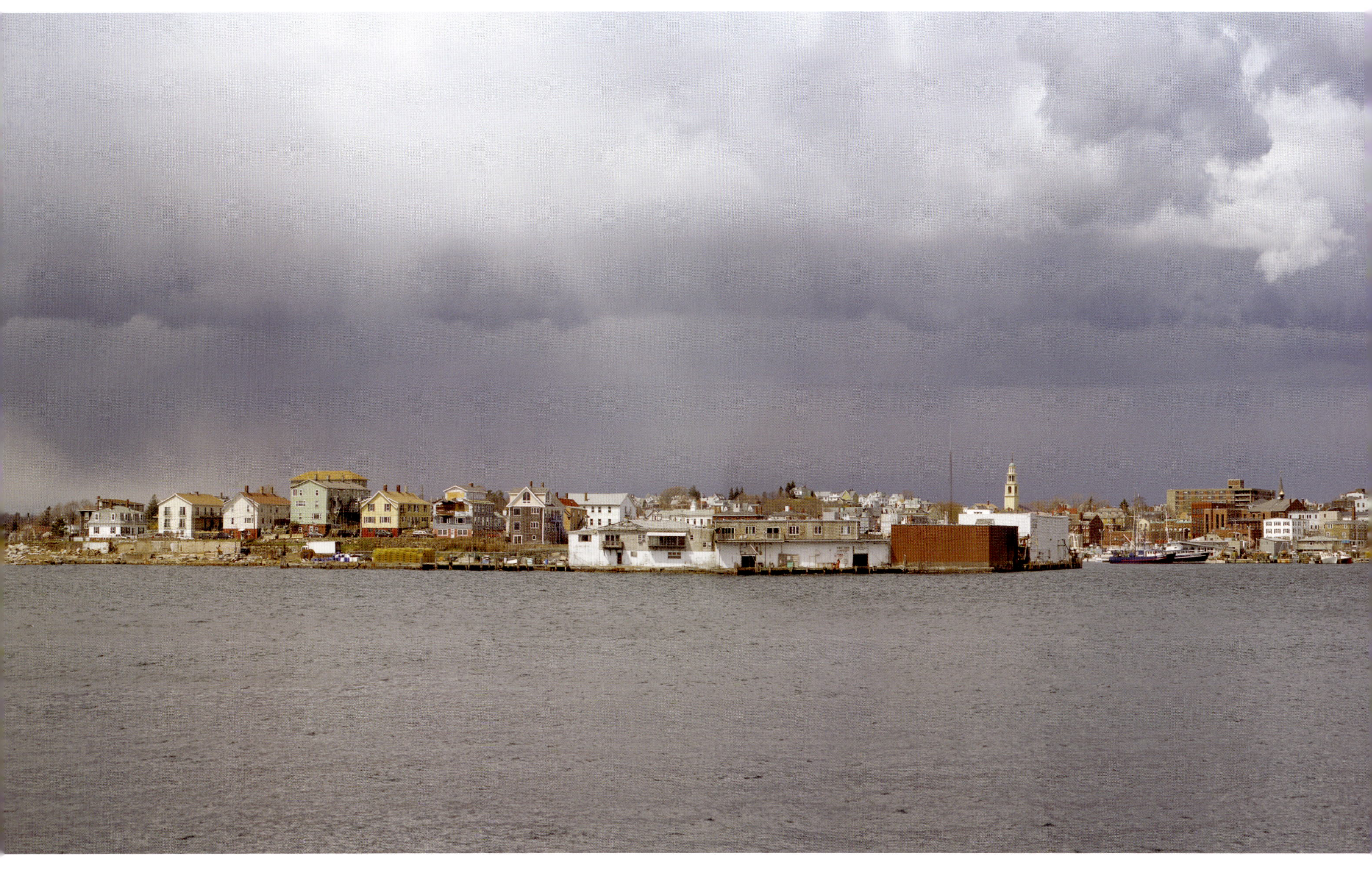

Port of Gloucester

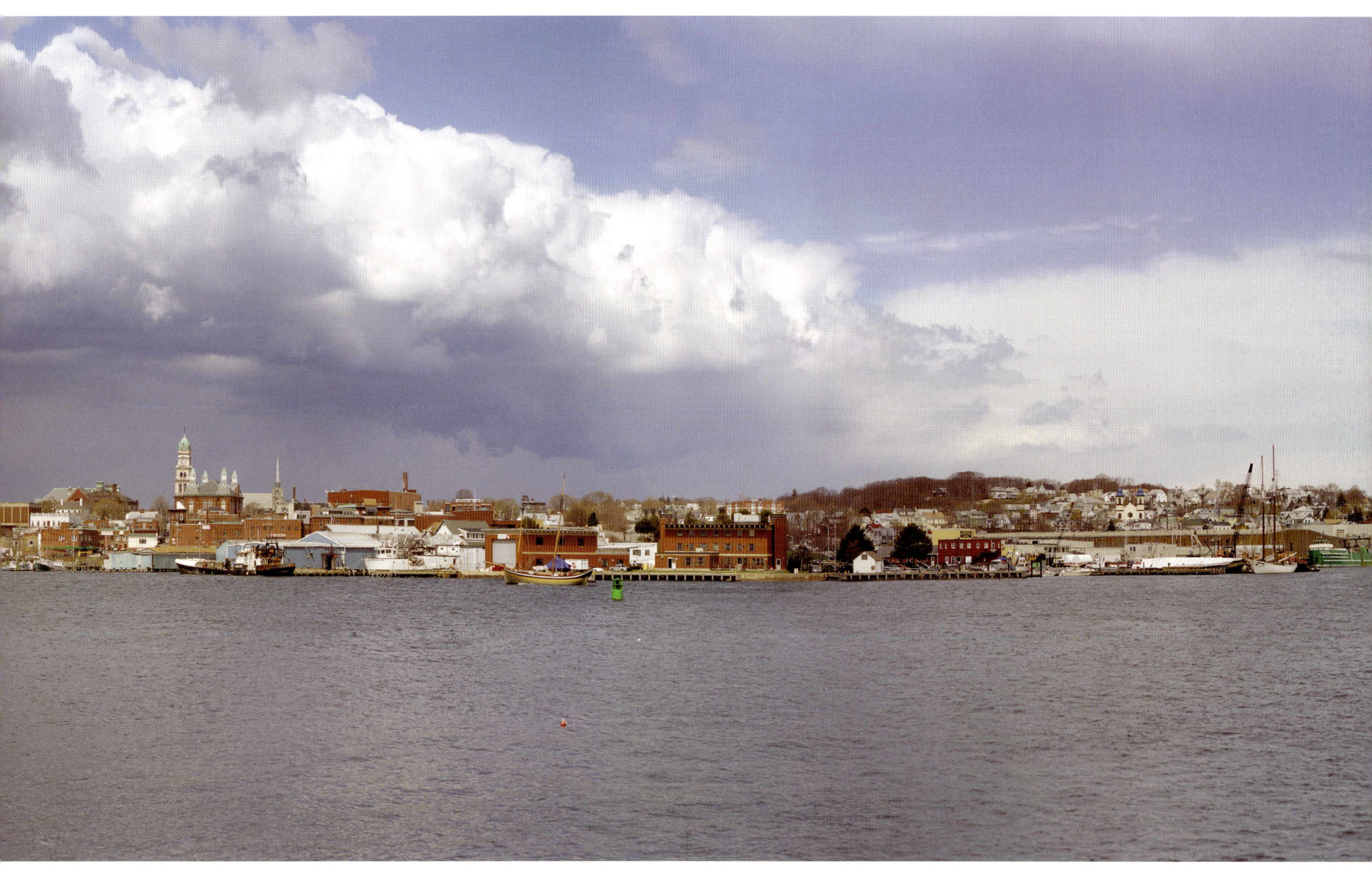

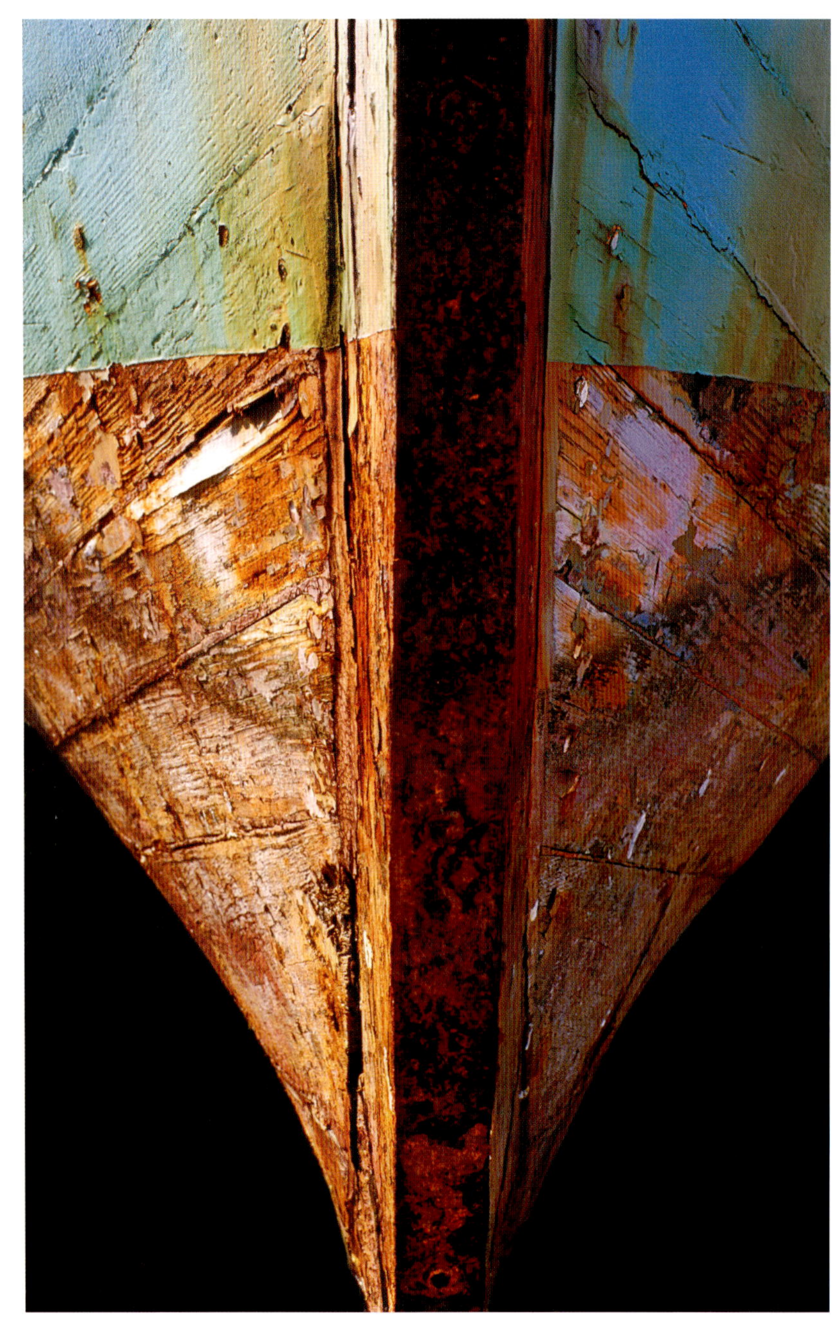

Fisherman's lament: "She was one hull of a boat, I tell ya."

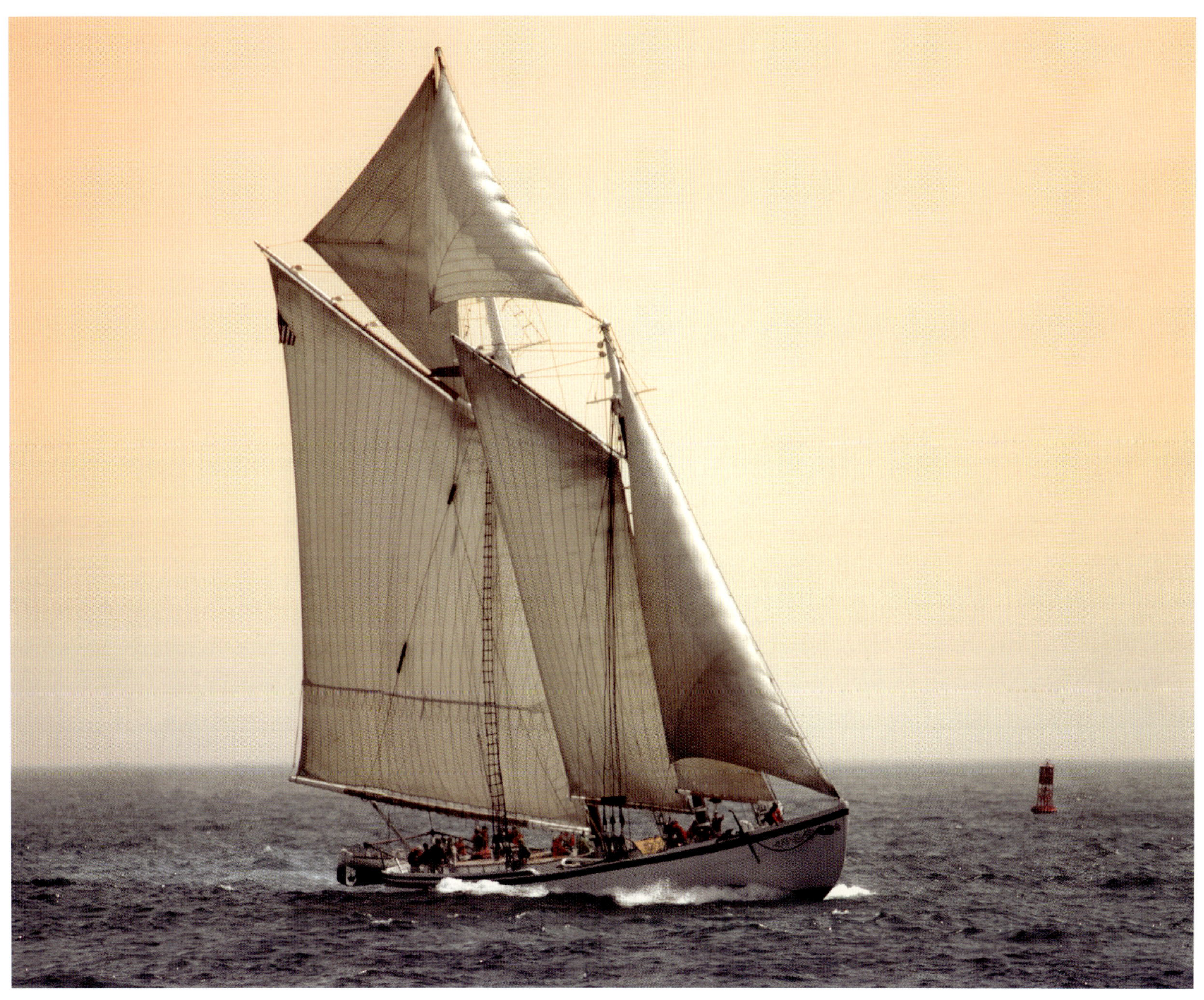

*Adventure,* the last of the "Gloucestermen," a 122-foot fishing schooner built in Essex in 1926. In 1988 she came home to Gloucester and swept the fleet in the Gloucester schooner race. Here she crosses the finish line off Eastern Point with everything flying.

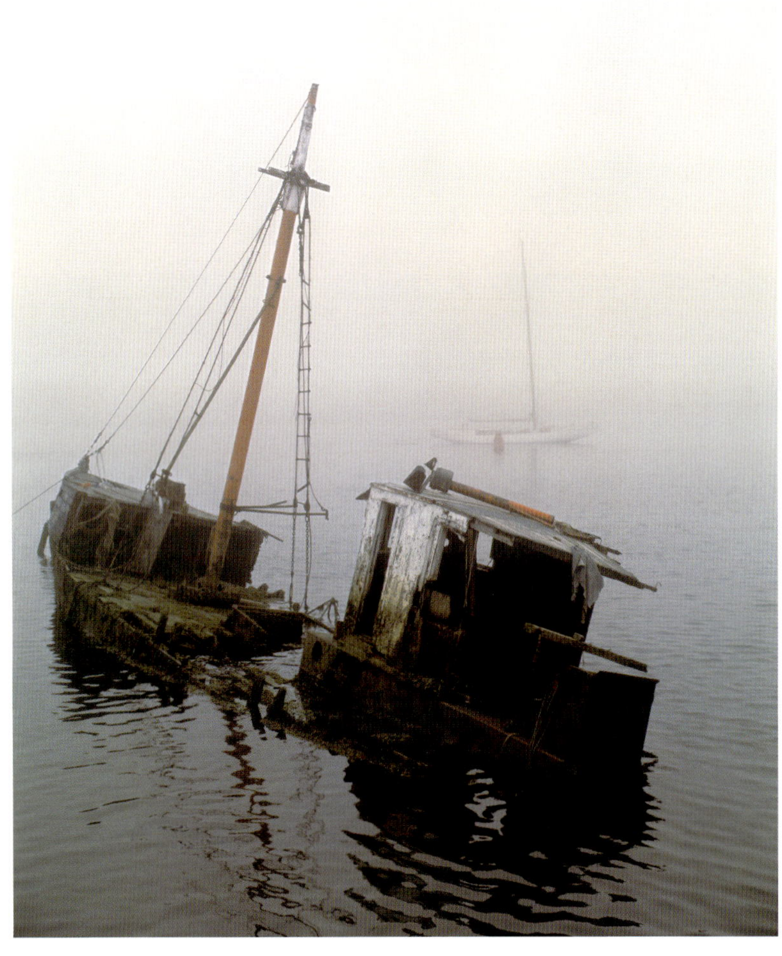

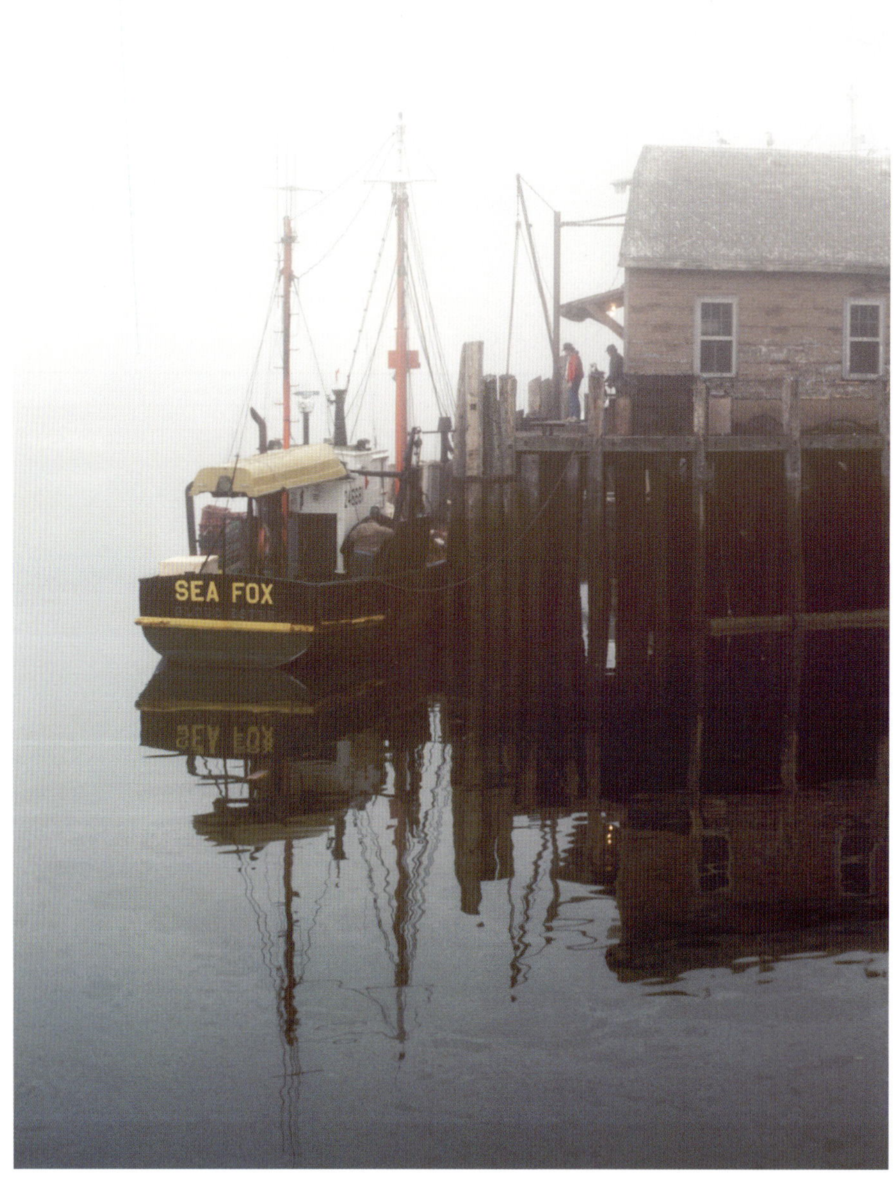


*Above:* Wreck of *Rosalie* off Rocky Neck
*Right: Sea Fox* getting under way after taking on ice.

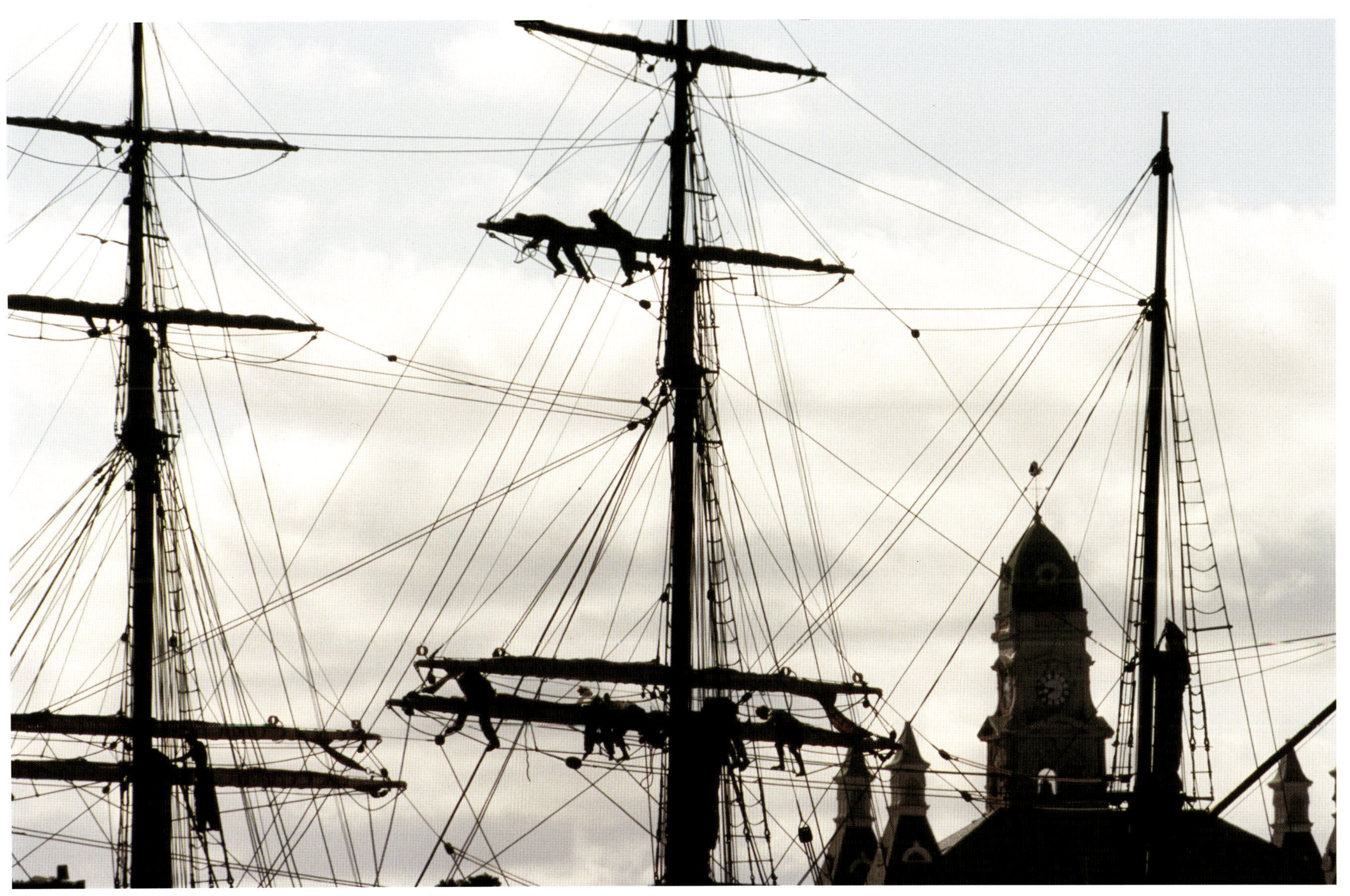

The tall ship *Picton Castle,* with crew on the yardarms

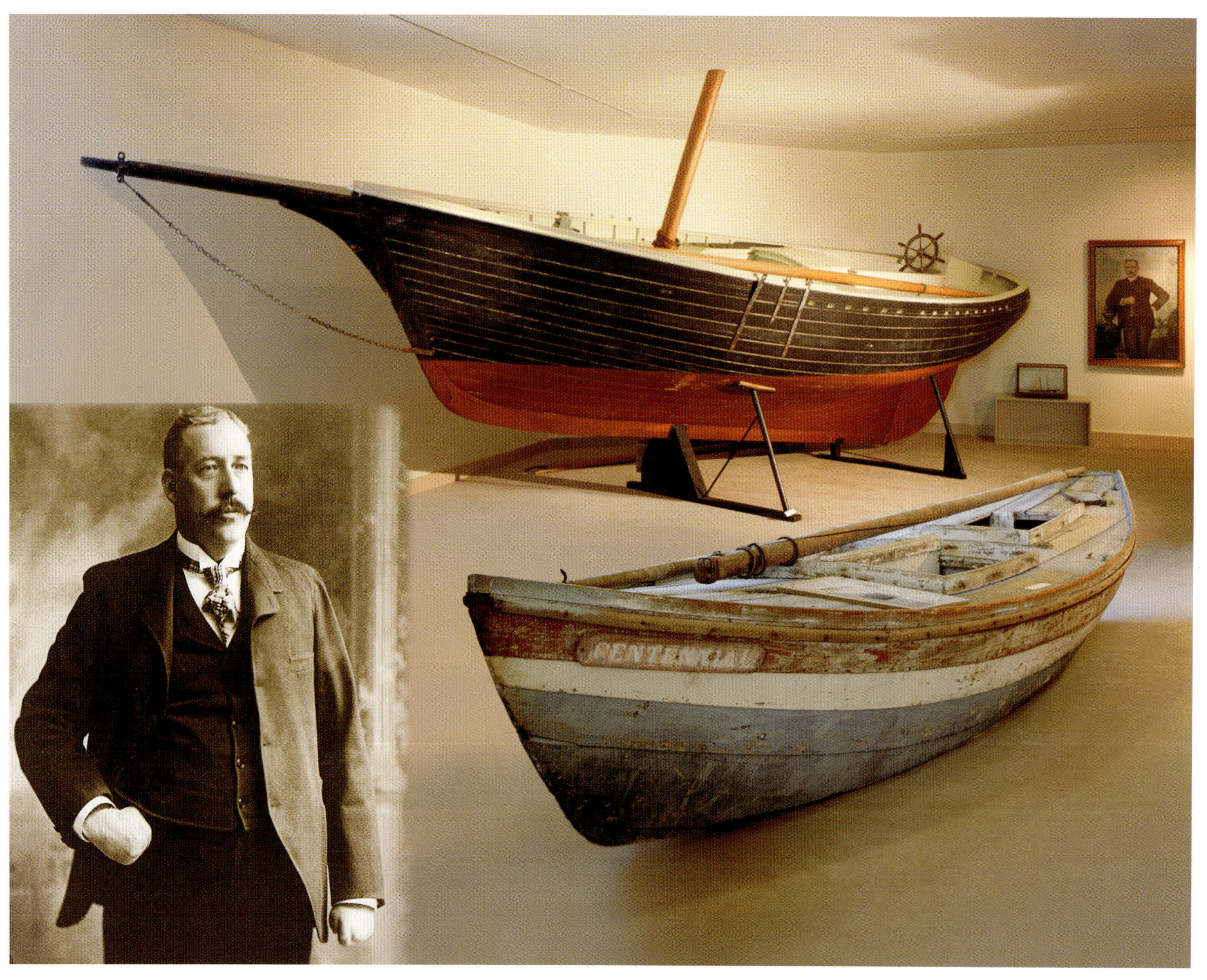


Howard Blackburn, the "hero of Gloucester" who lost his fingers sailing in a blizzard (inset), and his *Great Republic* (larger vessel), Cape Ann Historical Museum. Despite his loss of fingers, Blackburn sailed the Atlantic solo twice, once (in 1901) in the *Great Republic*. In 1876, Gloucester schooner captain Alfred Johnson had been the first person to sail across the Atlantic alone, in the twenty-foot dory *Centennial* (foreground).

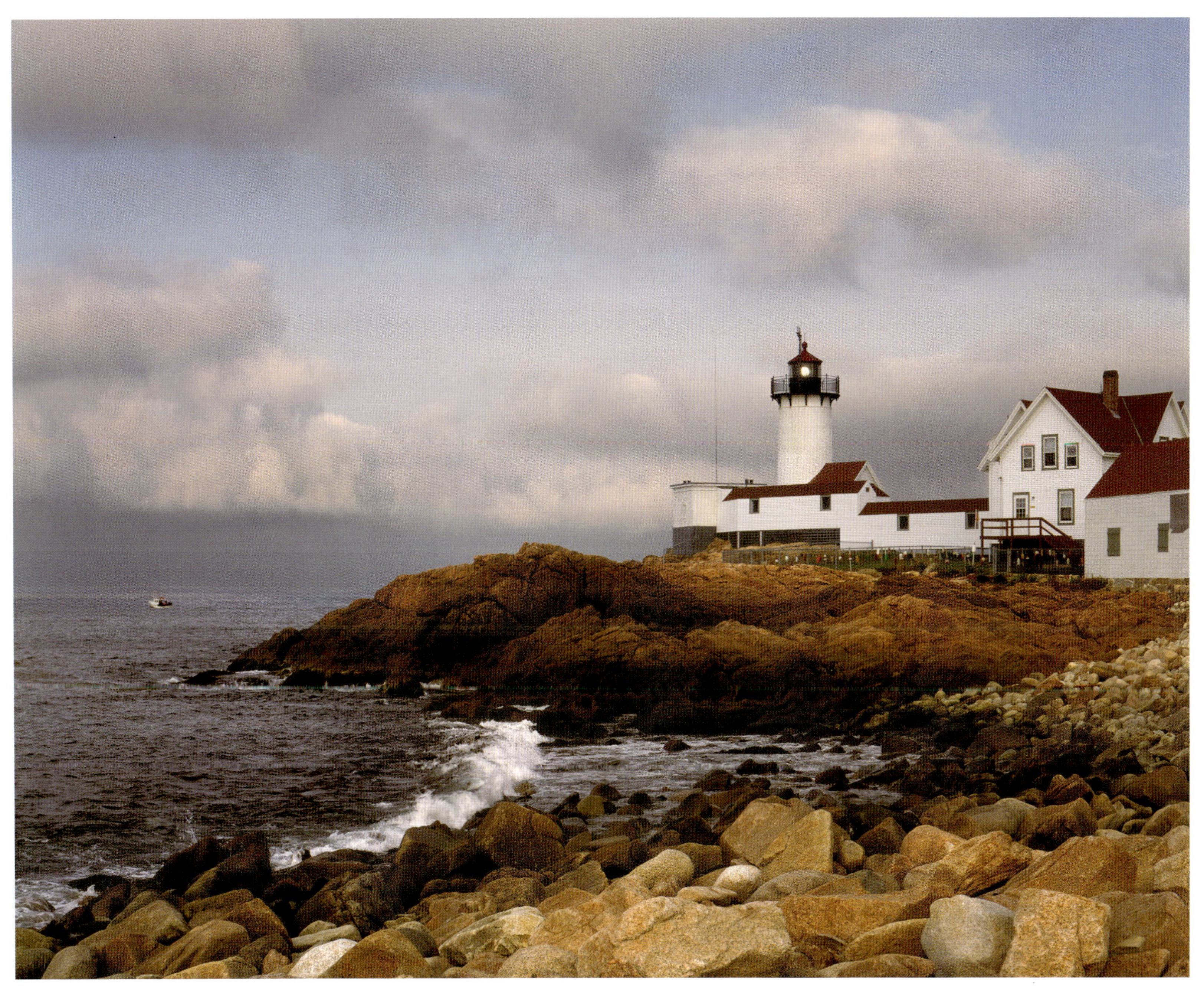

Eastern Point Light

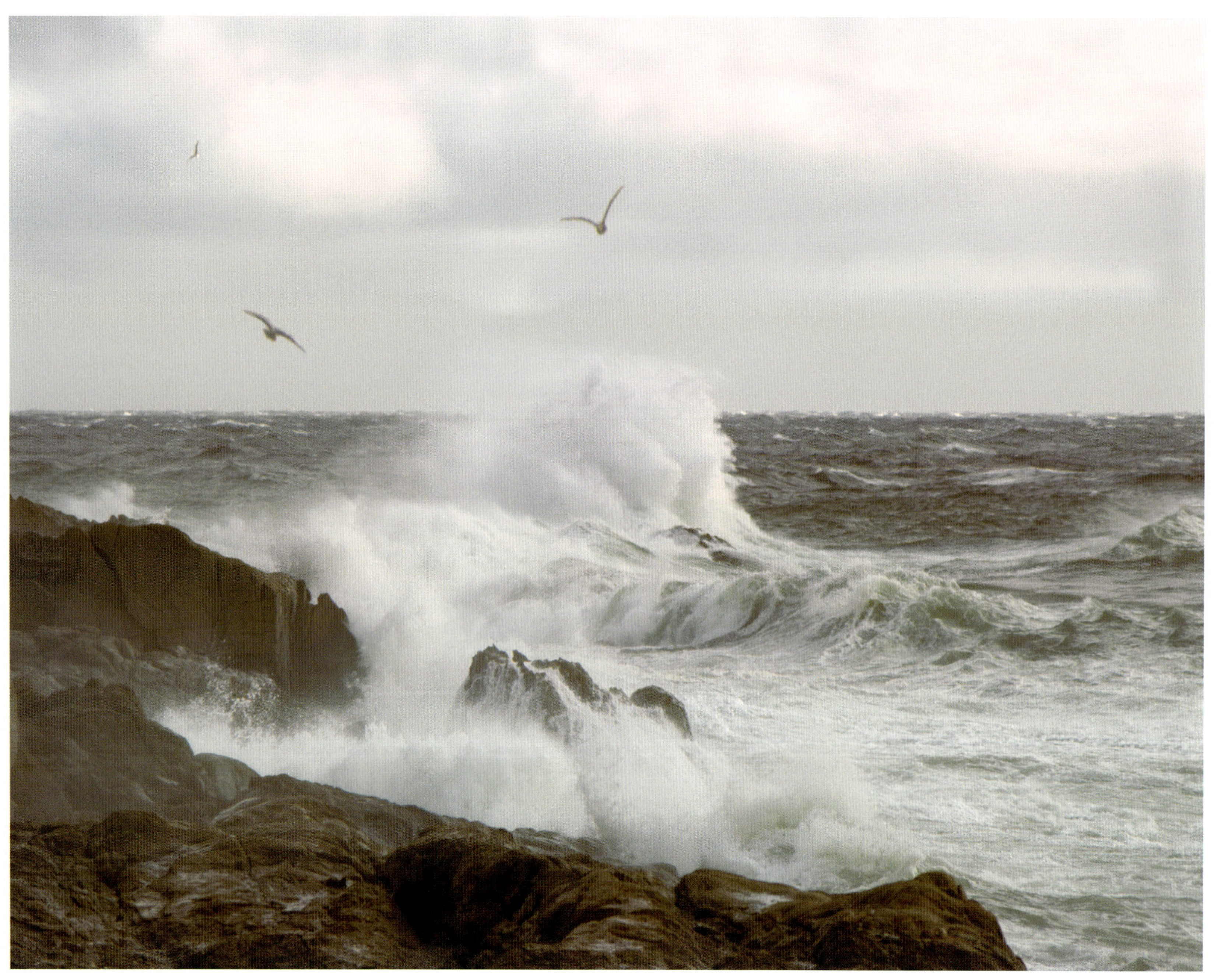

Winter gale, Atlantic Road

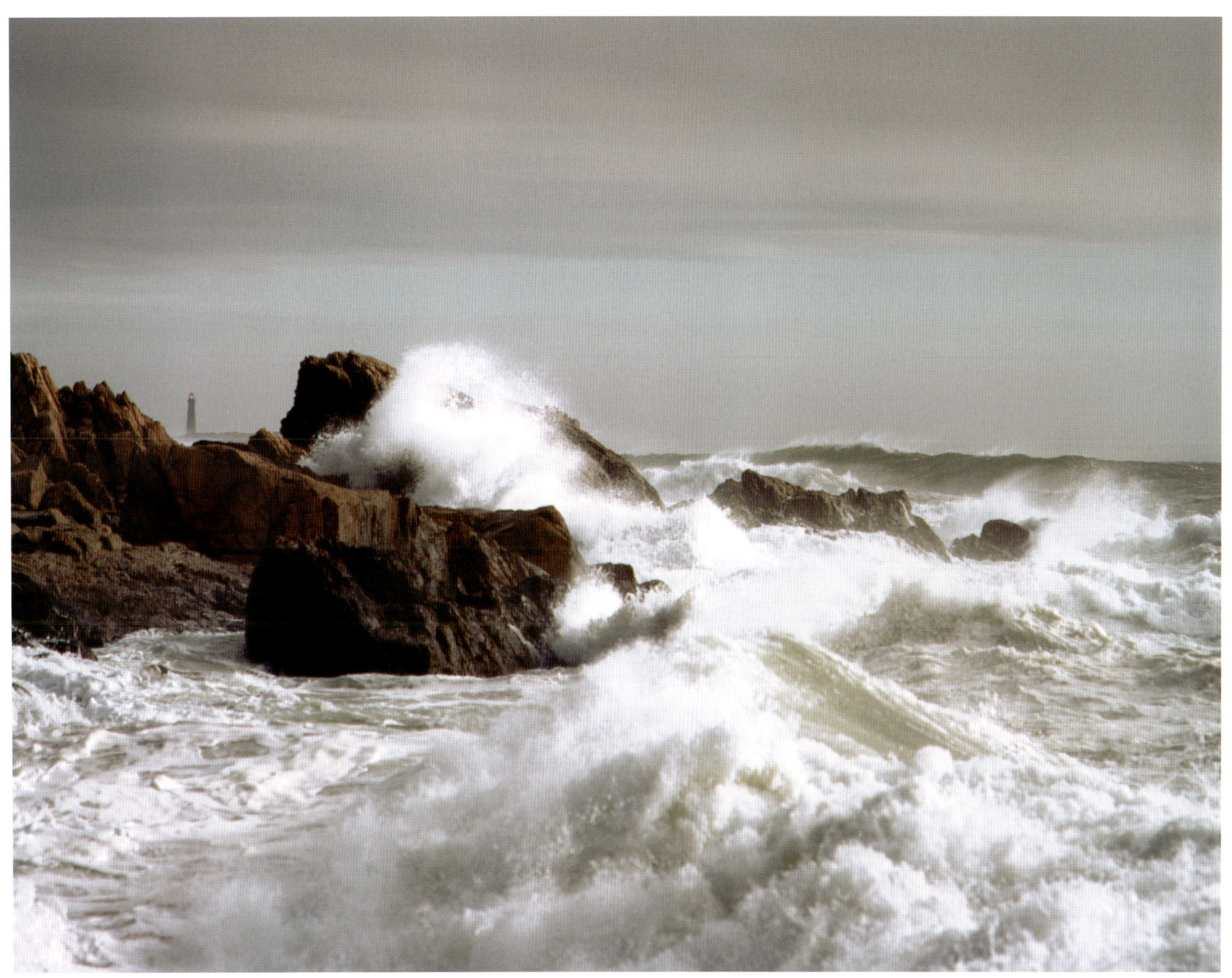

Atlantic gale, Bass Rocks

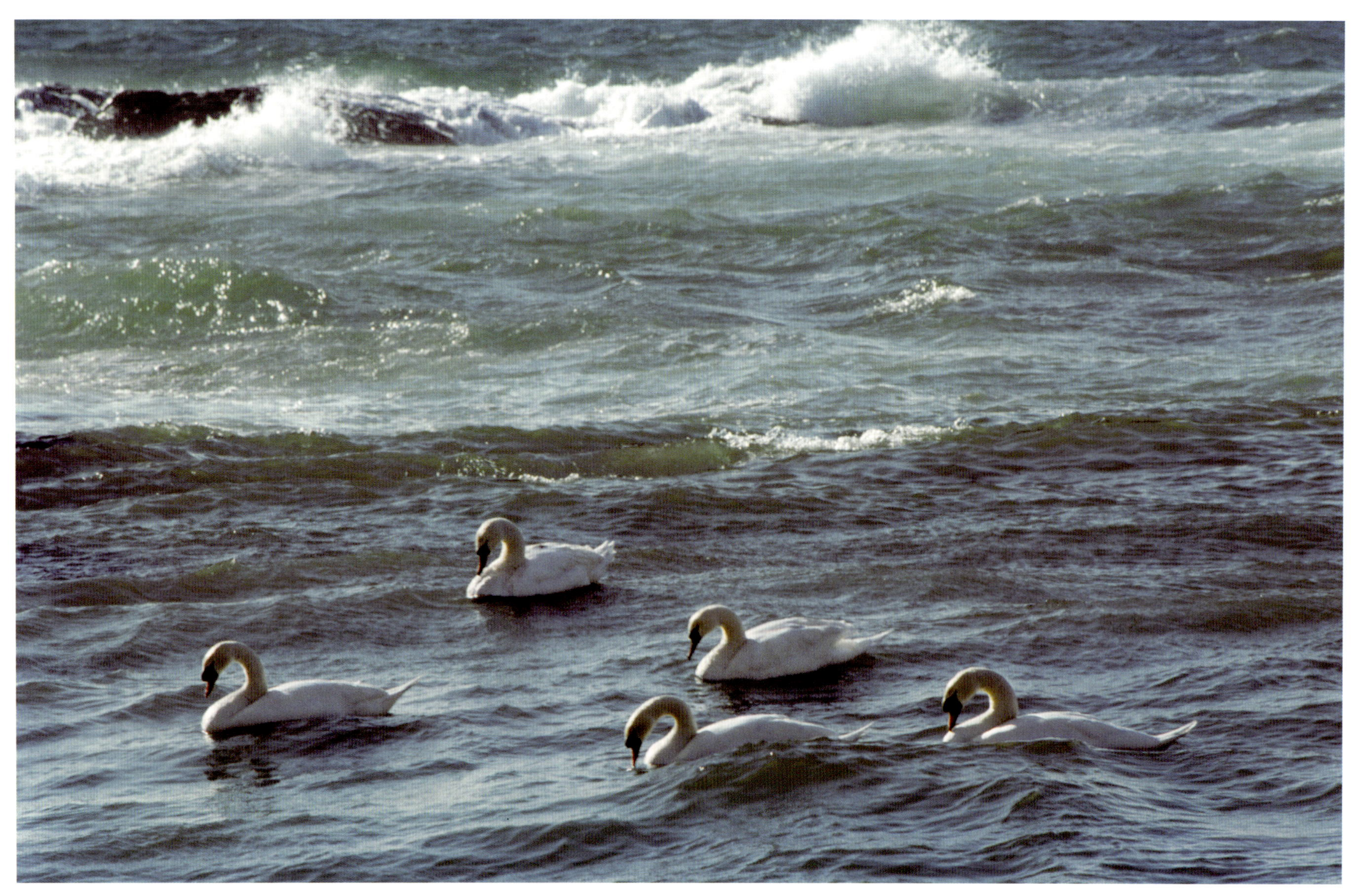

Mute swans, swimming heads-down in the lee of a storm, Wonson Cove

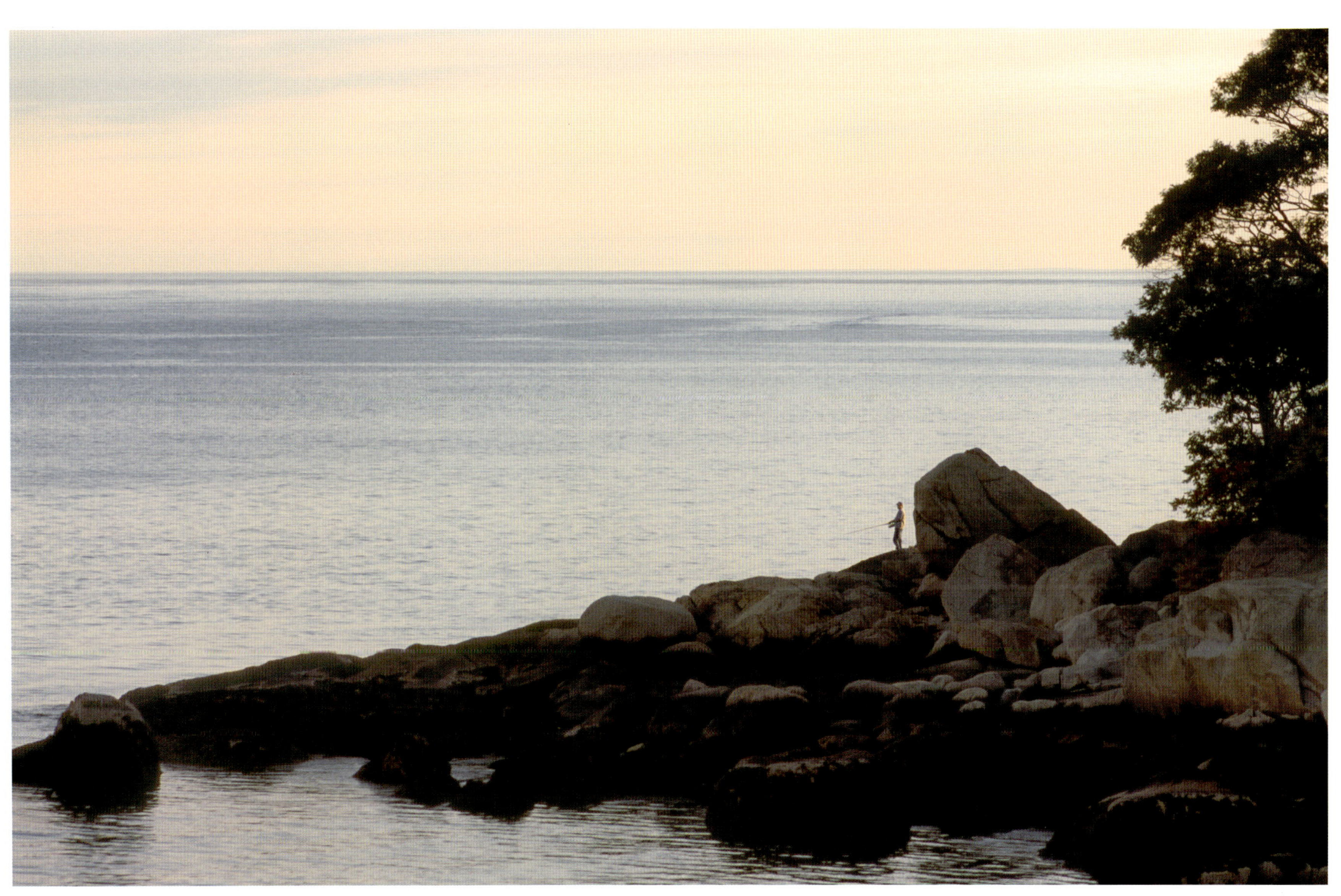

Alone but not lonely: fishing at Stage Fort Park

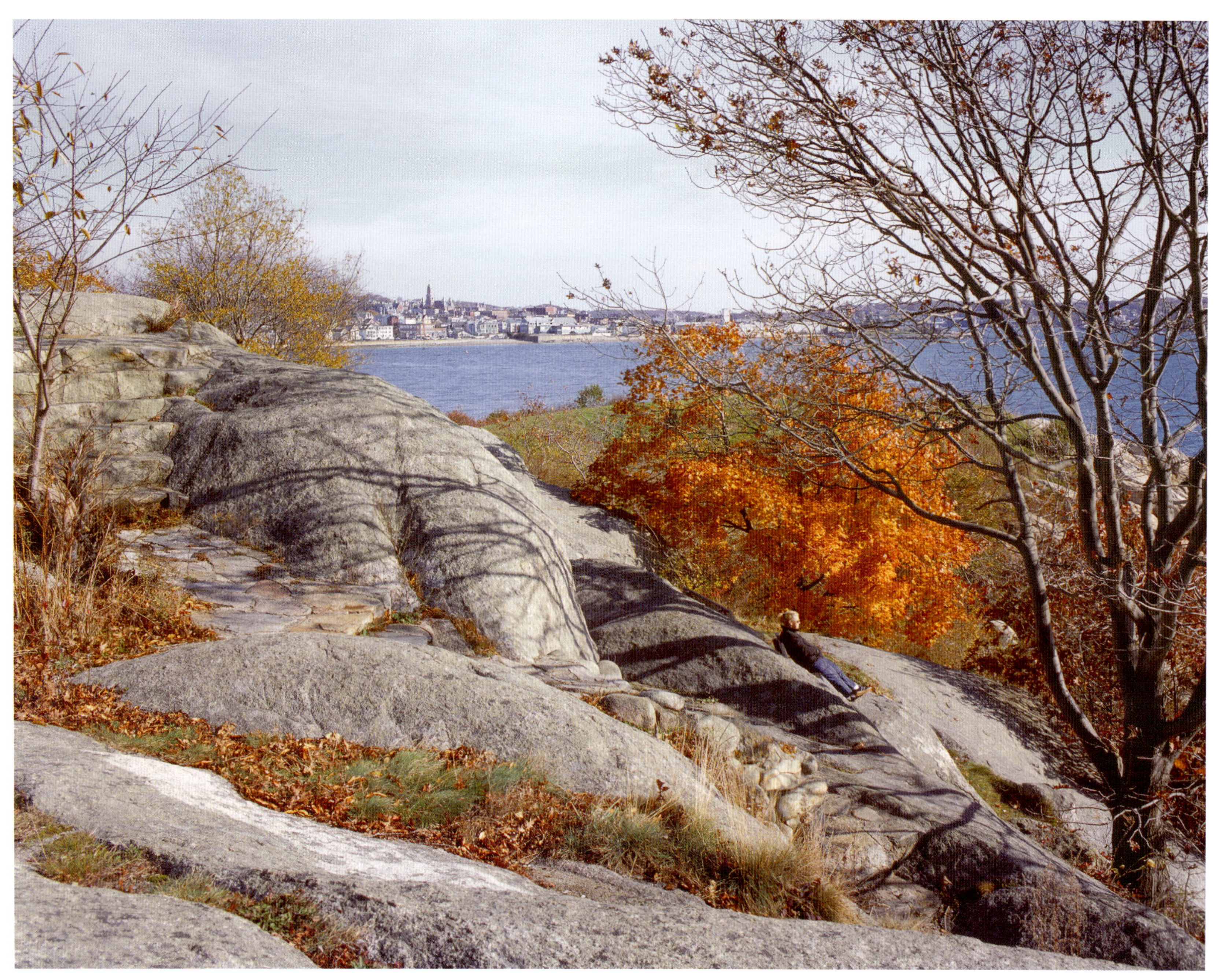

Warm autumn sun and a view by the sea, Stage Fort Park

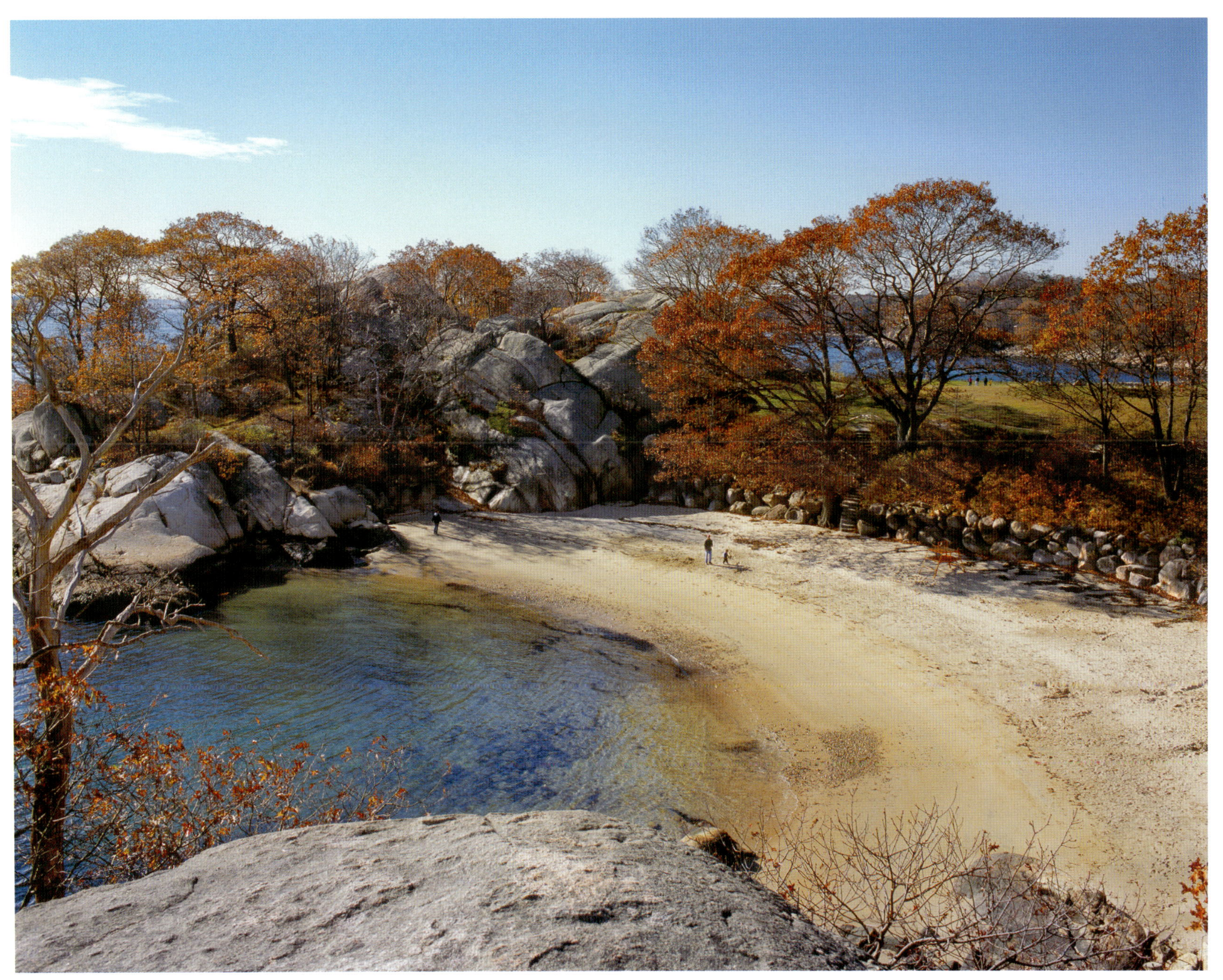

Half Moon Beach, Stage Fort Park

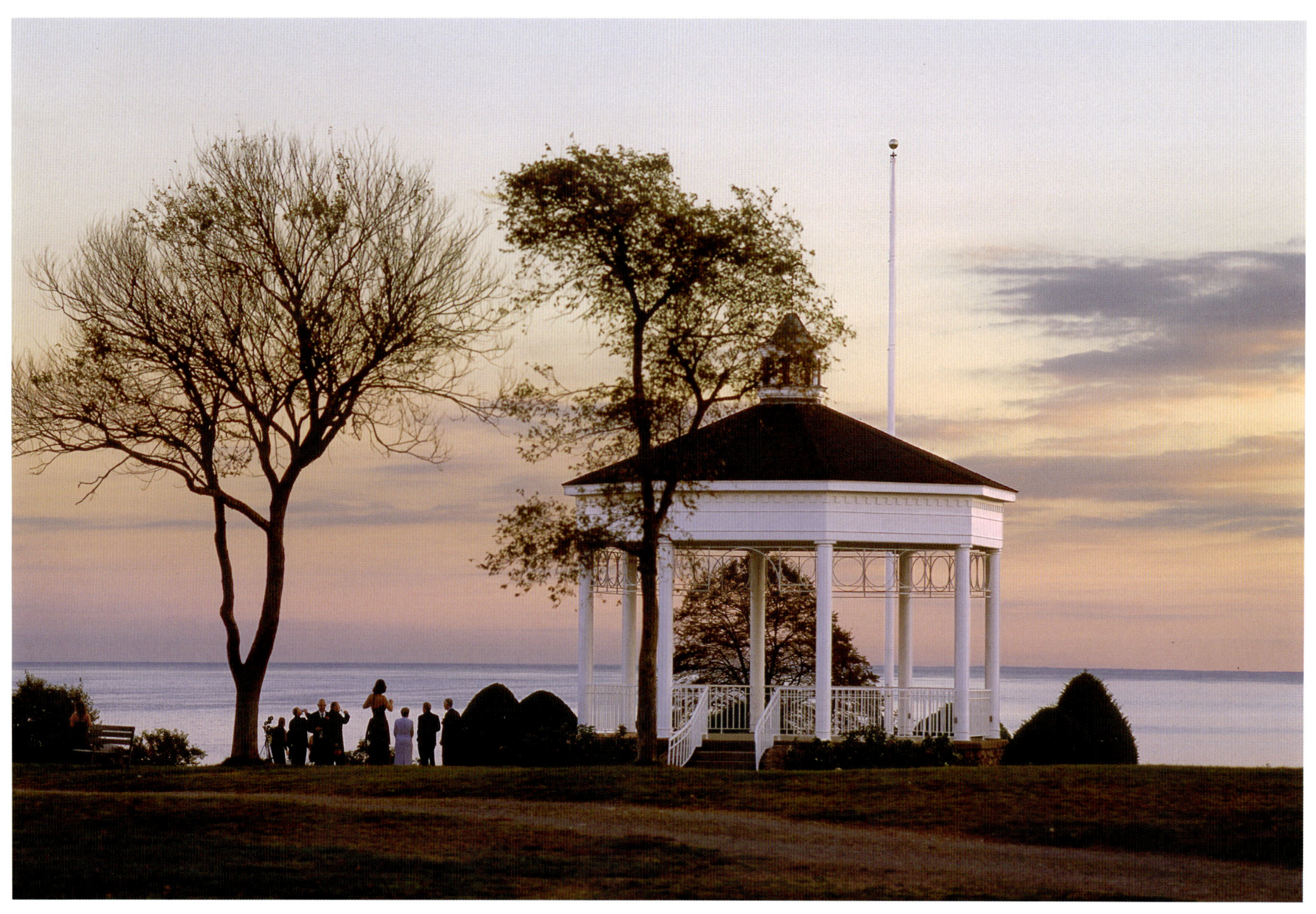

Wedding party, Stage Fort Park

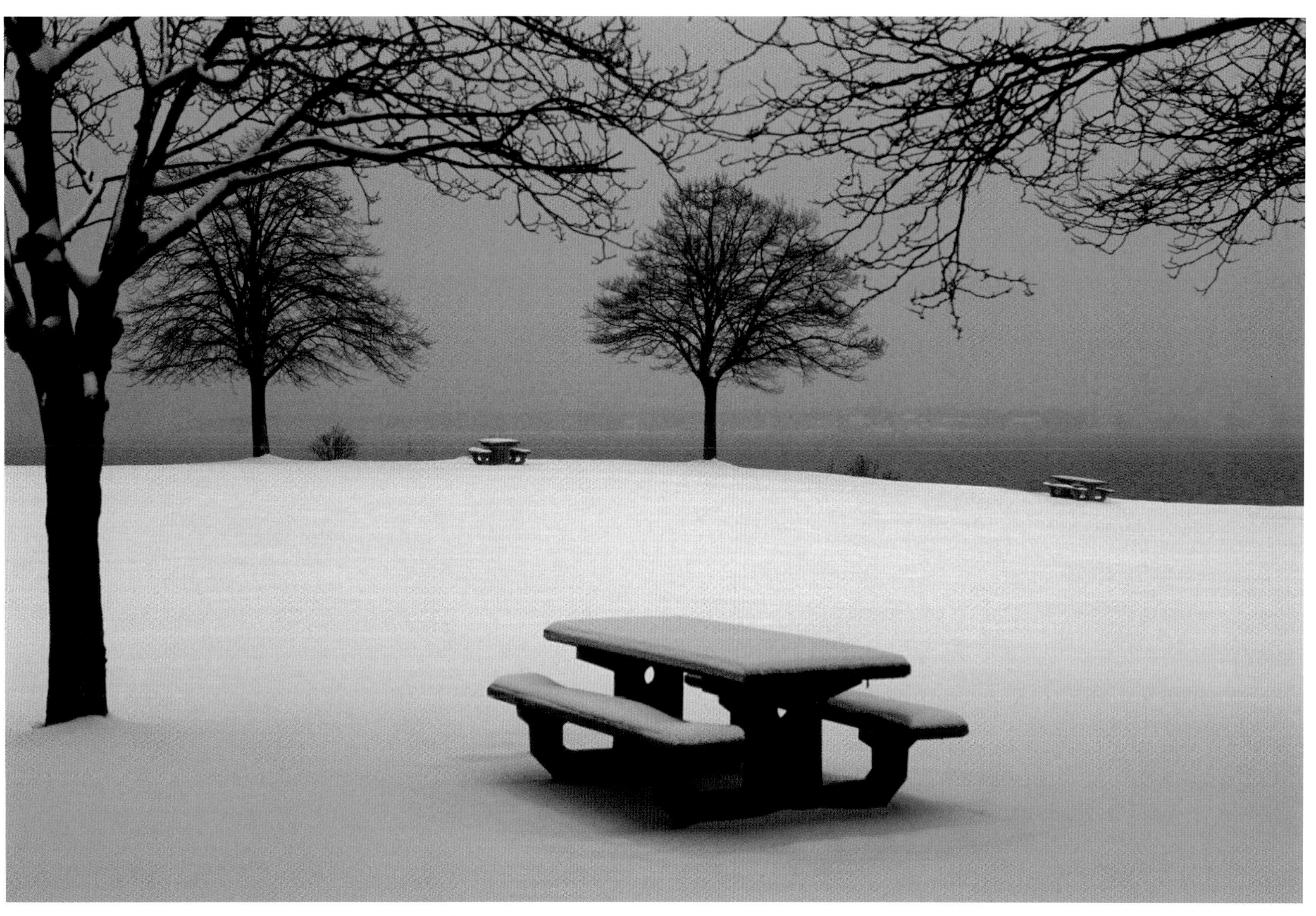

Dormant in winter, I listen to the silence.
People laughing, children playing
warm smoky air currents
sizzling hot dogs and hamburgers.
All faint sounds of summer past
at Stage Fort Park.

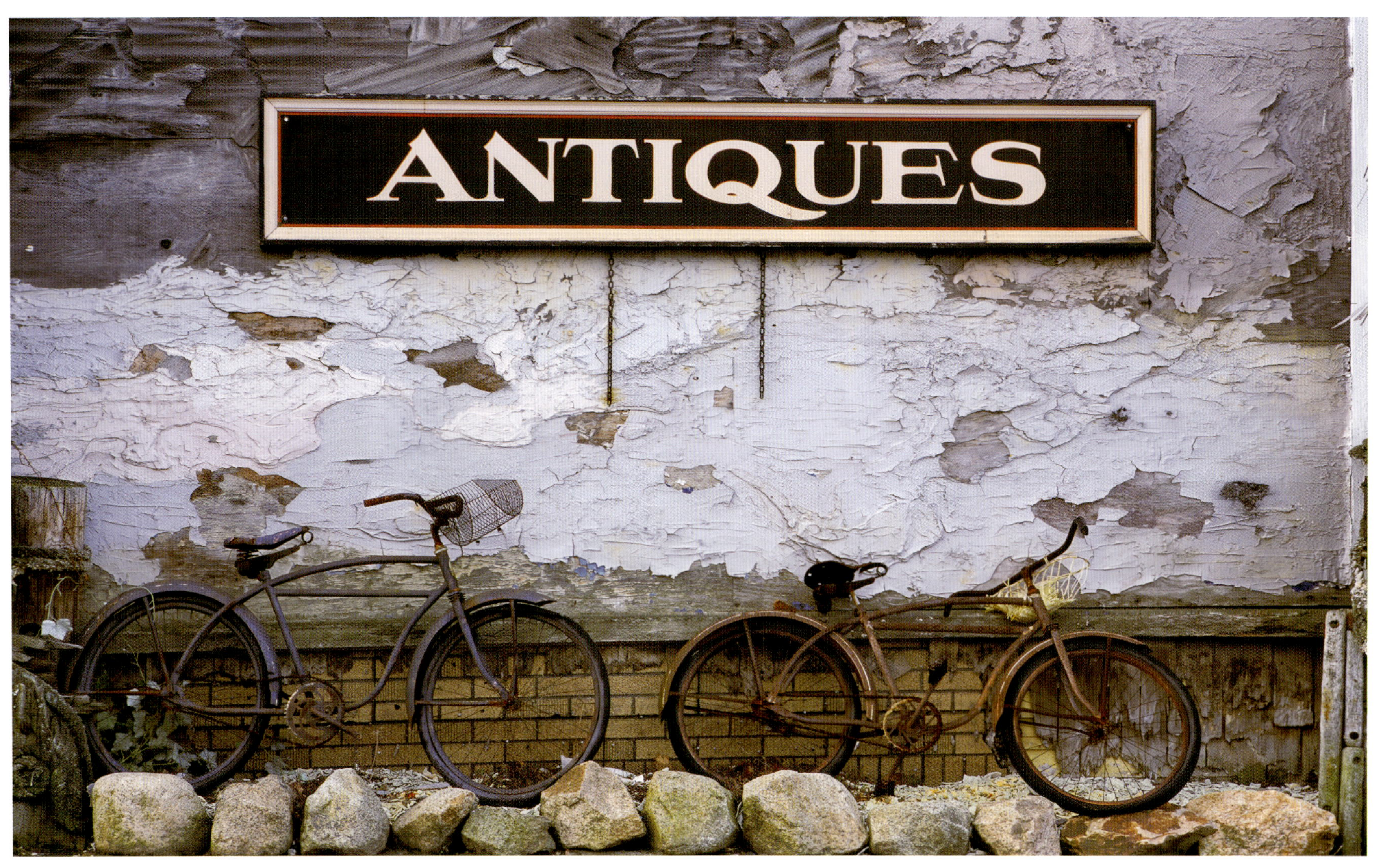


Antique shop, Magnolia

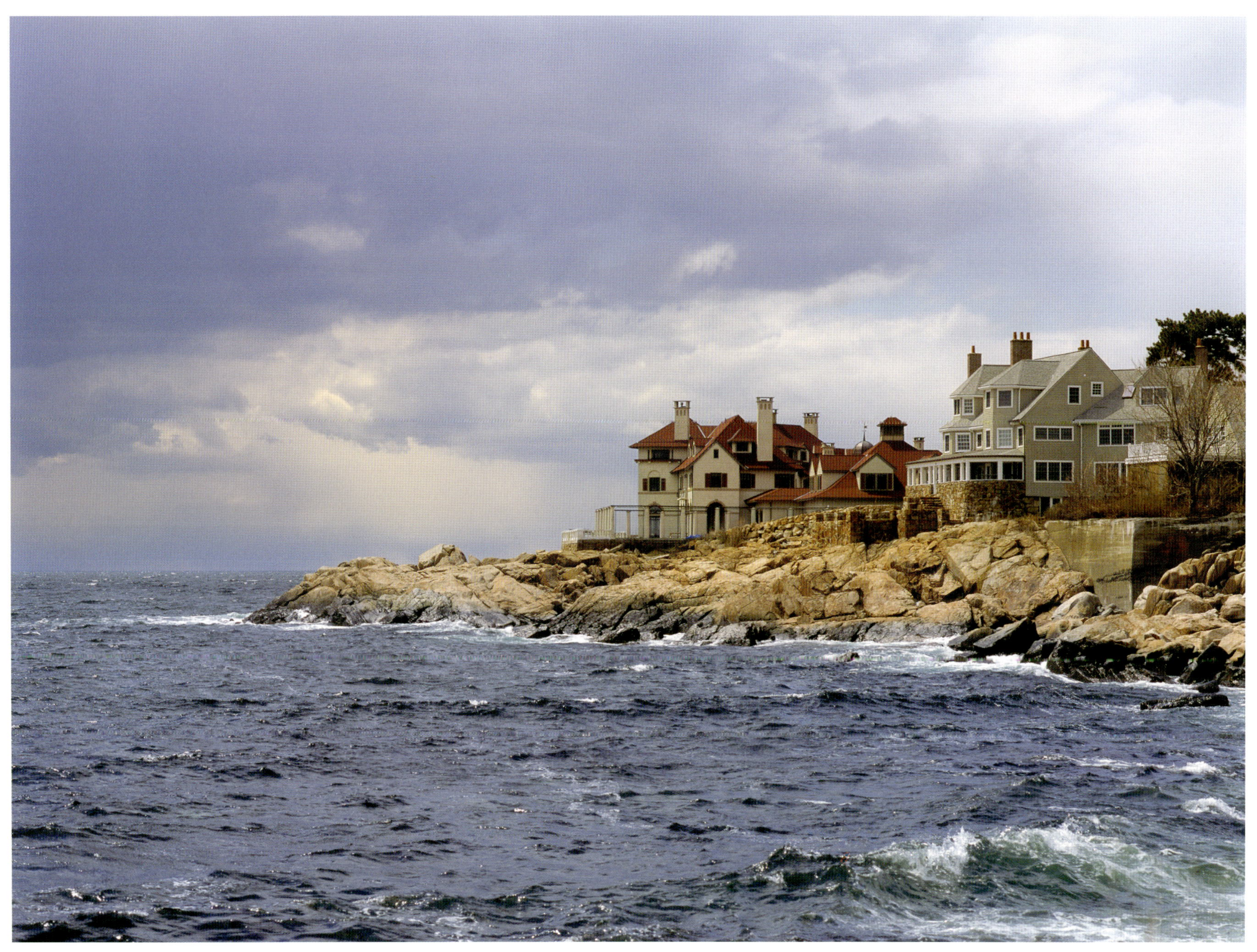

Mansions on Shore Cliff, Magnolia

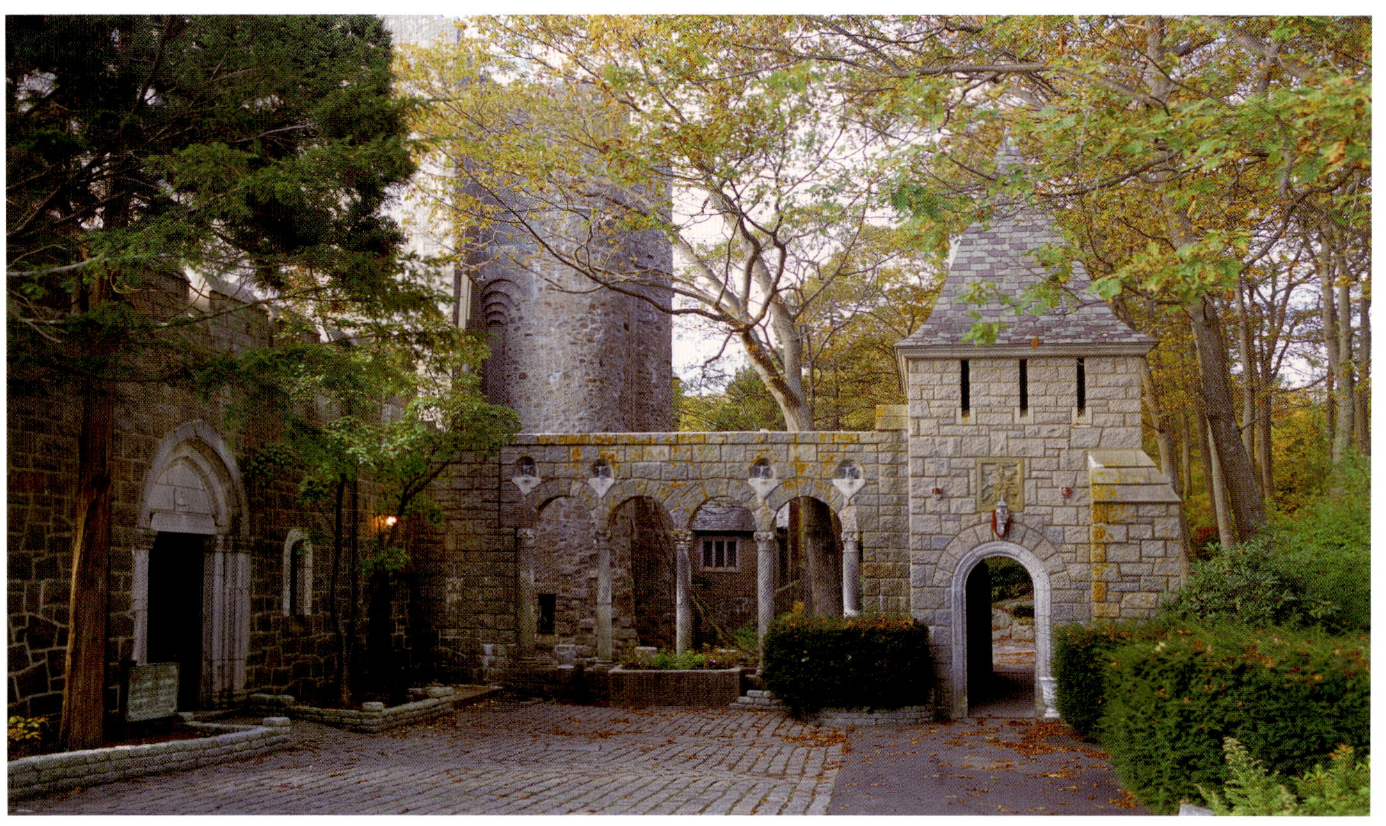

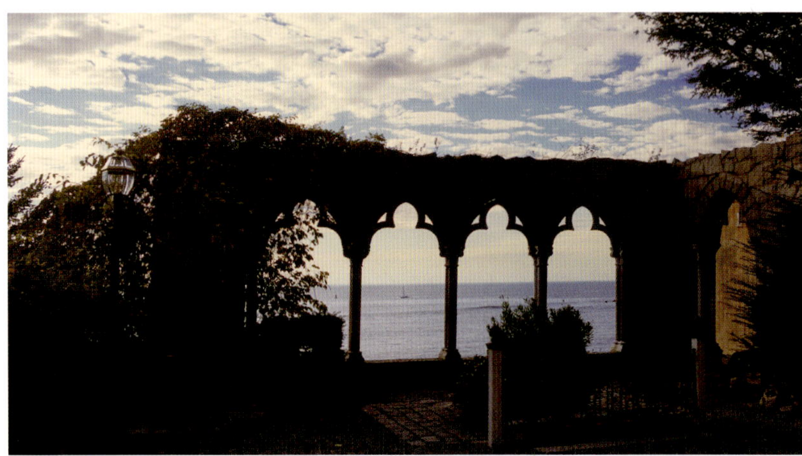

Hammond Castle Museum, built in the 1920s by the inventor John Hays Hammond as a home and a showcase for his collection of artifacts

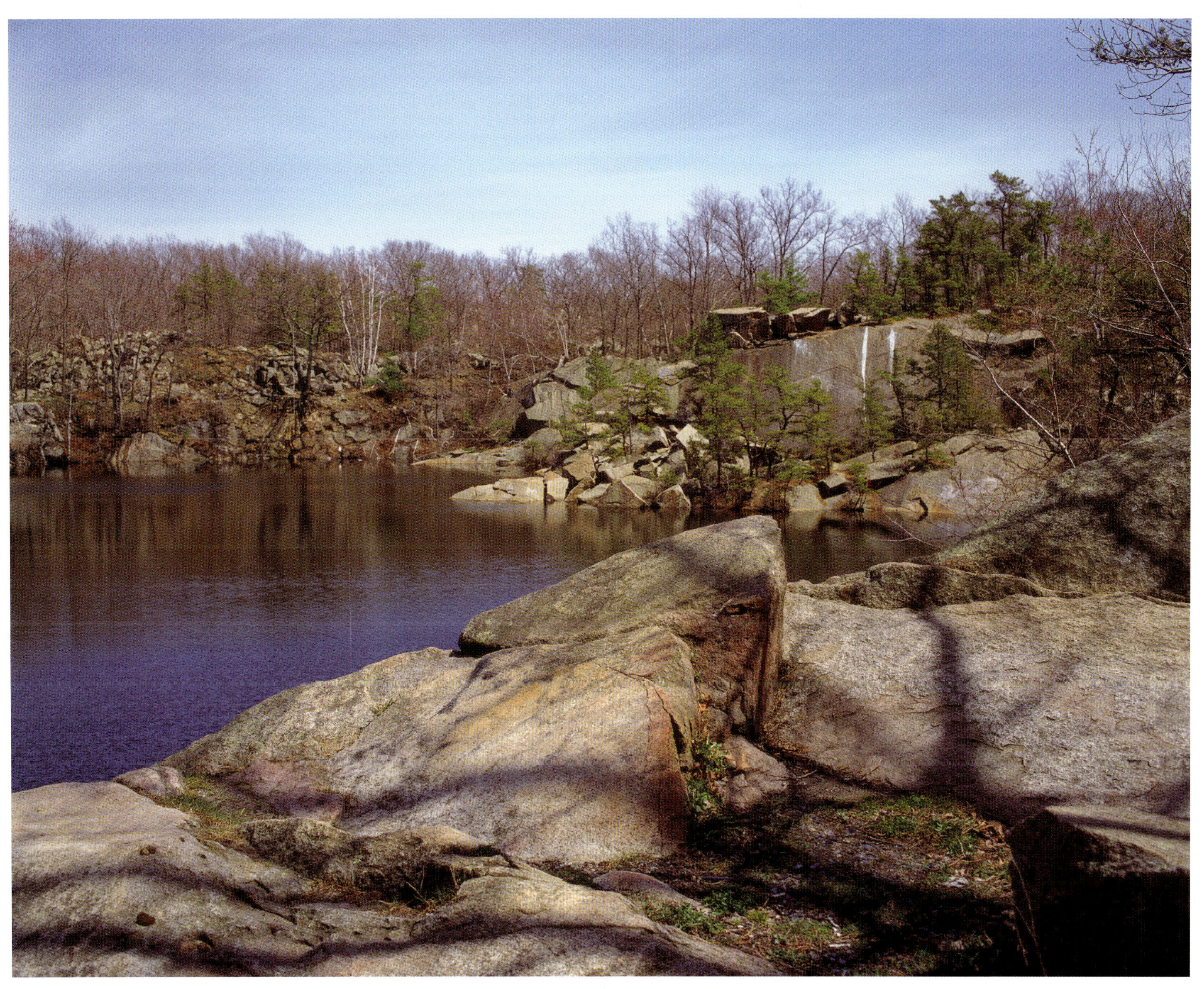

One of Dogtown Common's many quarries and trails

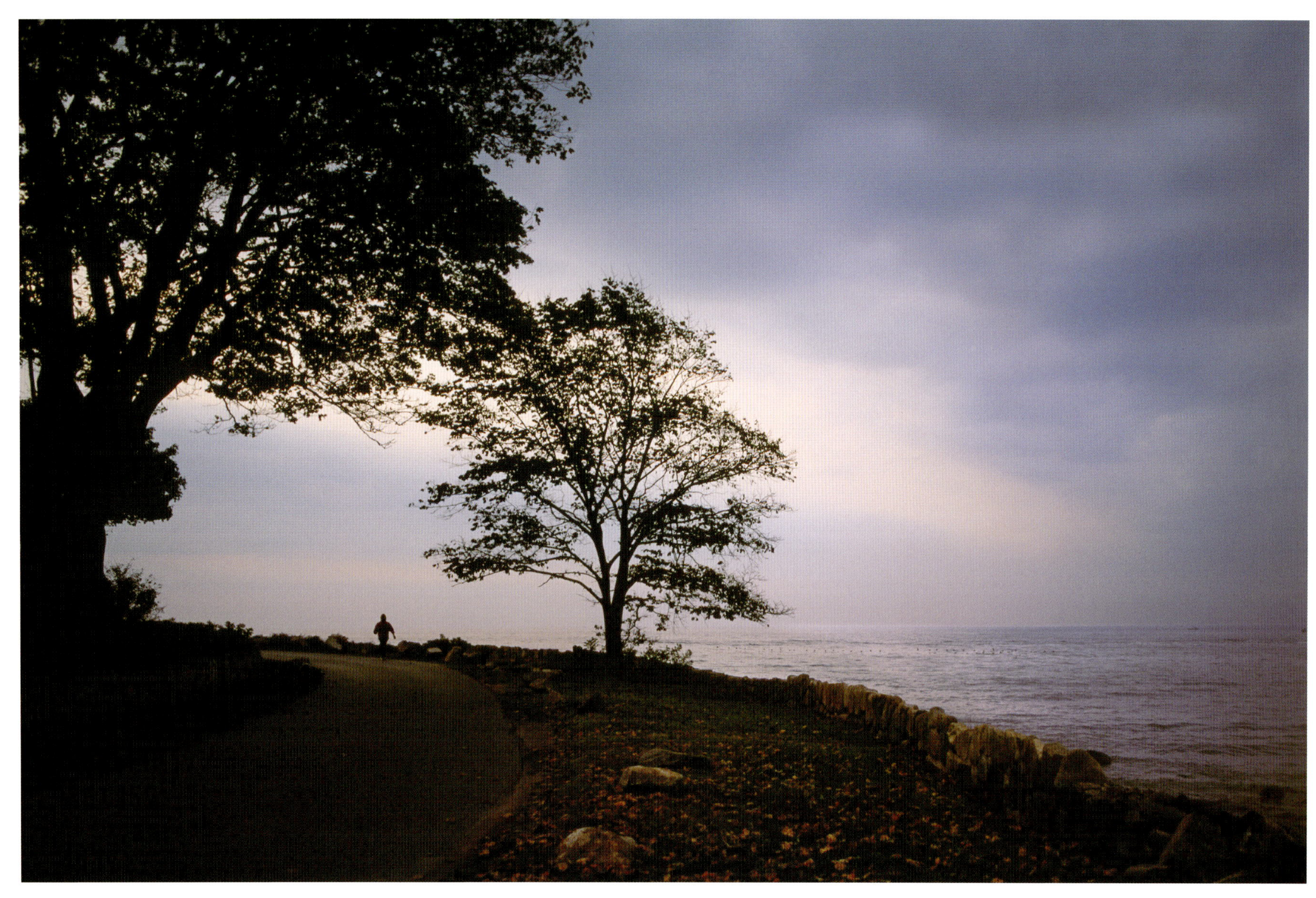

Walking around Shore Road to Hesperus Avenue, Magnolia

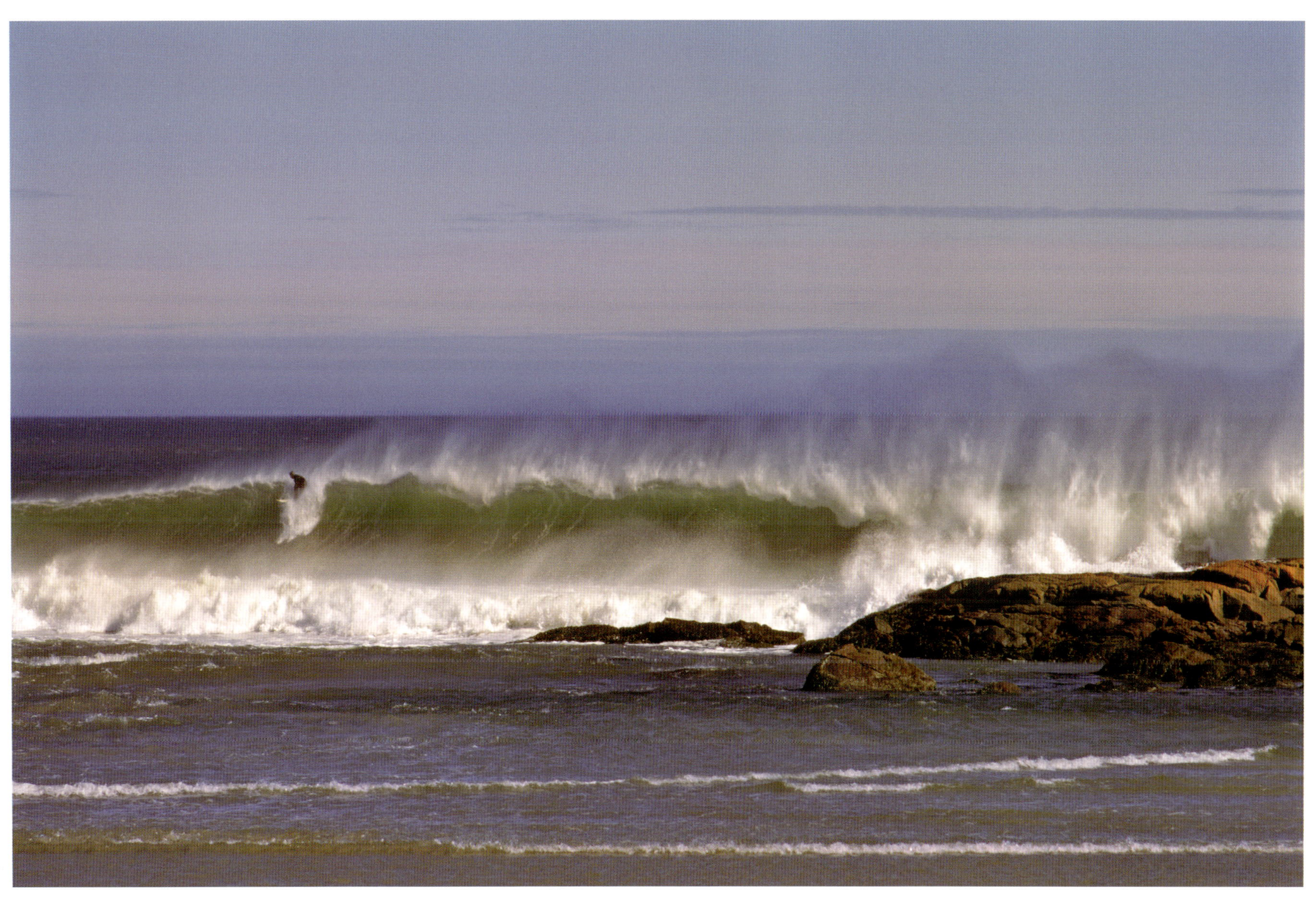

Lone February surfer, Good Harbor Beach

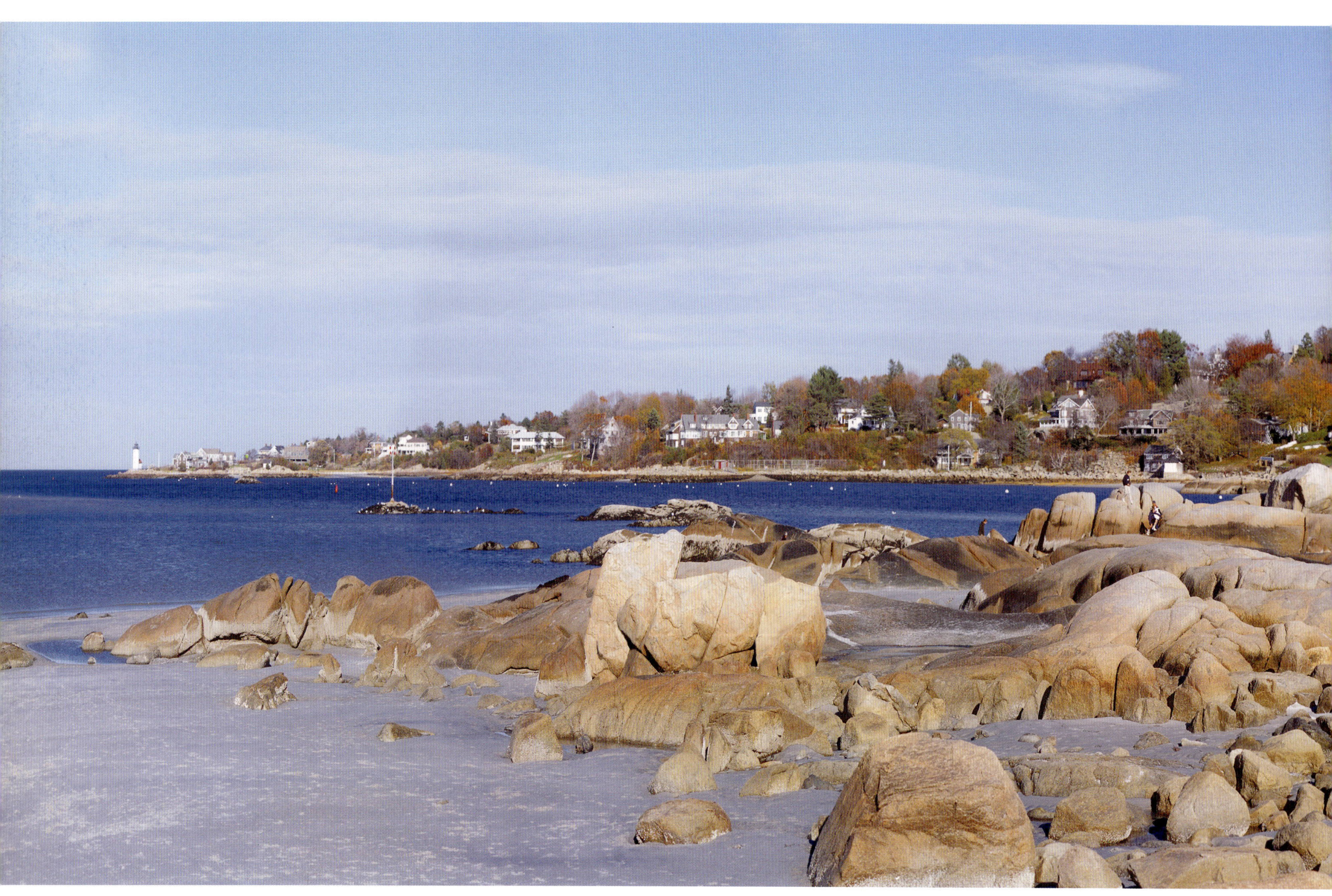

The weathered smooth rocks and fine white sand of Wingaersheek Beach, along the Annisquam River

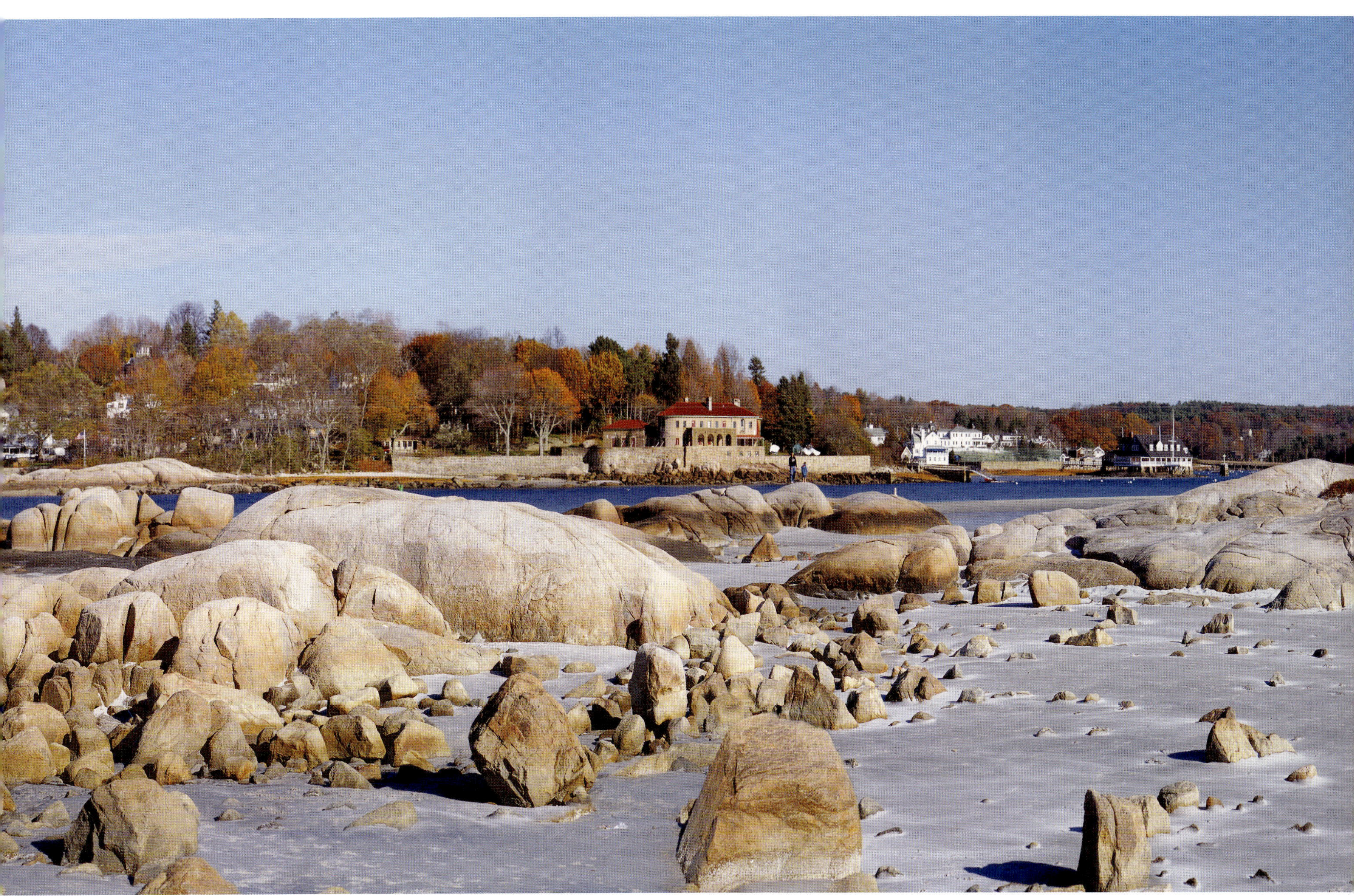

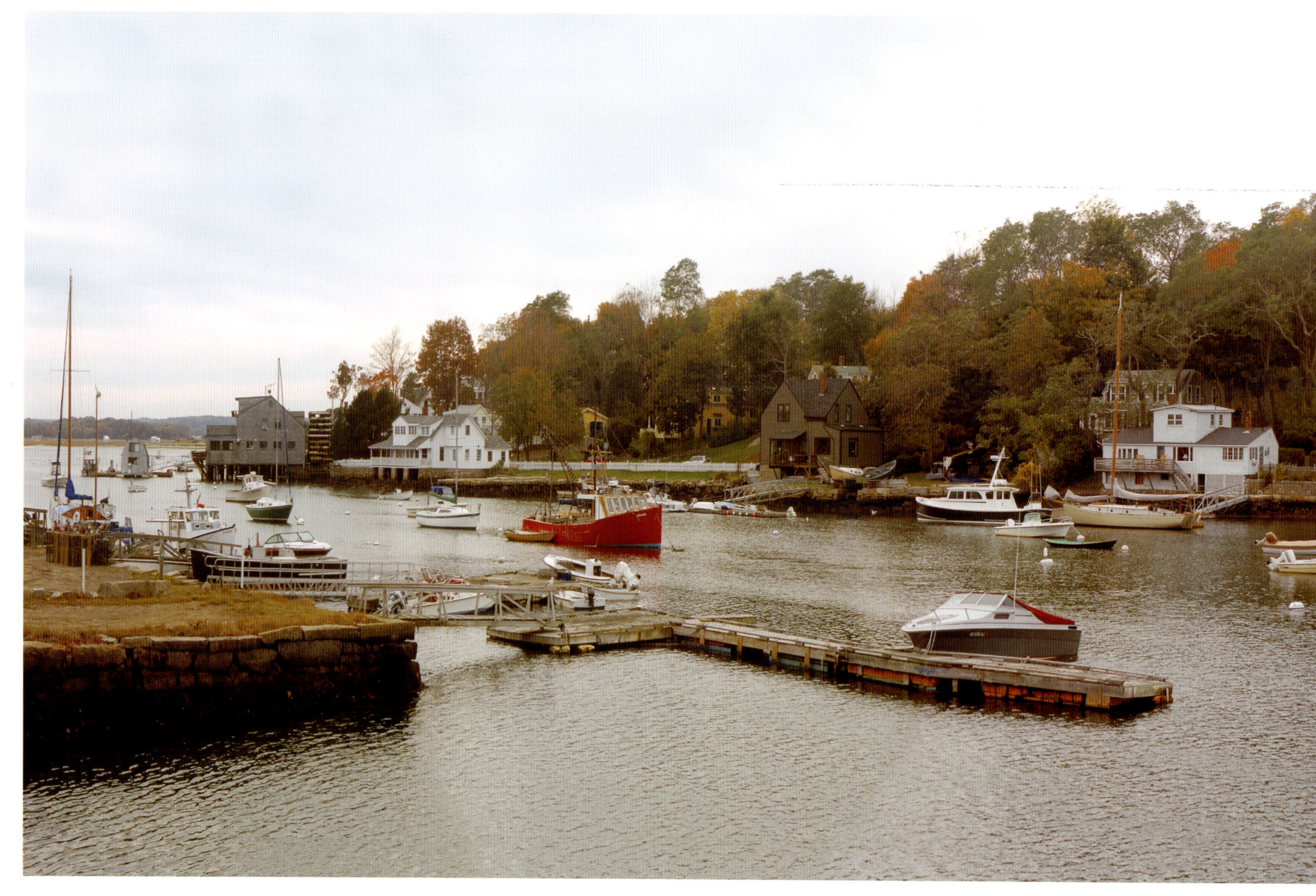

Annisquam Harbor

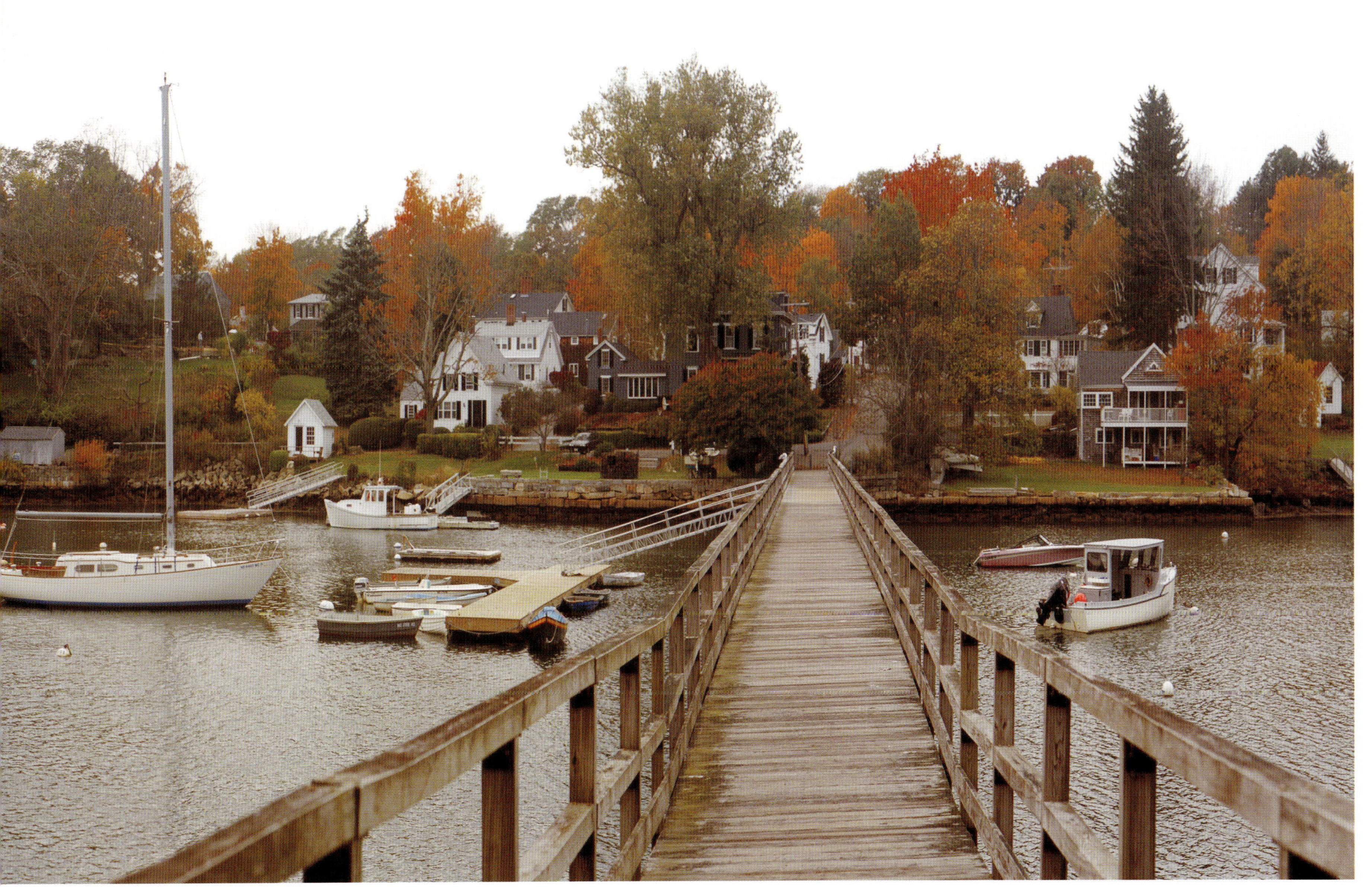

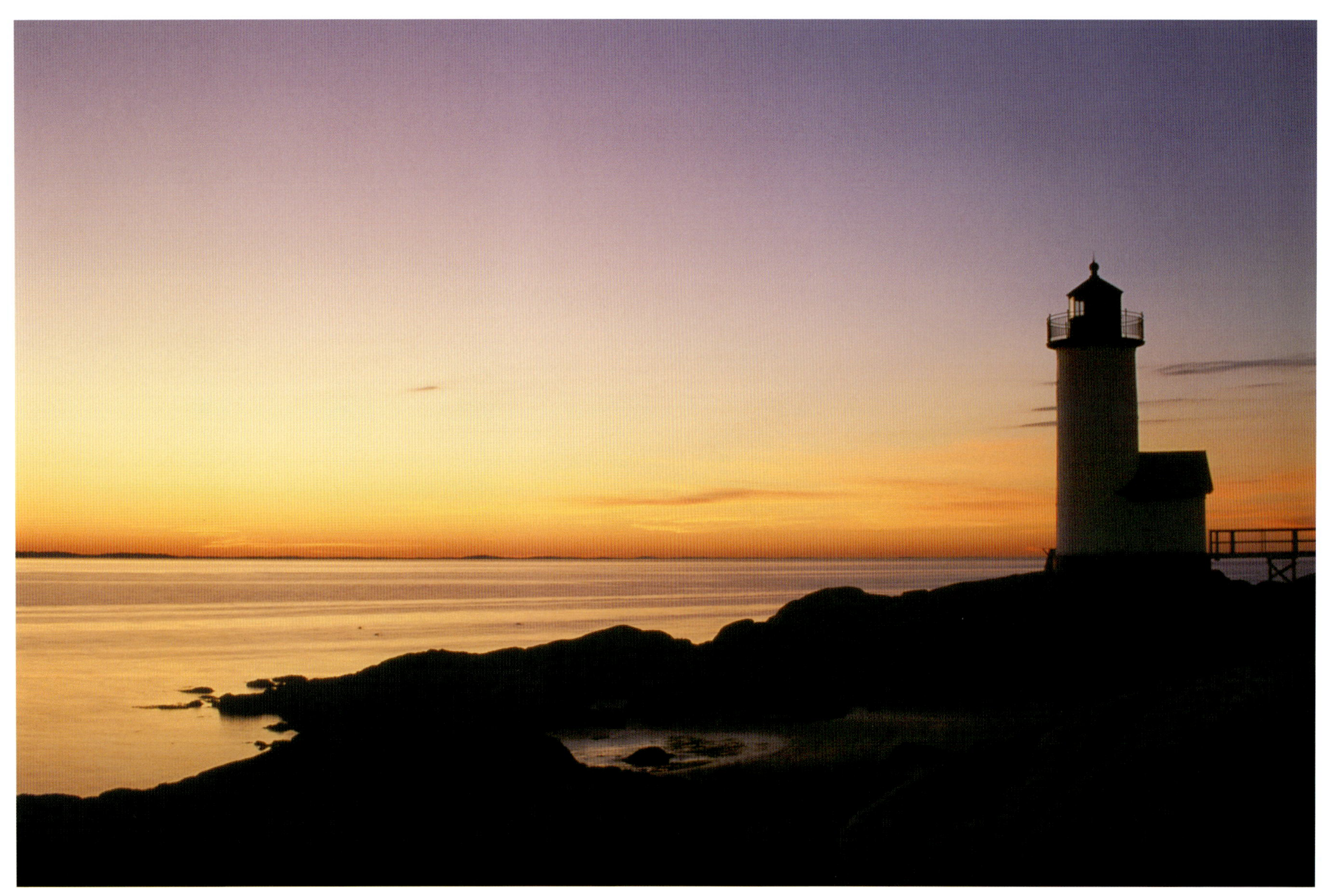

The sunset side of Cape Ann: Annisquam Light over Ipswich Bay

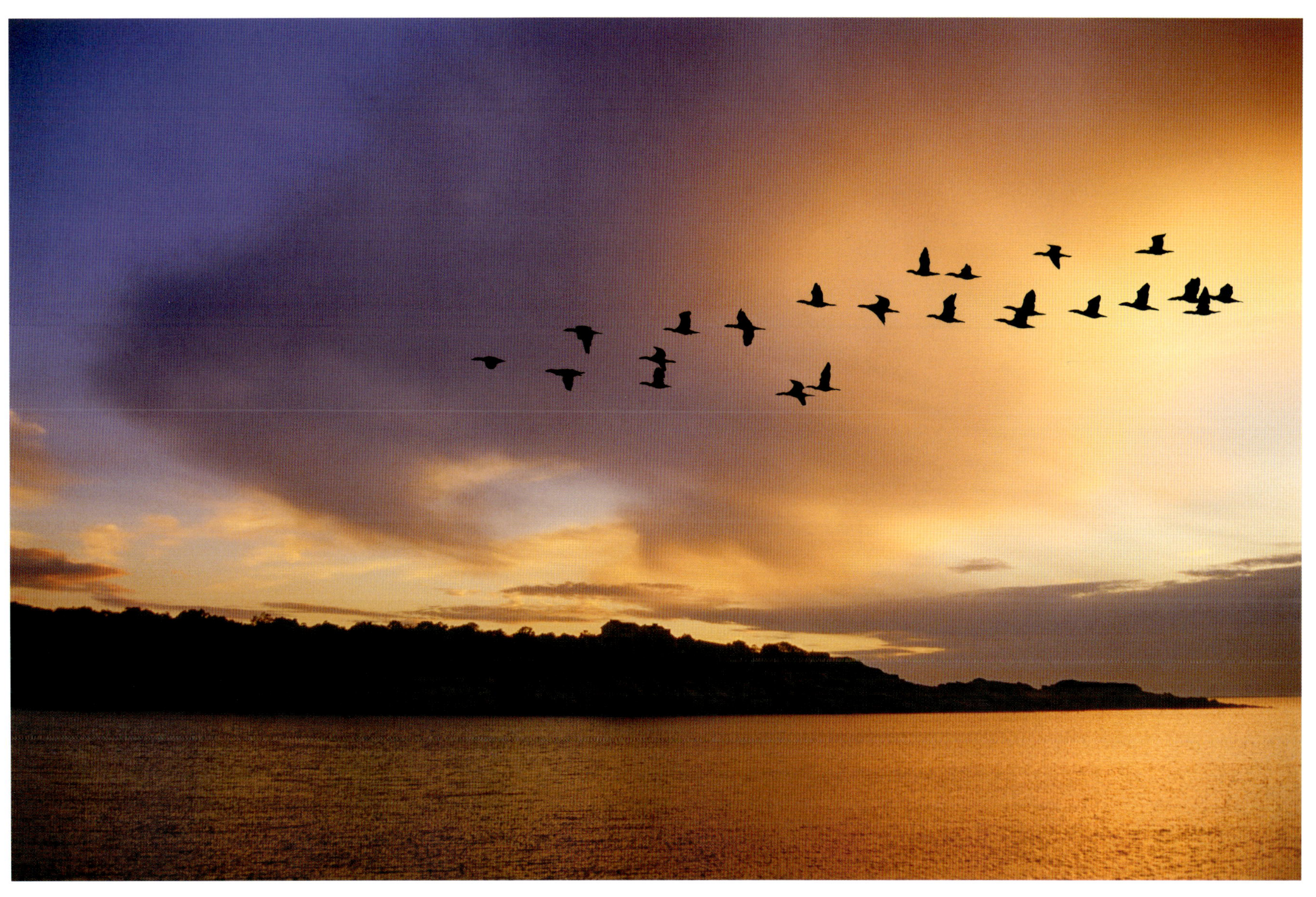

Folly Cove sunset

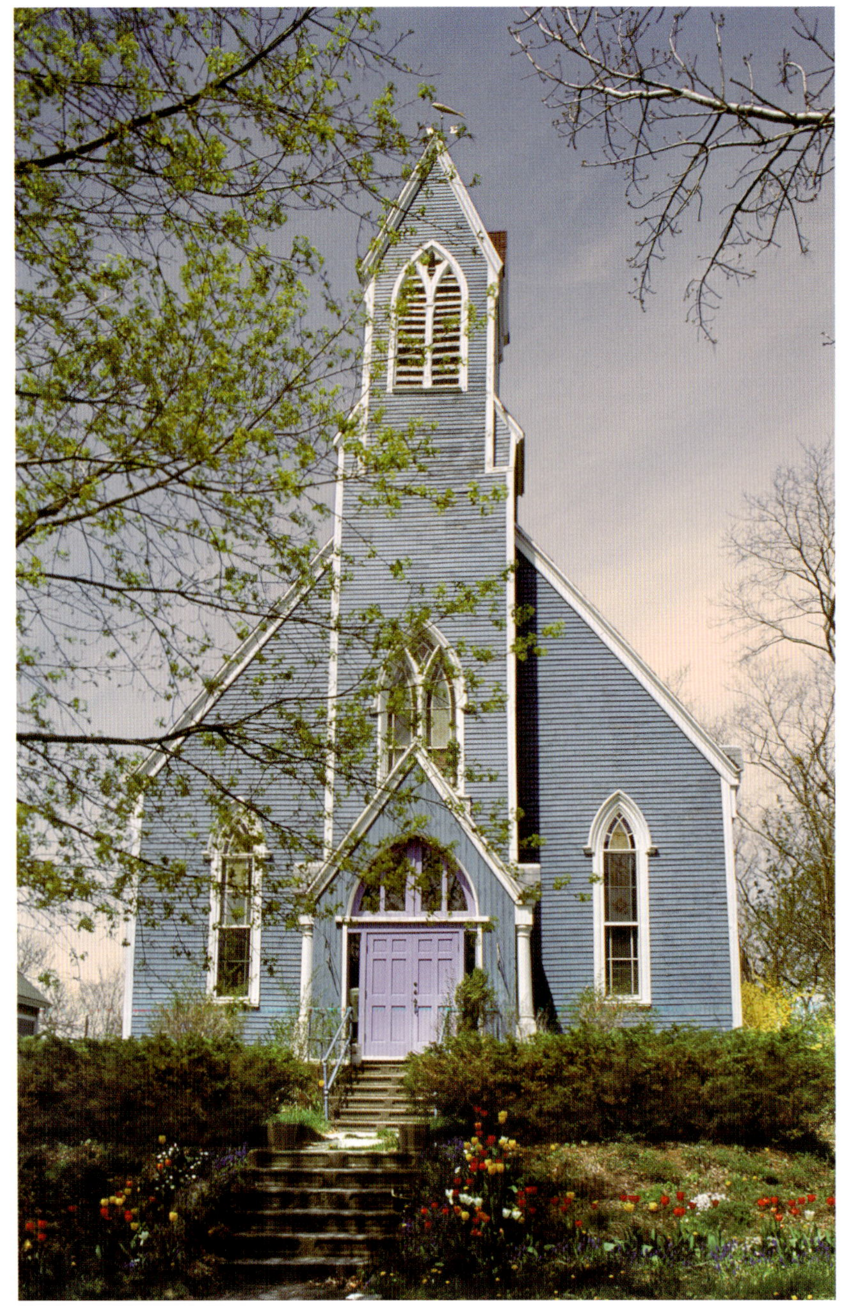

Blue church, Lanesville, now a private home

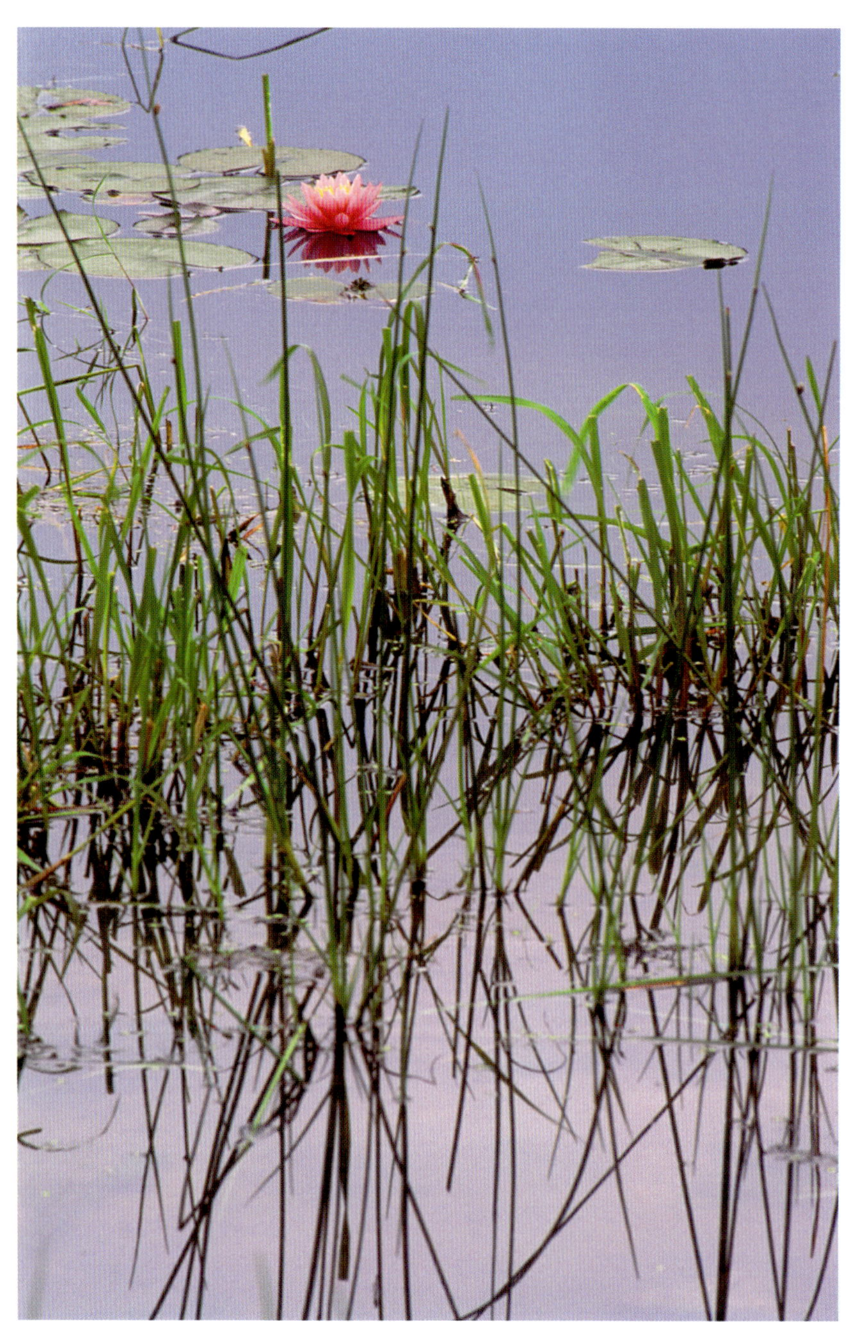

Days Pond

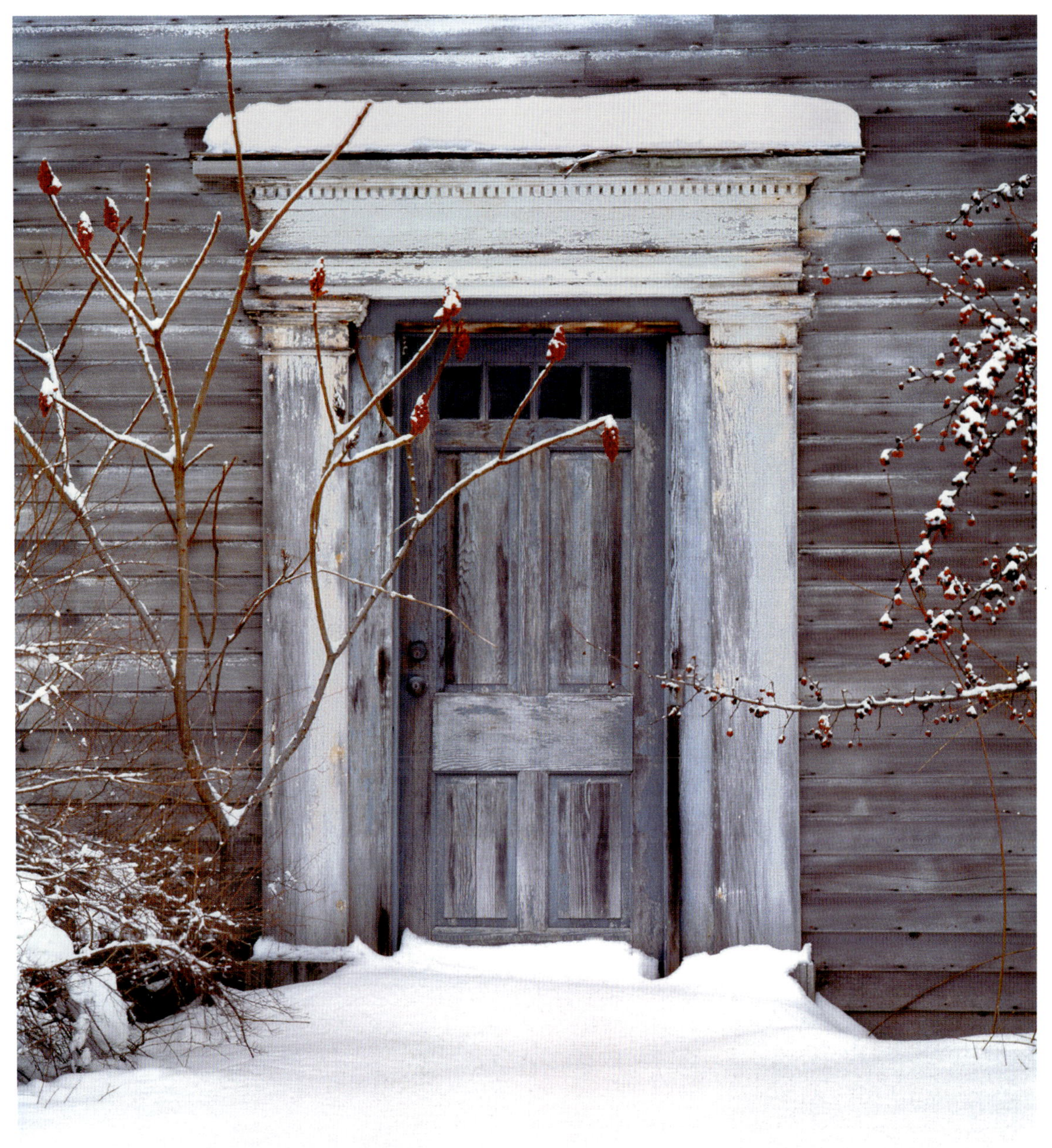

This old house, West Gloucester

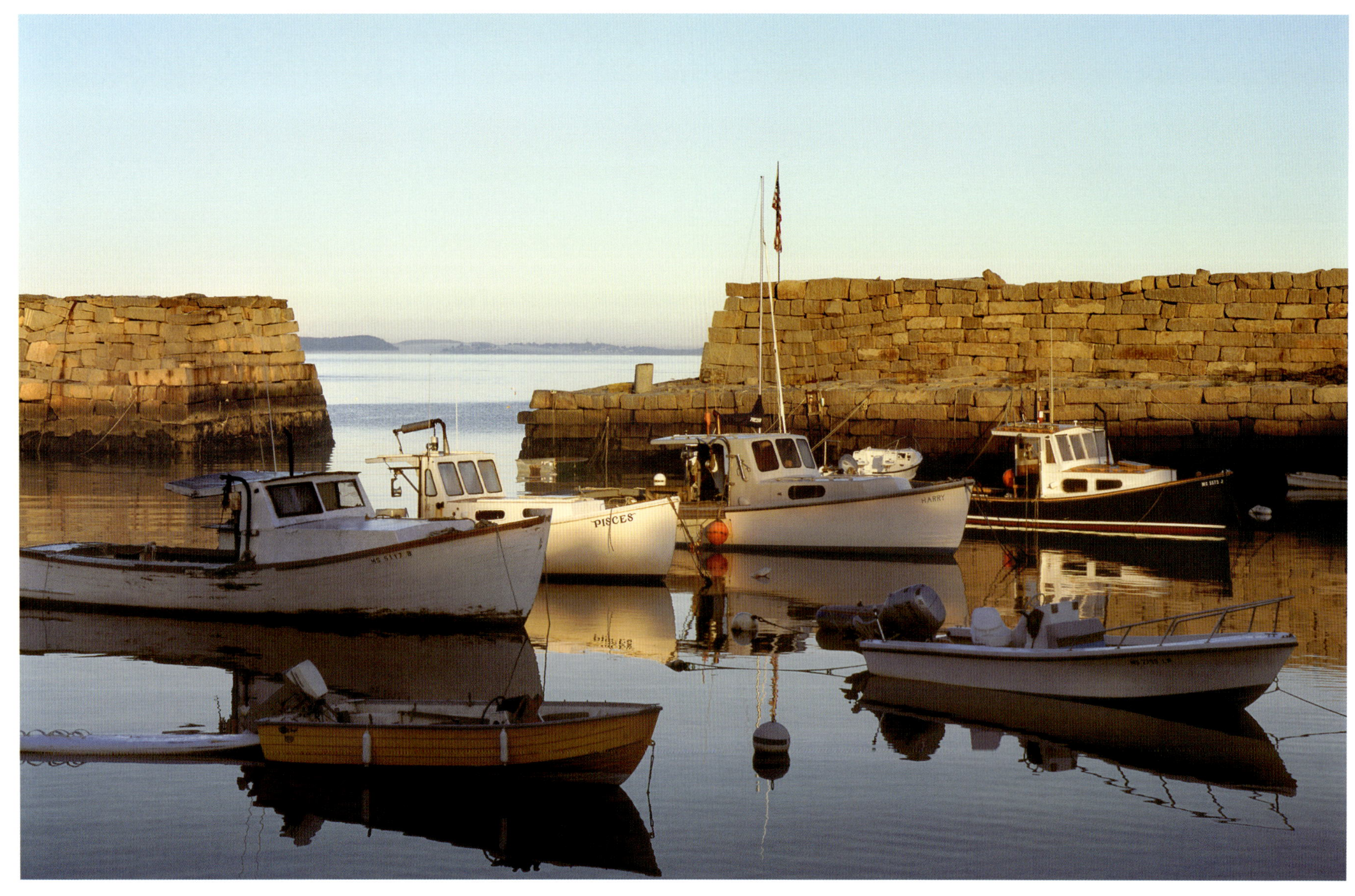


Lane's Cove

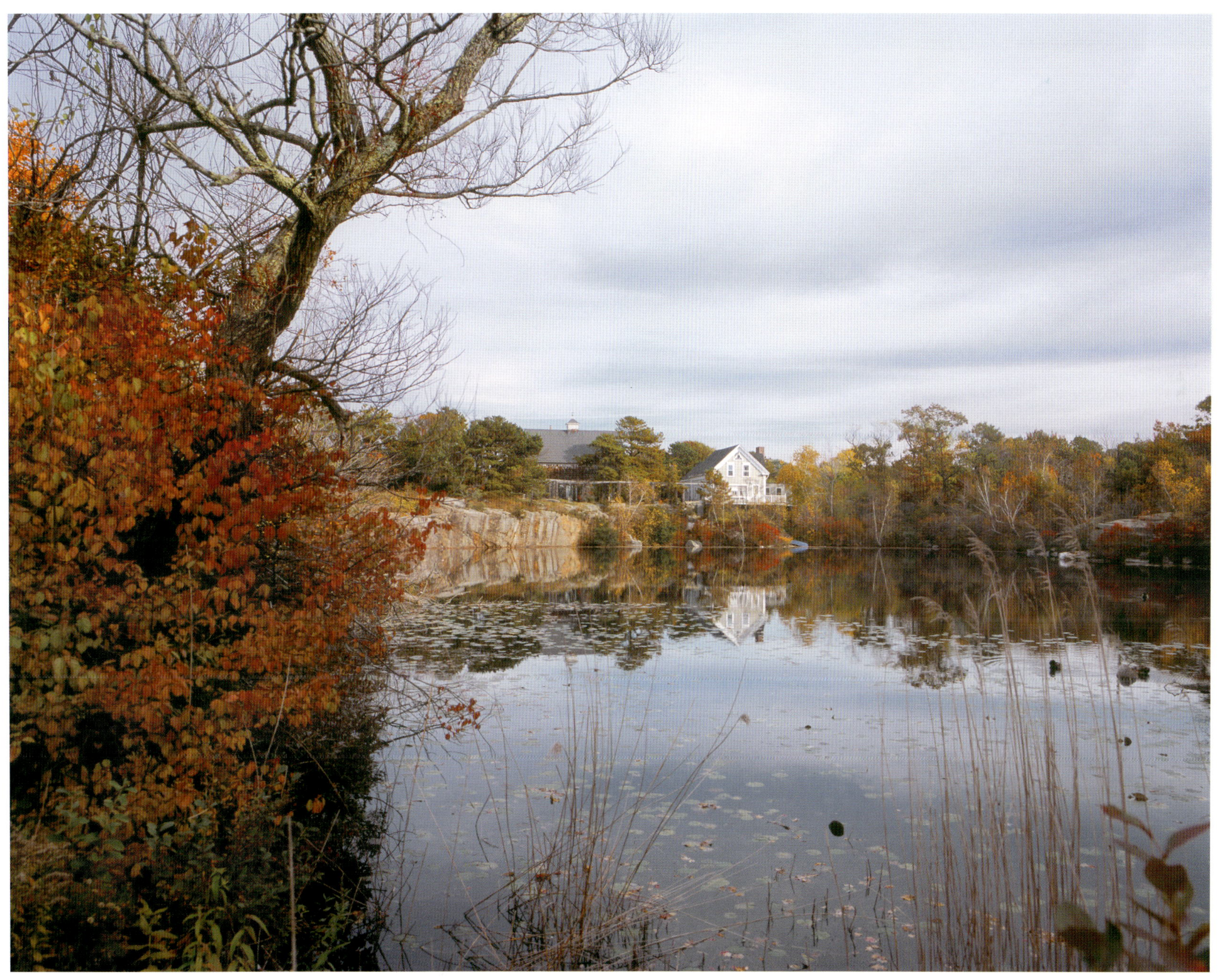

Butman Quarry, Lanesville

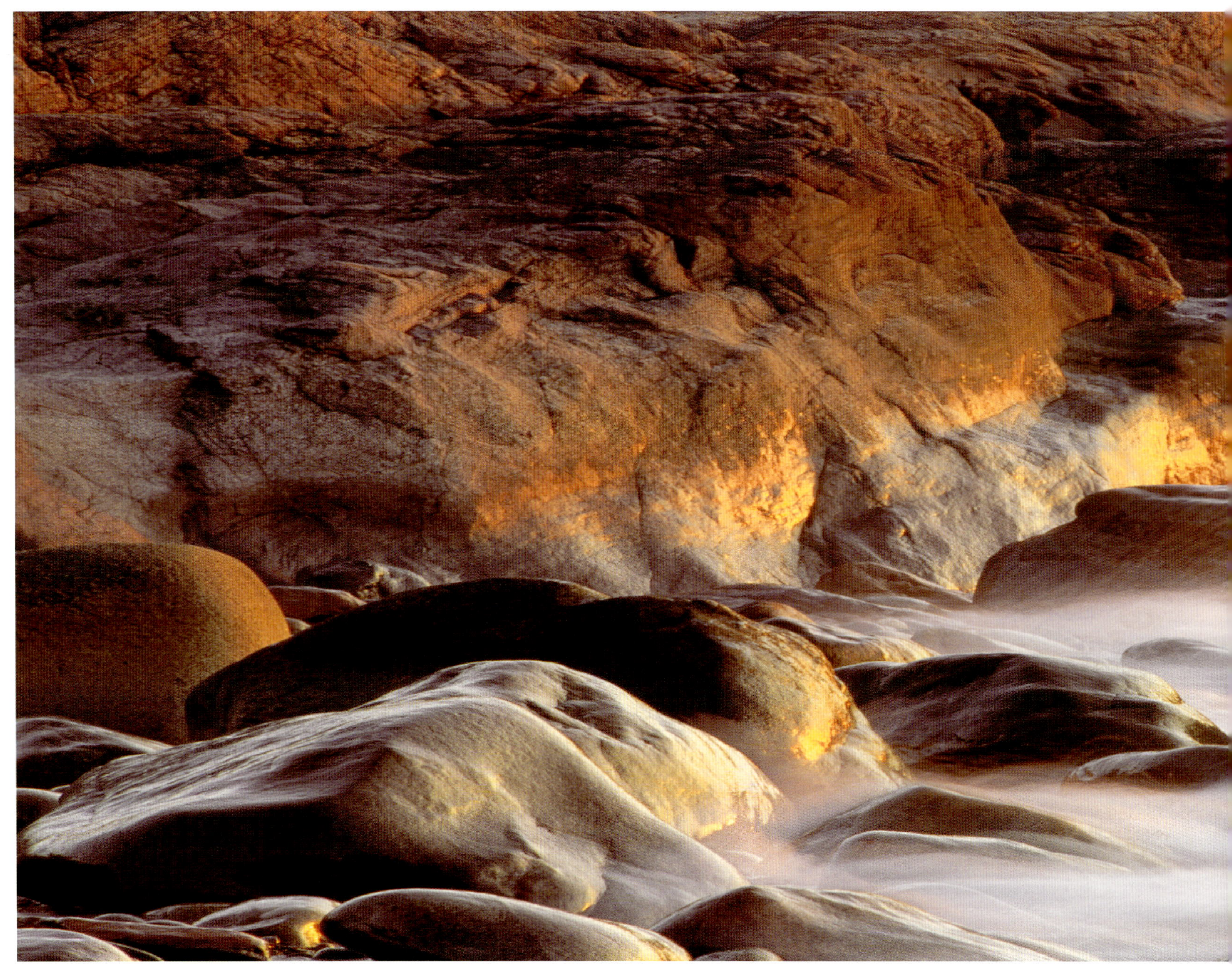

First light—Rock of Ages, off Atlantic Road

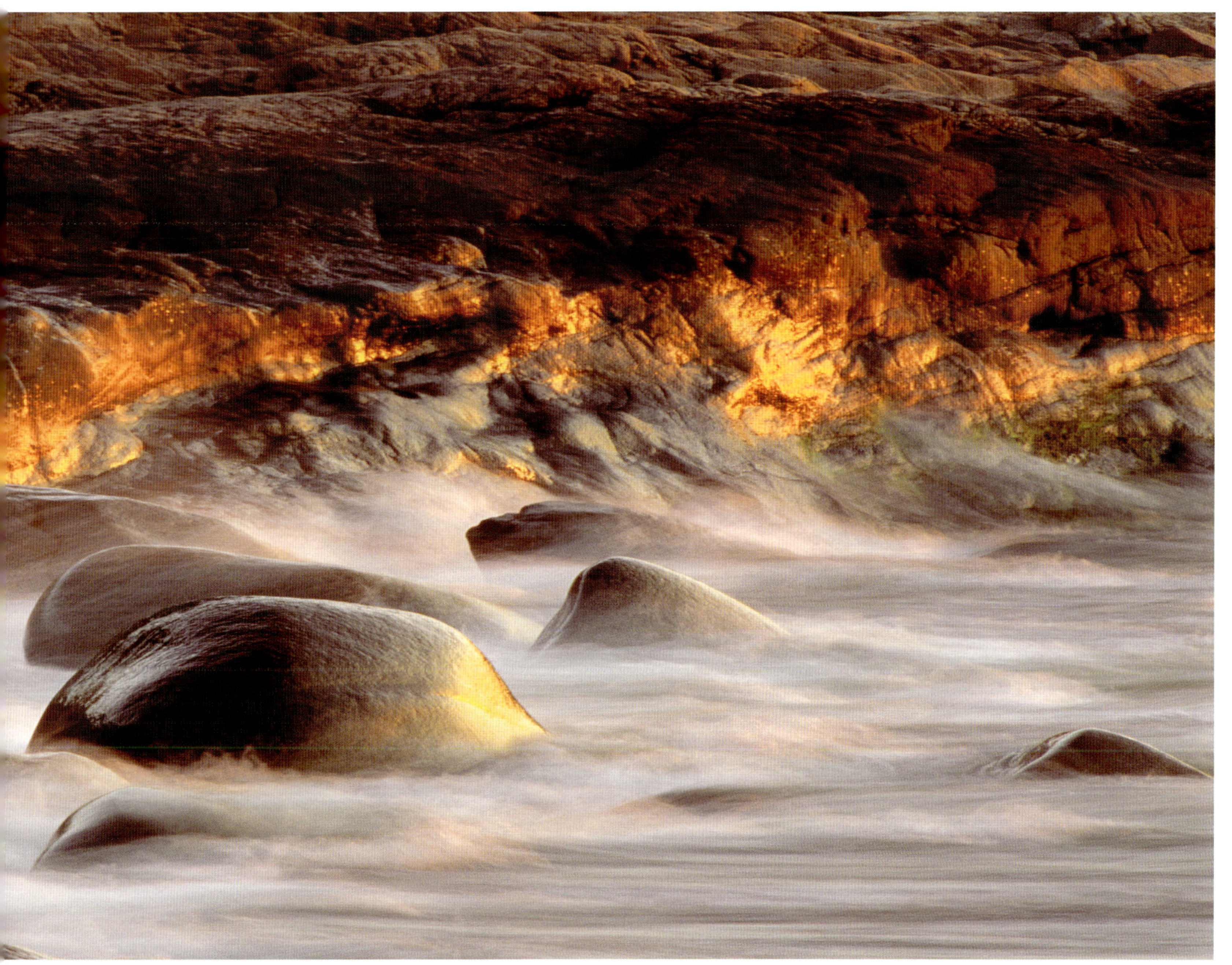

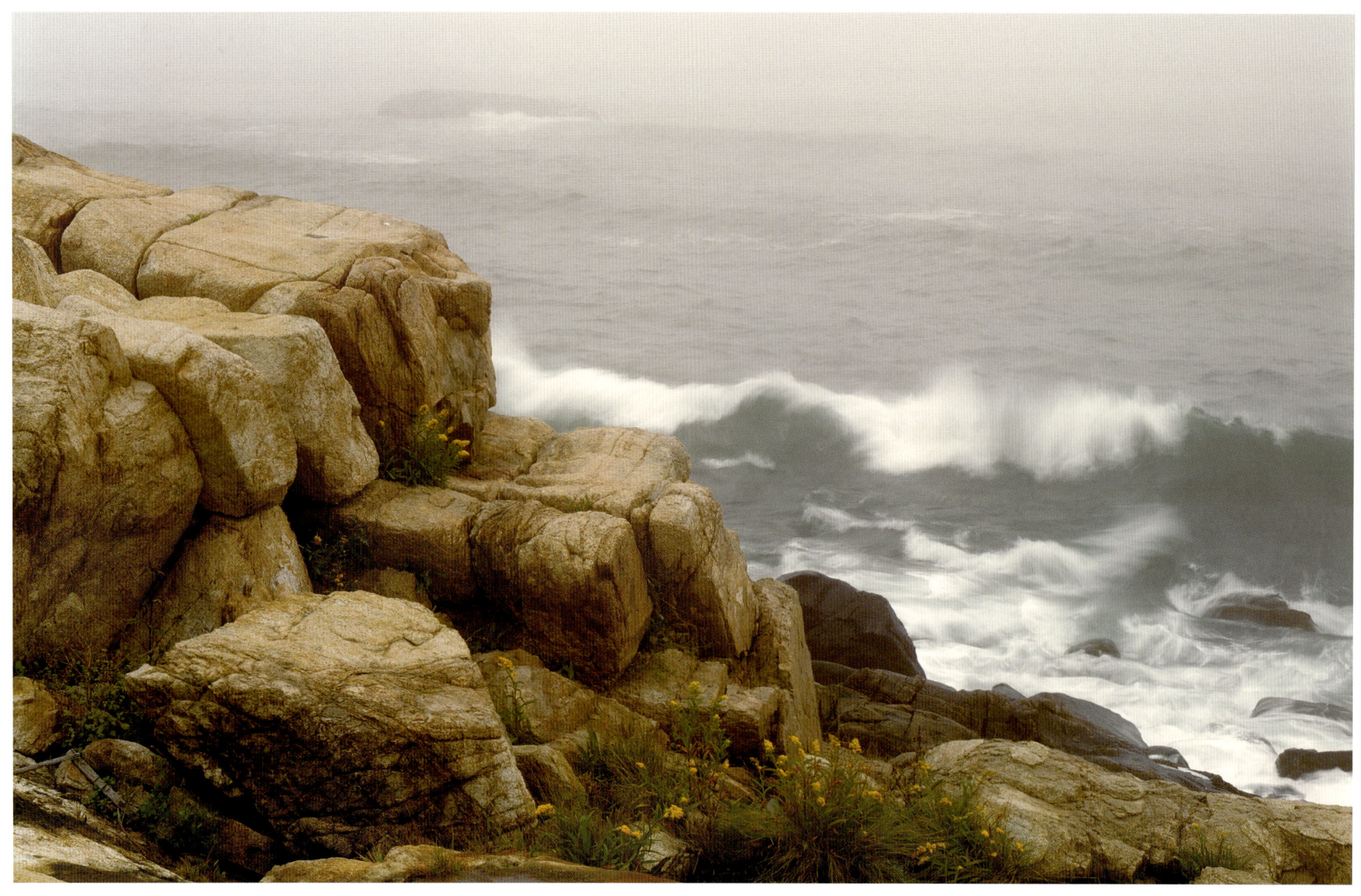

The Wishing Rock, Atlantic Road

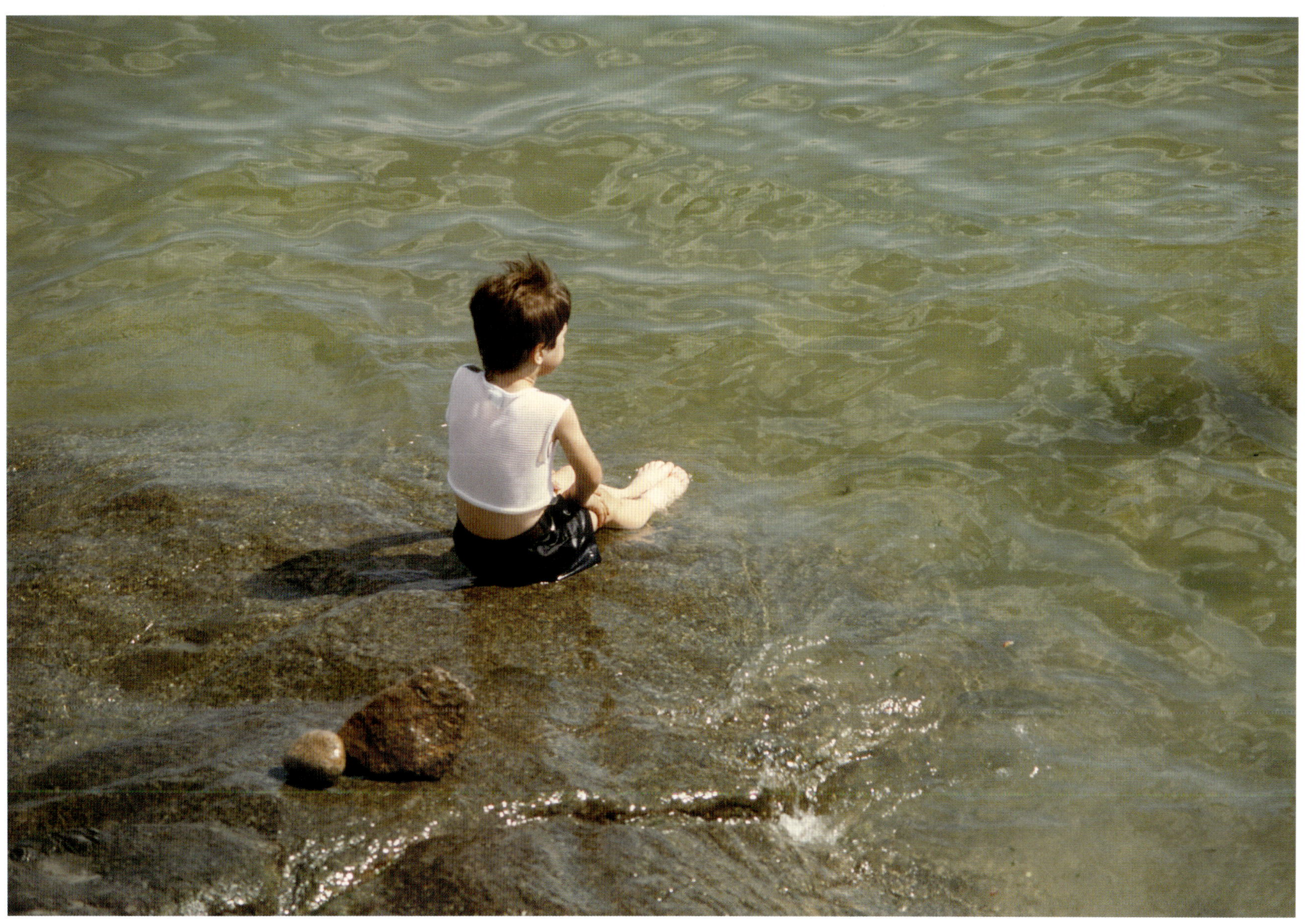

This young boy caught my eye. For nearly an hour at low tide, he struggled to lift, roll, and push a rock nearly his own weight onto a ledge. Exhausted, he brought a smaller stone to mark his claim. Seemingly satisfied with his work, he climbed up on the ledge to rest. He sat motionless for a long time, mesmerized by a big sky and the sea. (It was at that point that I took this image.) With a cooling breeze and a rising tide, he shivered but did not leave his perch until a swell forced him off the ledge to the beach. When he was leaving with his parents, the boy looked back several times to where his "claim" had been as the sea swept clean his retreating footprints in the sand.

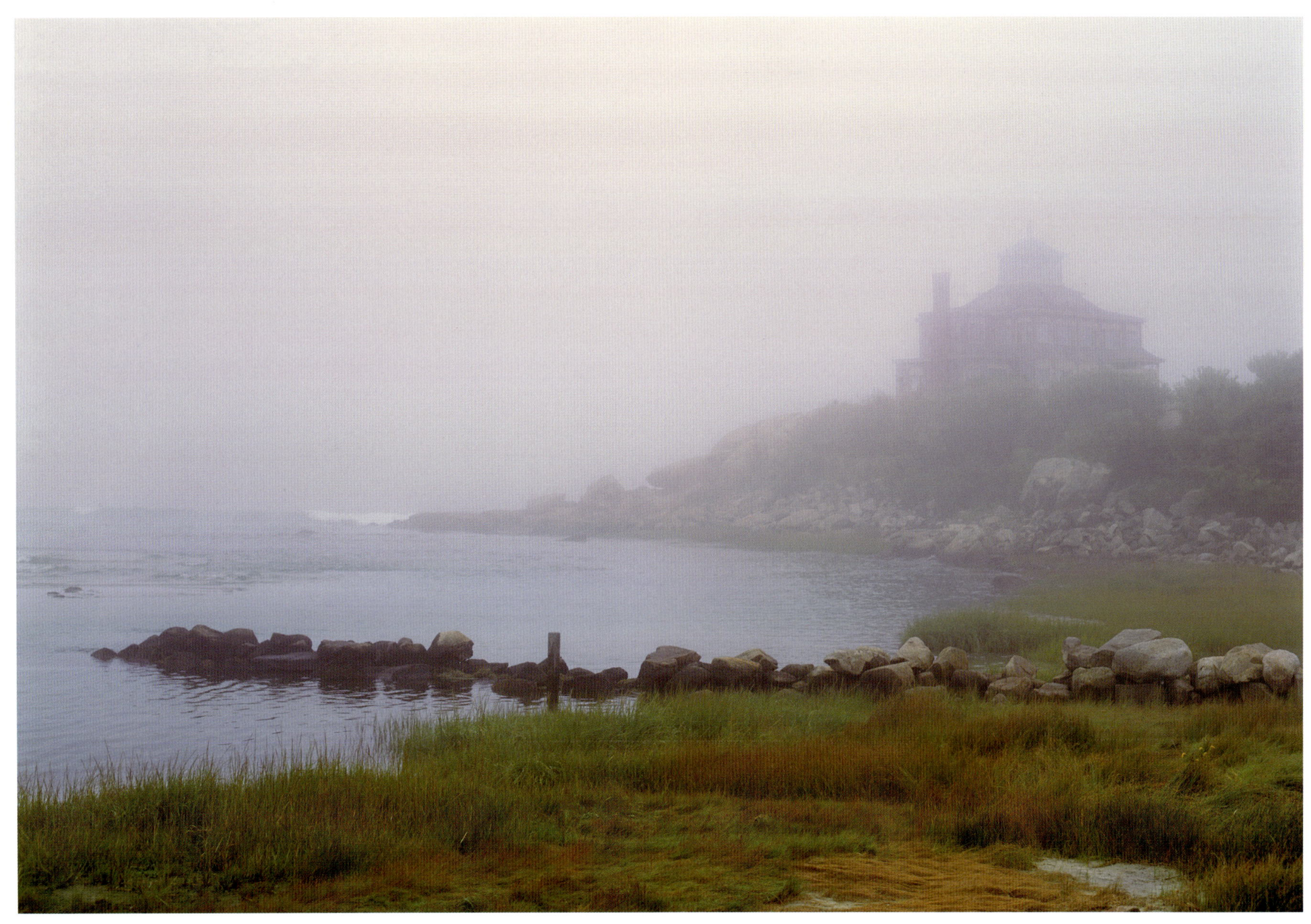

The House on Good Harbor, in the fog . . .

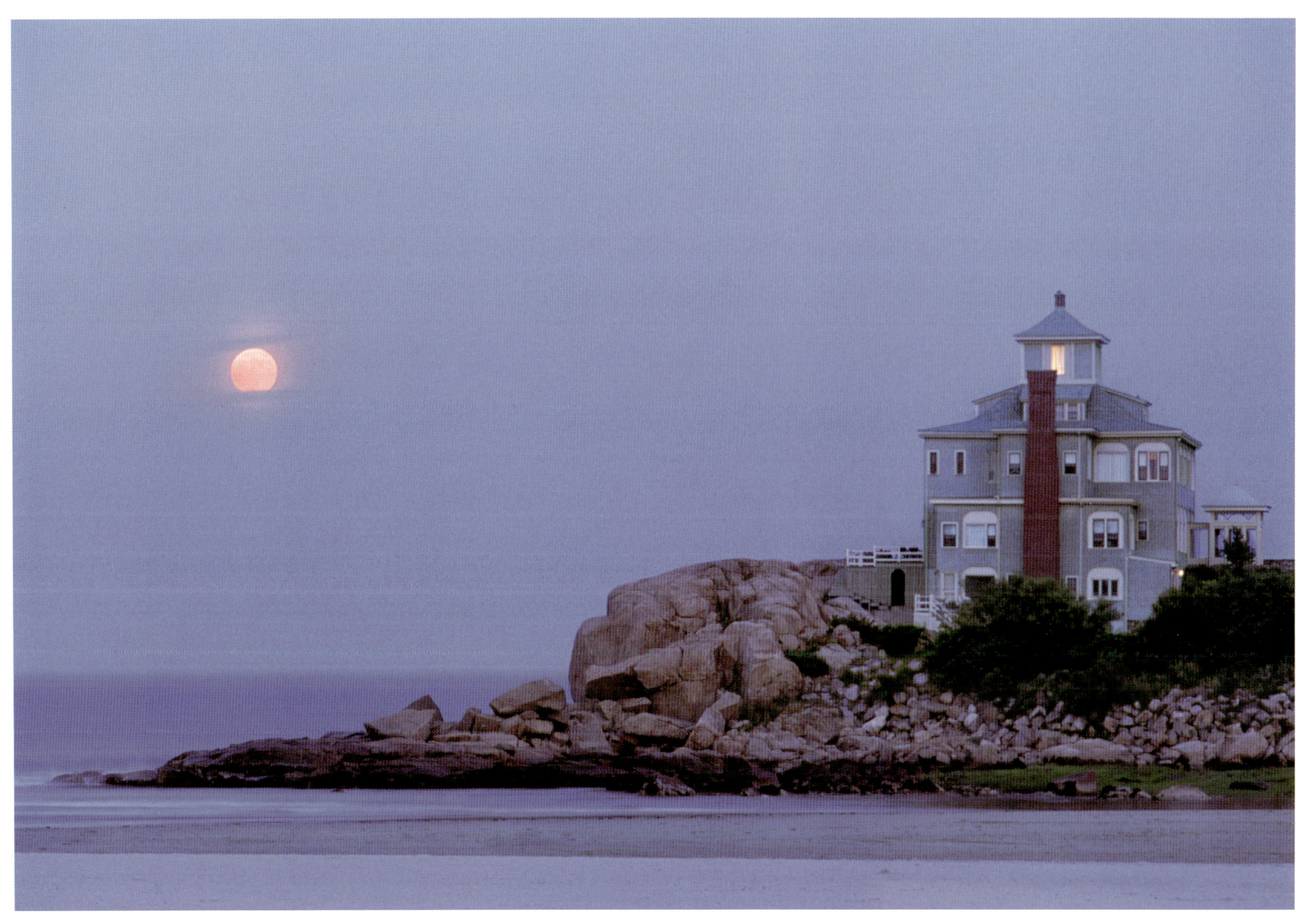

. . . and at moonrise

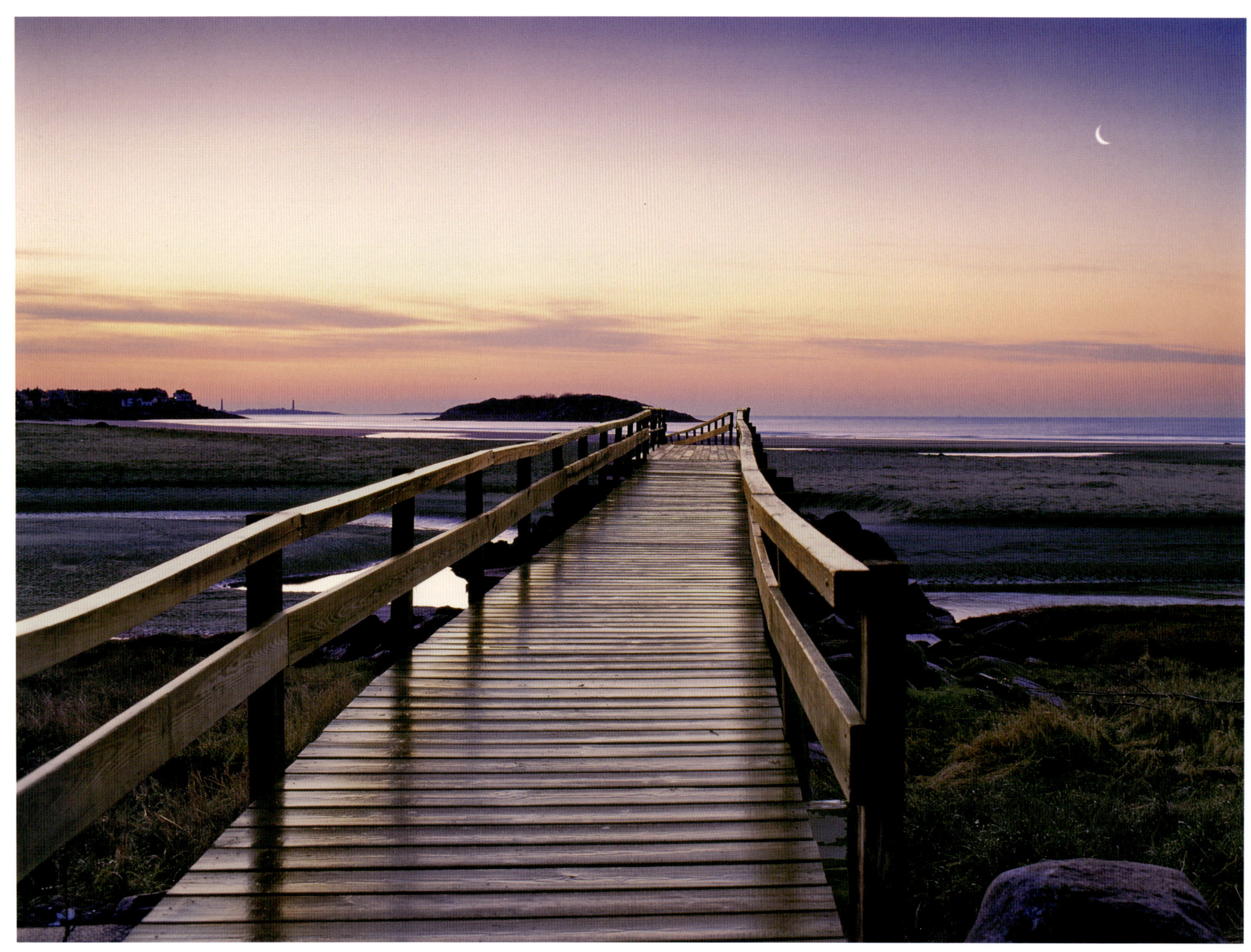

Boardwalk and bridge to Good Harbor Beach

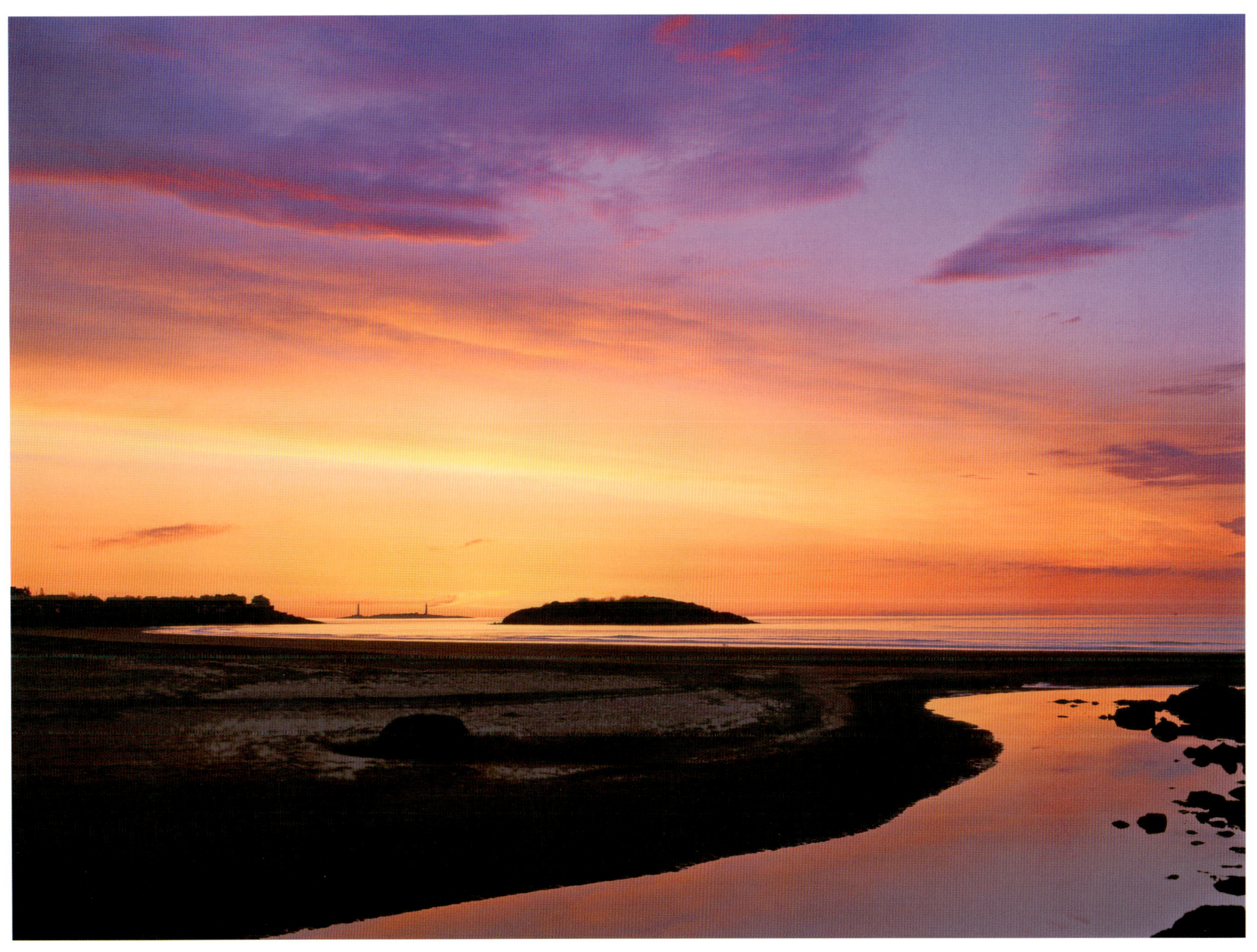

Sunrise, Good Harbor Beach

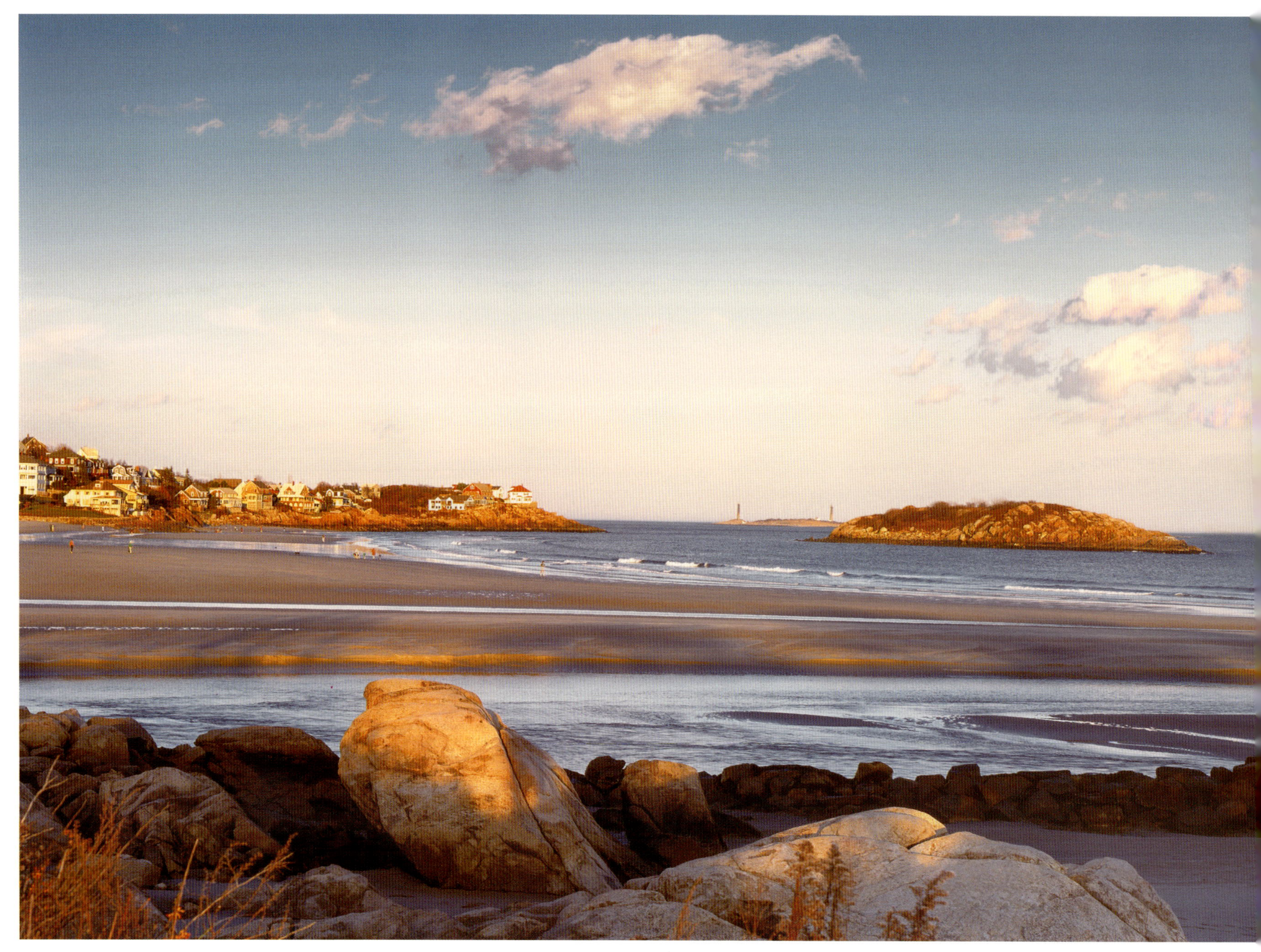

Good Harbor

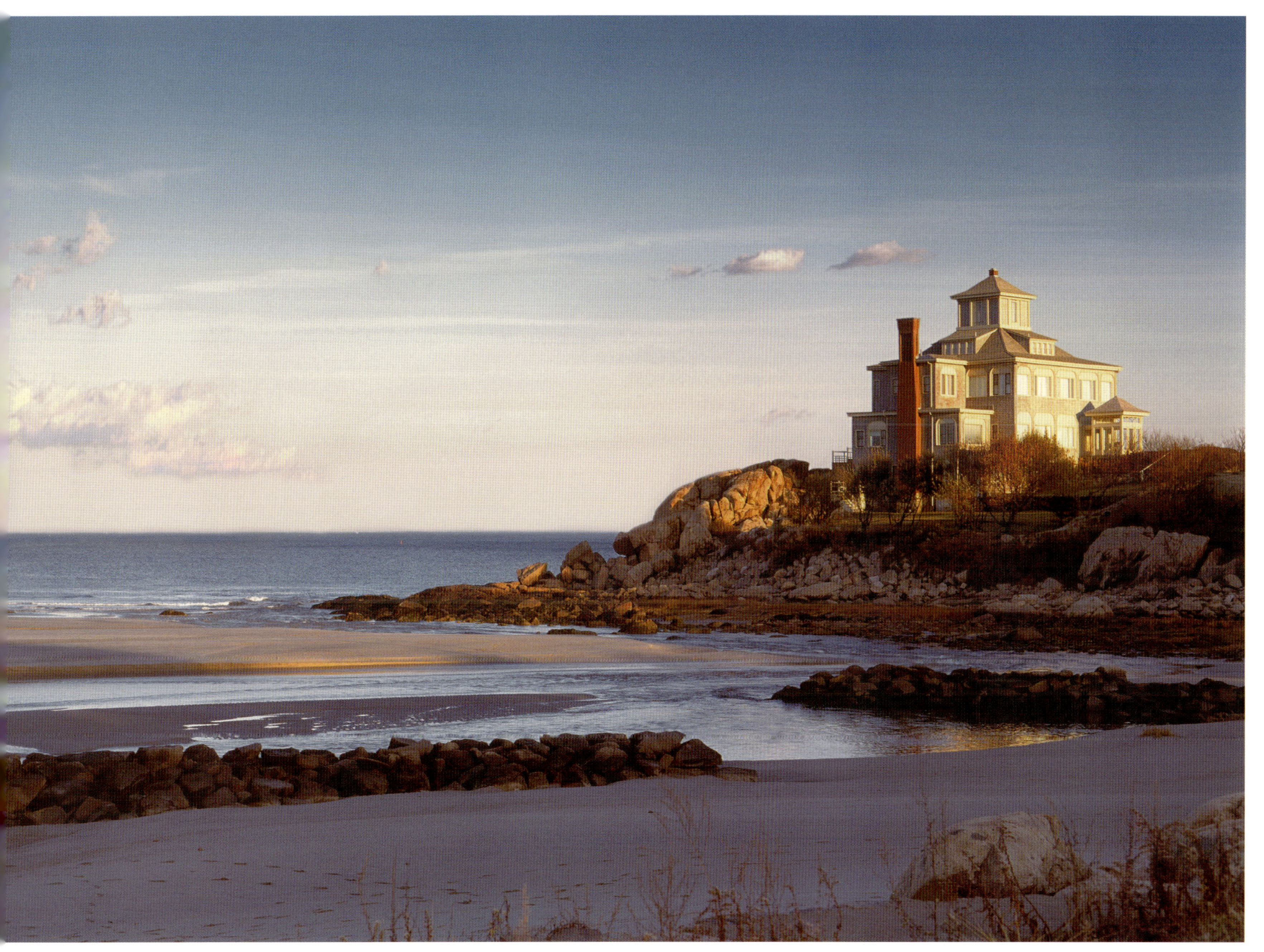

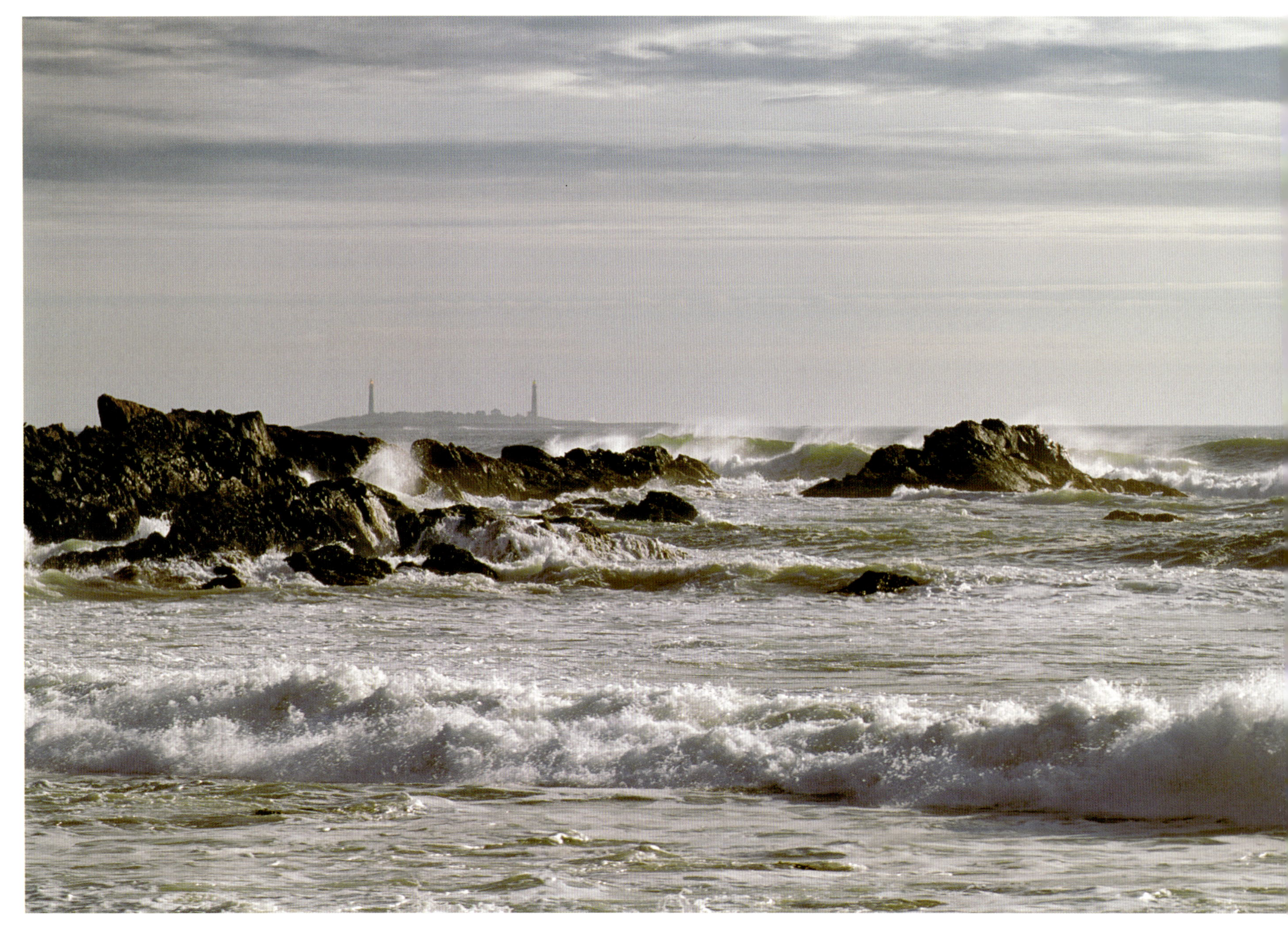

Bass Rocks, with Thacher Island in the distance

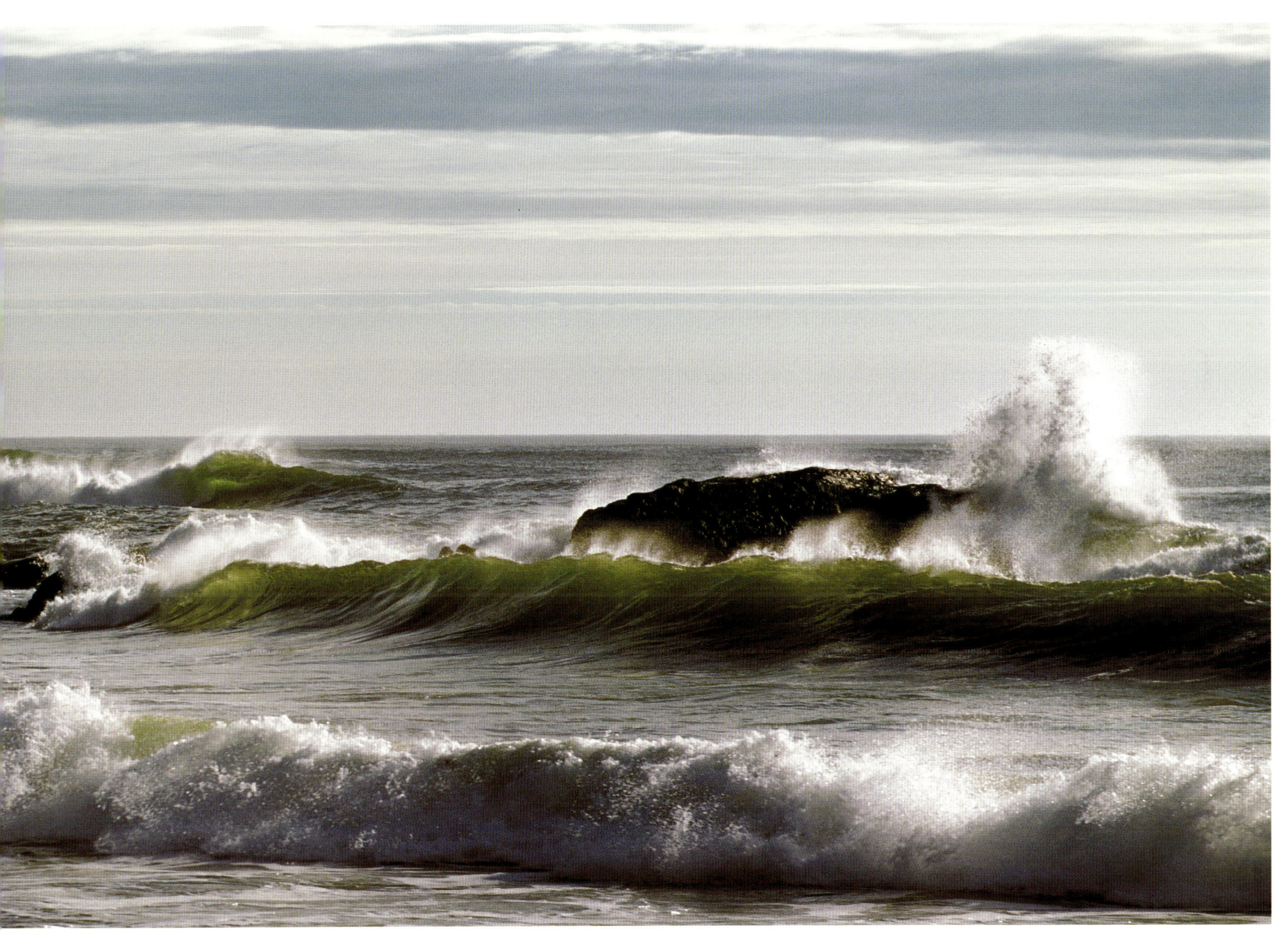

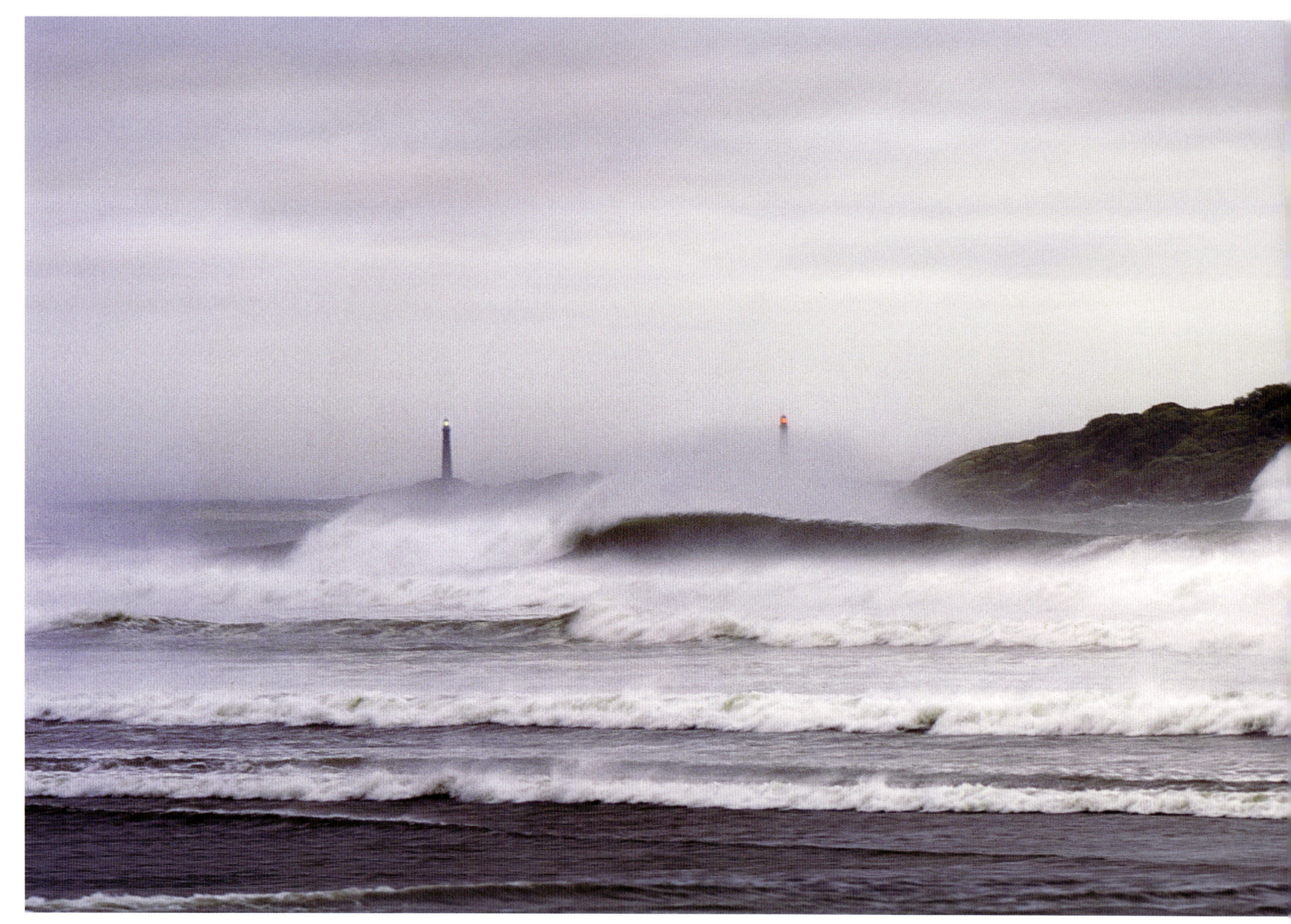

The tail end of Hurricane Bob, 1991

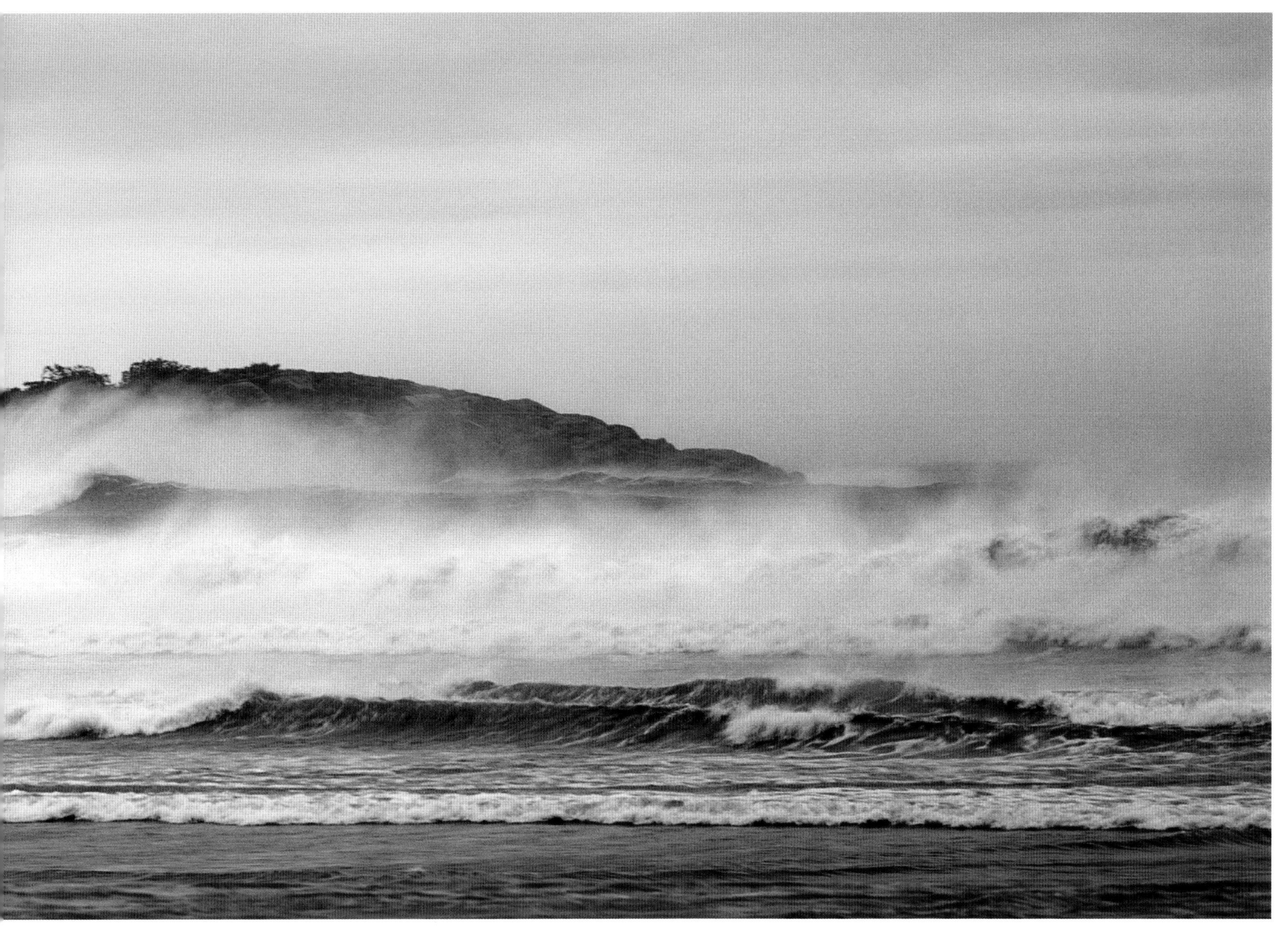

# ROCKPORT

*Tragabizanda* is a mouthful. It's a good thing John Smith's 1614 name for Rockport didn't stick. The first shipwreck in our colonial history occurred here in 1635 when Anthony Thacher and his family were hurled onto the island named for them. The Twin Lights, as much symbols of the town as the oft-painted Motif No. 1, help latter-day mariners avoid the Thachers' fate.

Once a parish of Gloucester and a fishing village, Rockport became a giant in granite when that building stone was quarried in the nineteenth century. Painters soon discovered the sun-splashed town and came here in droves. Ever since Hannah Jumper and her teetotaling supporters smashed every bottle of liquor they could find in the Women's Raid of 1856, artists and others have brought their own liquid refreshment to an oxymoron—a dry sea town.

Now adored as a summer haven at the end of the world, or at least Cape Ann, Rockport has decided to offer drink to the parched—though a swim in the drink, or a walk just about anywhere in this gorgeous village, has always been a great way to spend a summer's day.

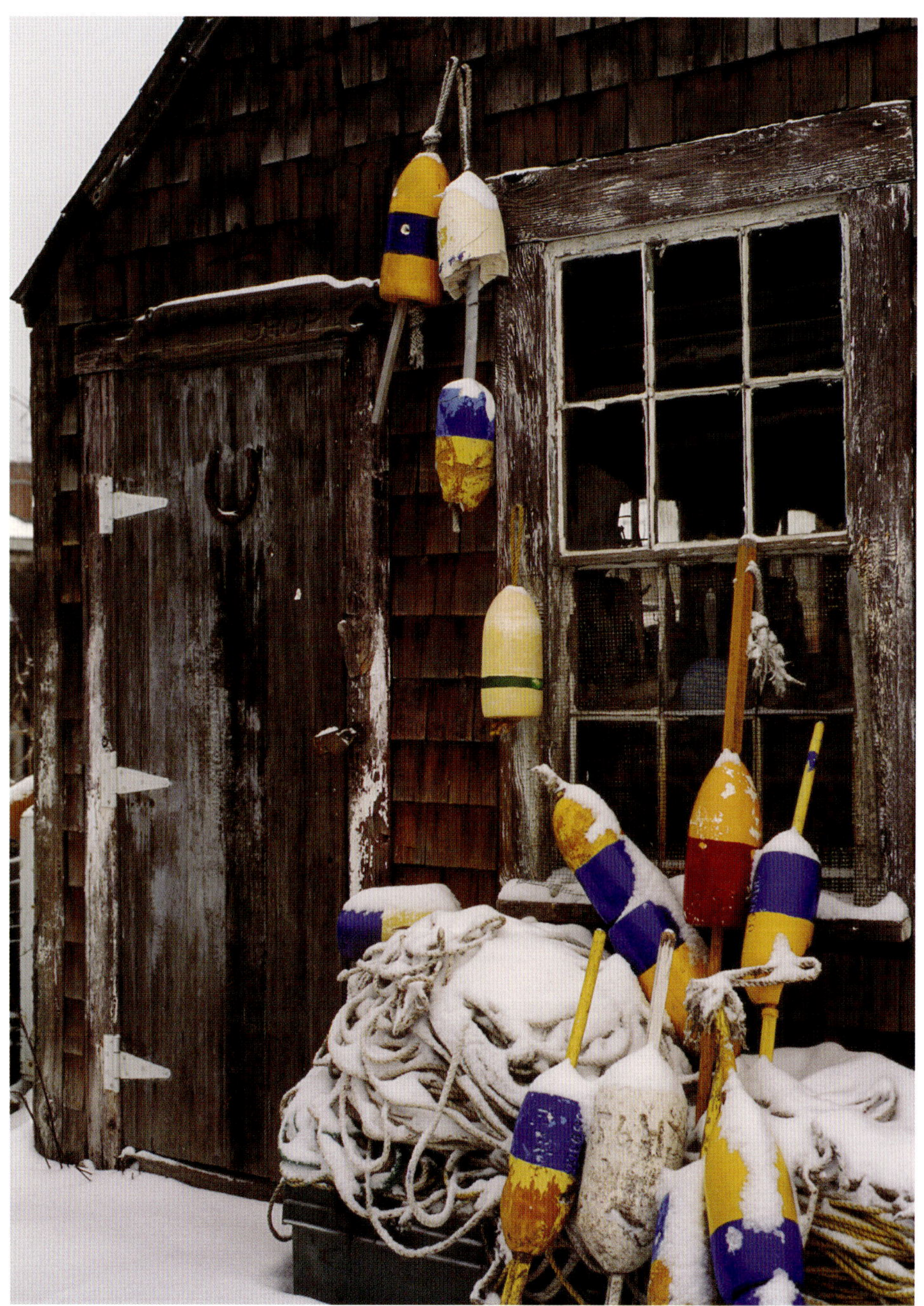

*Above:* Lobster shack
*Opposite: Spirit of Peace,* at Motif No. 1

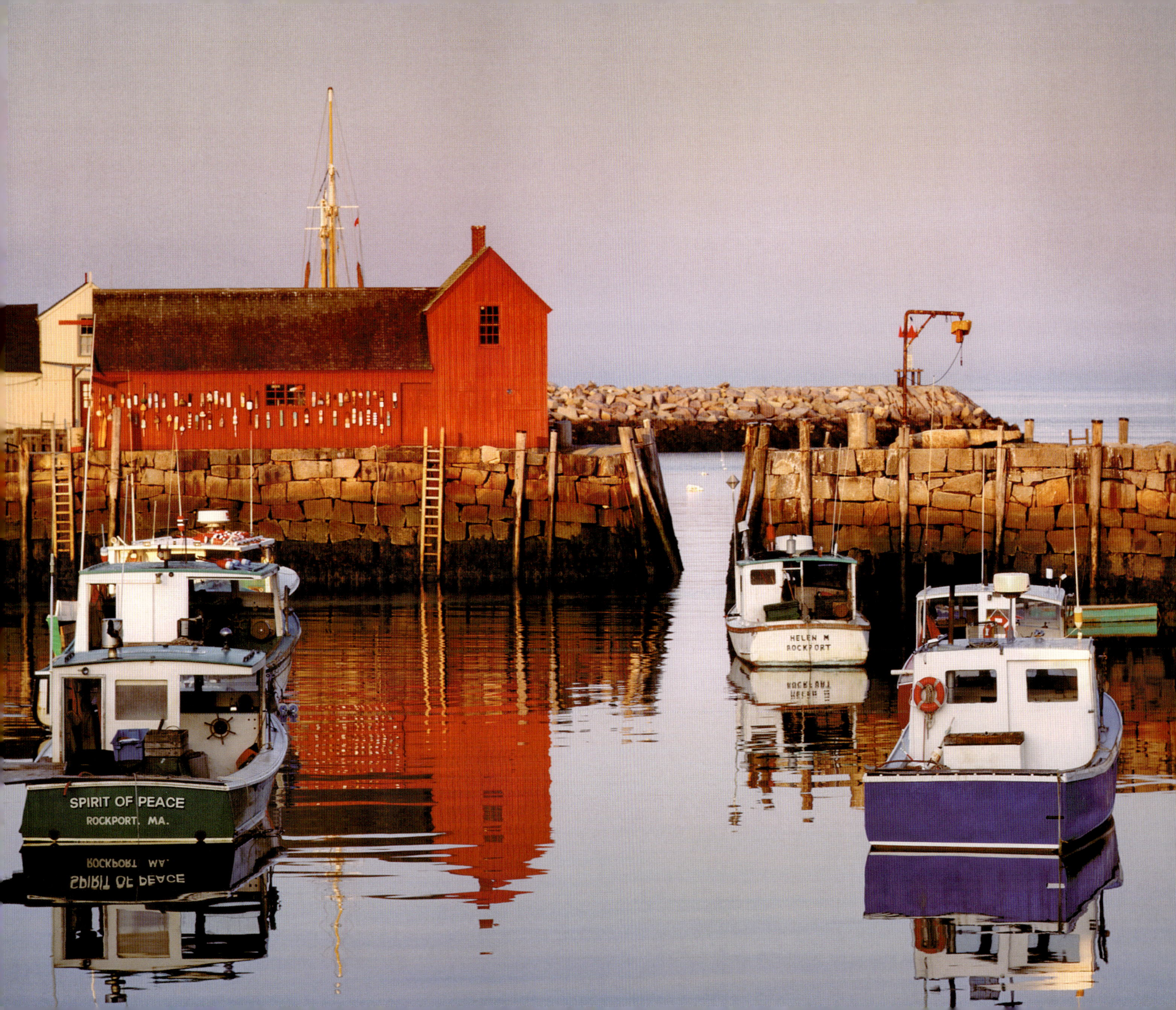
SPIRIT OF PEACE
ROCKPORT, MA.
HELEN M
ROCKPORT

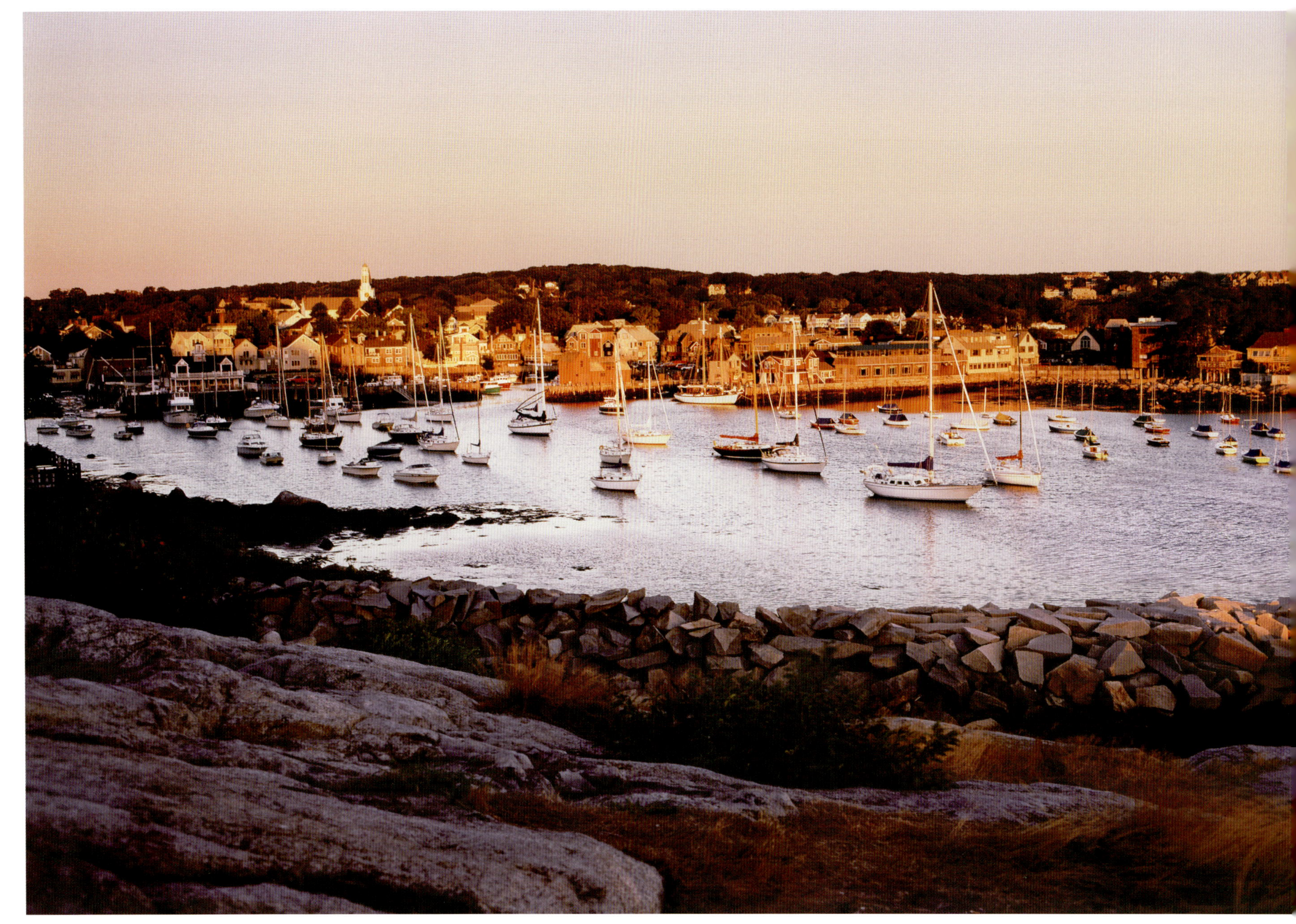

Rockport Harbor

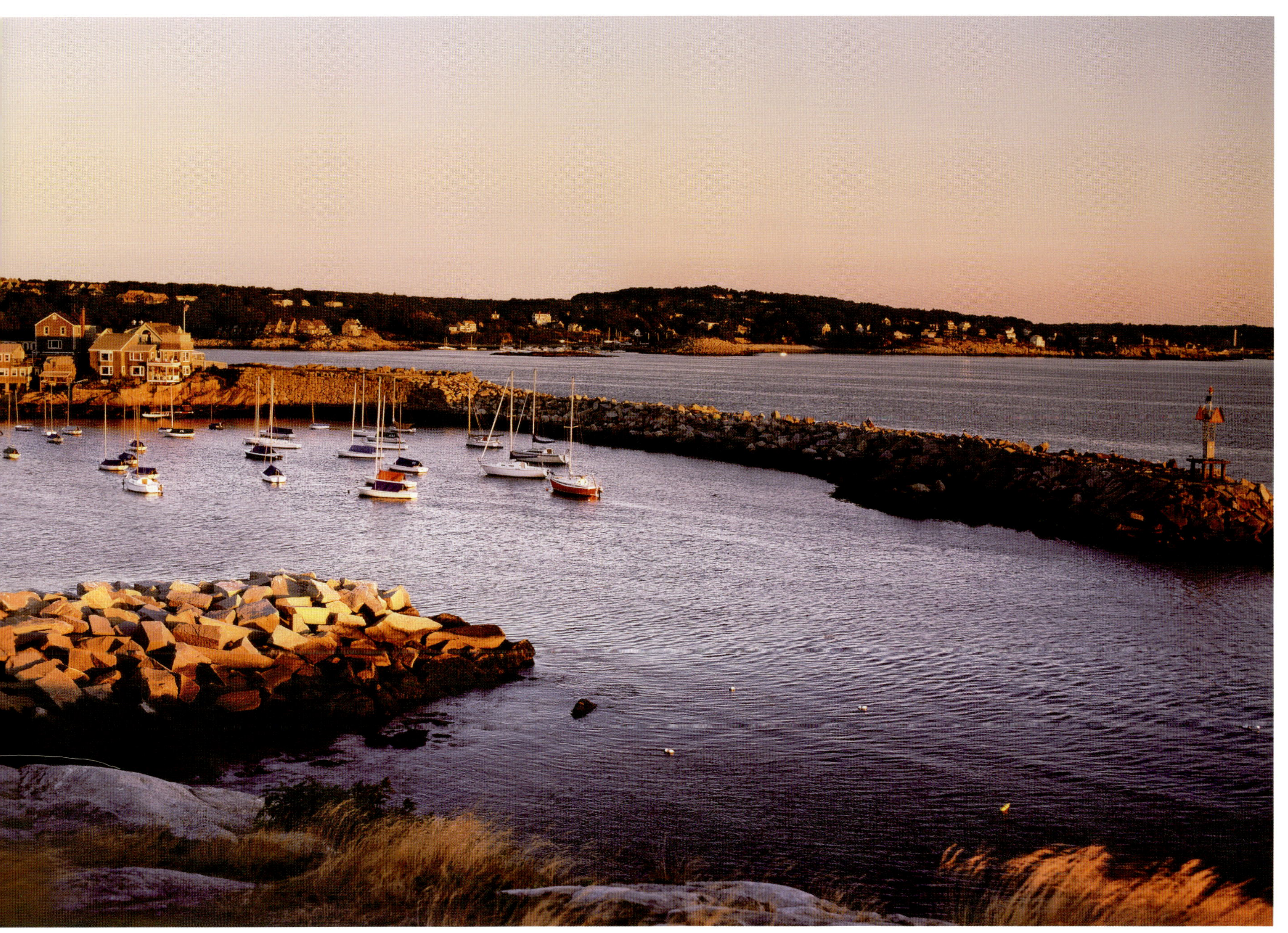

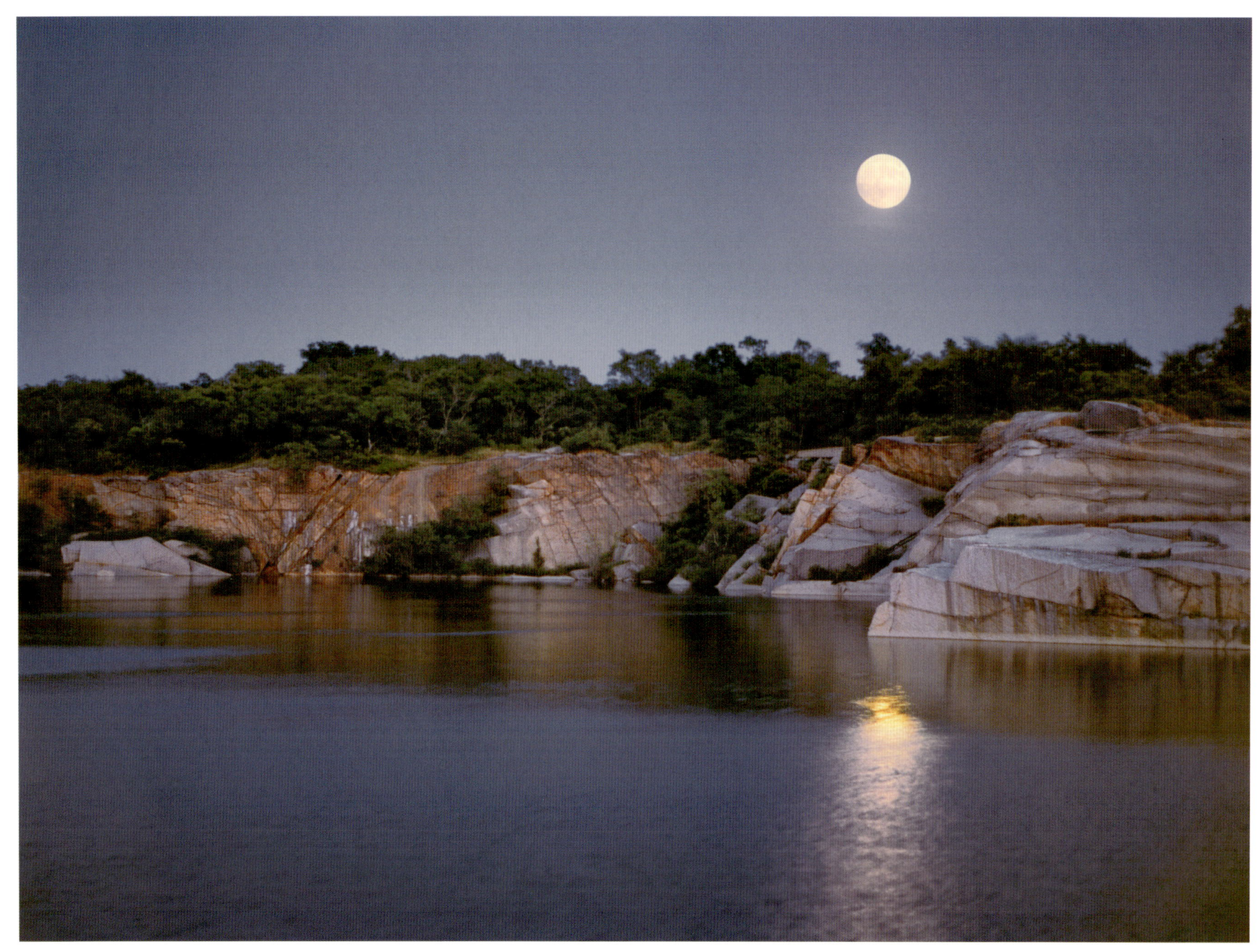

Moon over Halibut Point quarry

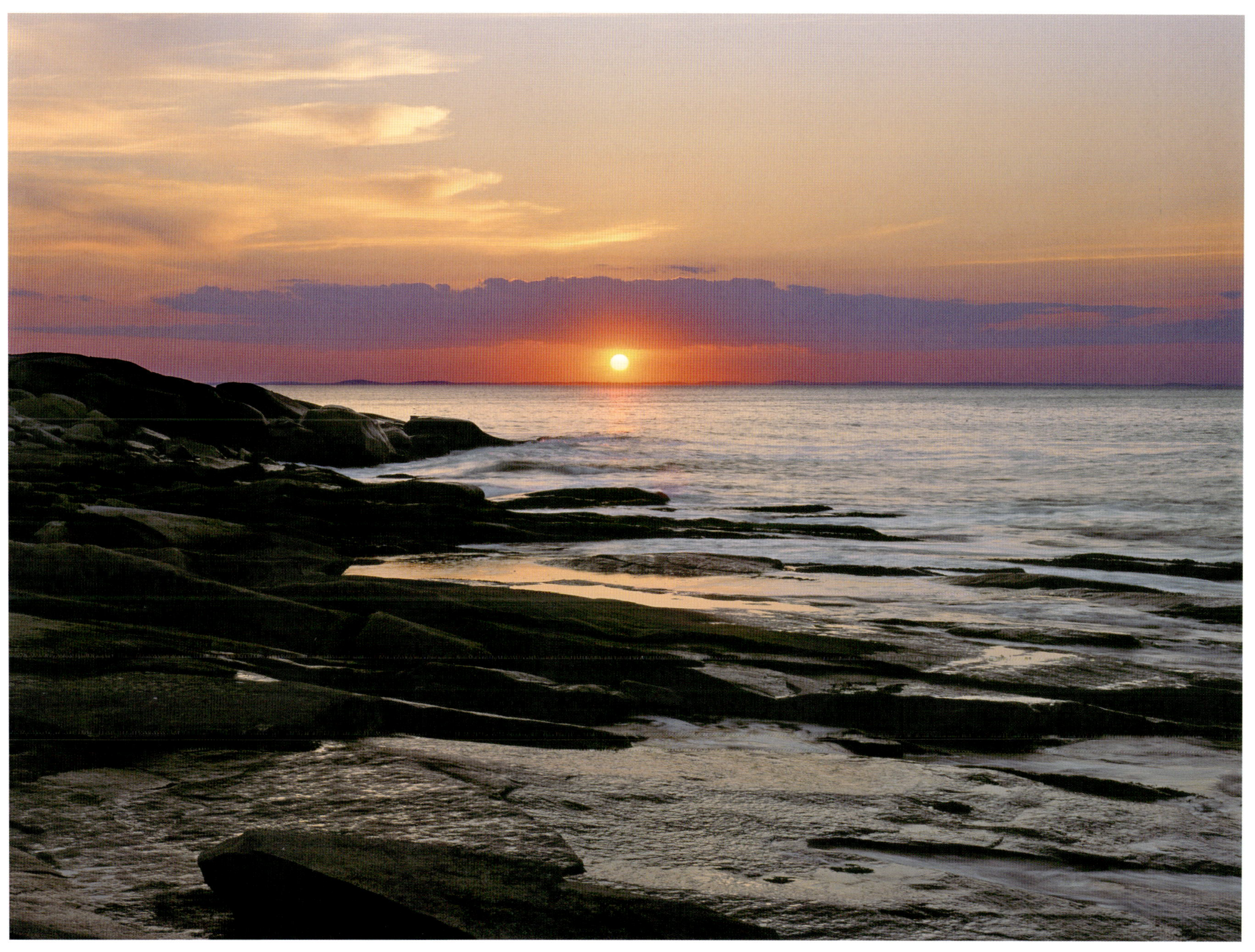

Halibut Point sunset

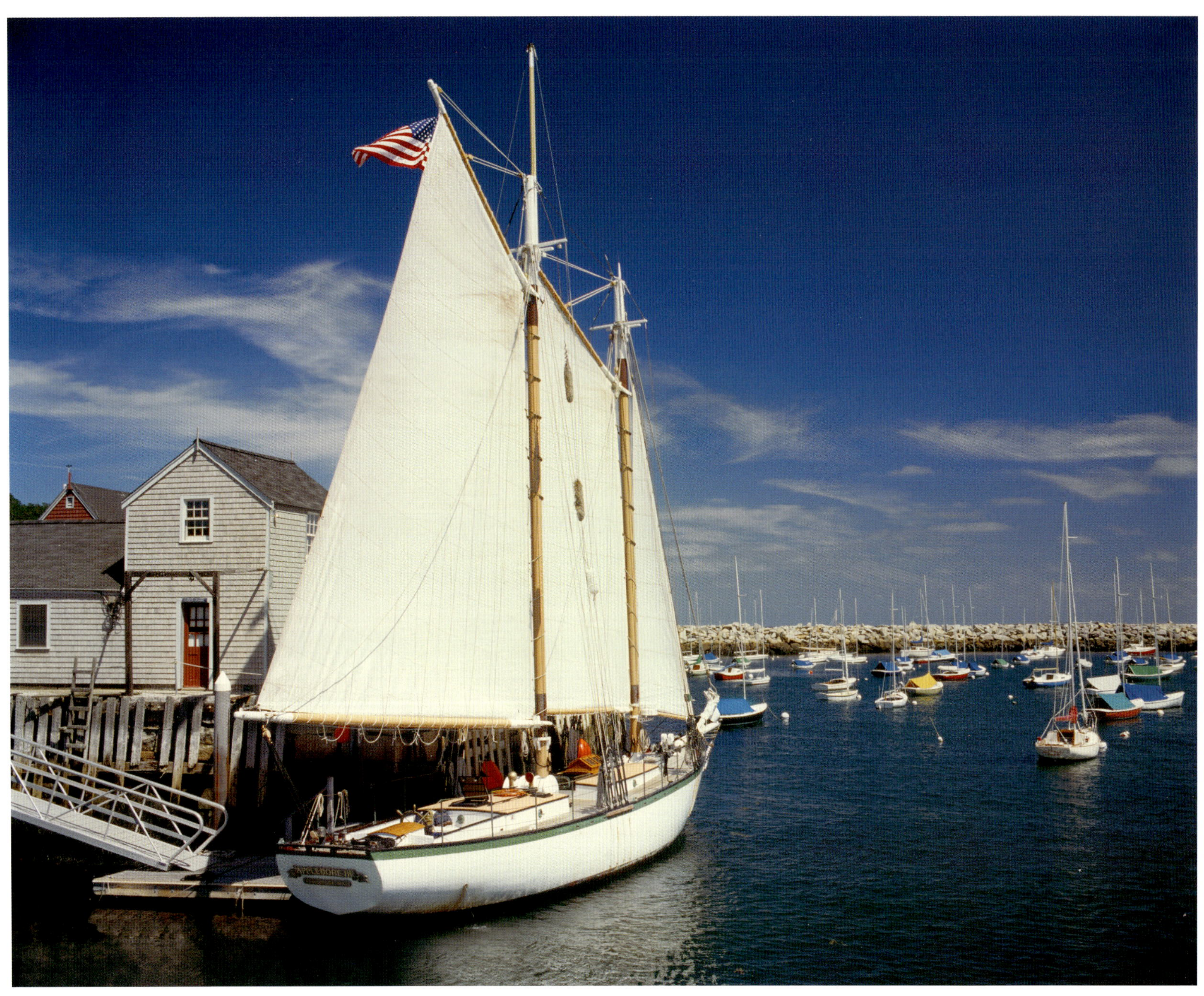

The schooner *Appledore III*, which sails from Rockport Harbor daily

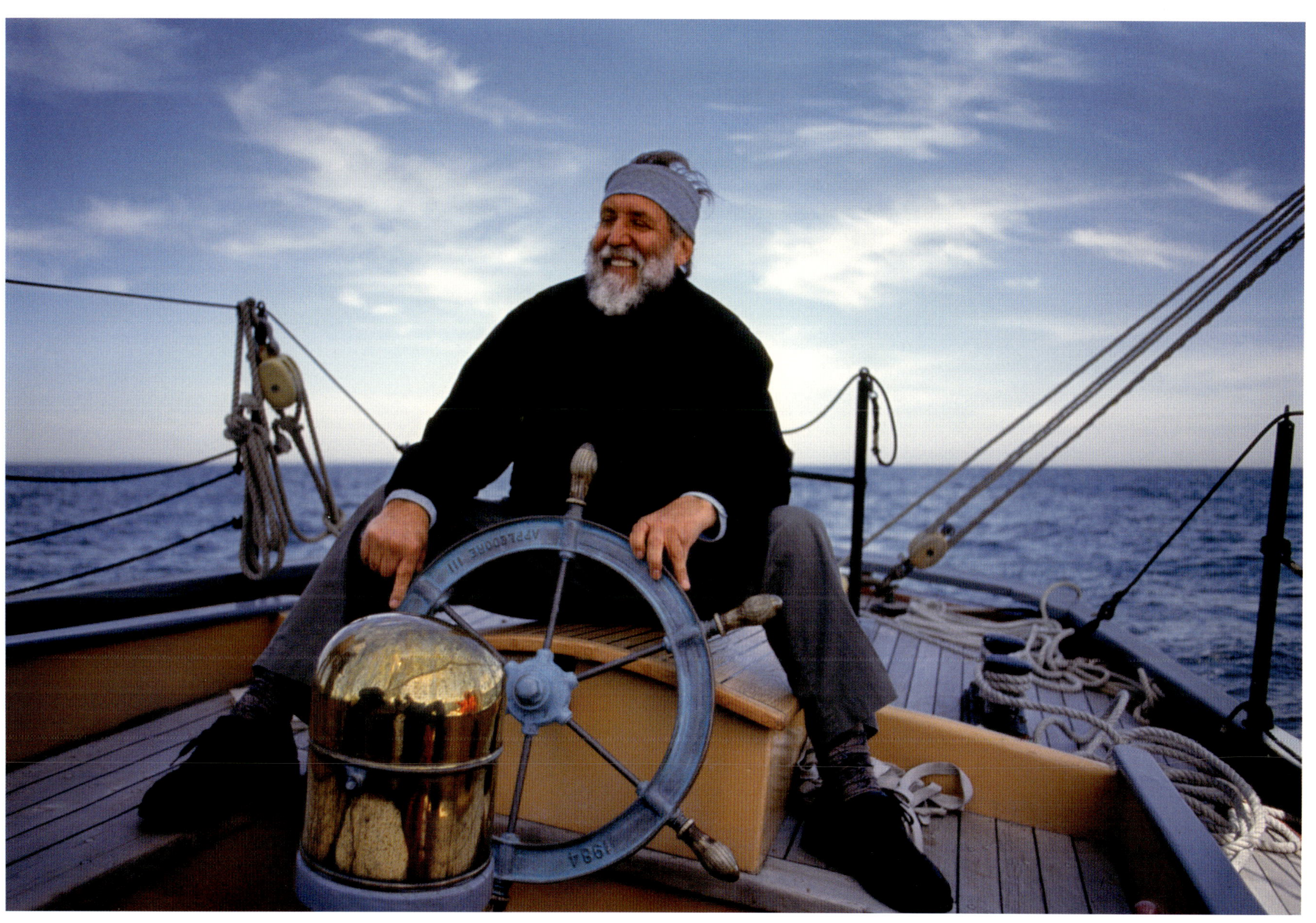


The man behind the wheel of *Appledore III:*
Dr. William Bradley epitomizes John Masefield's poem "Sea-Fever" like no other.

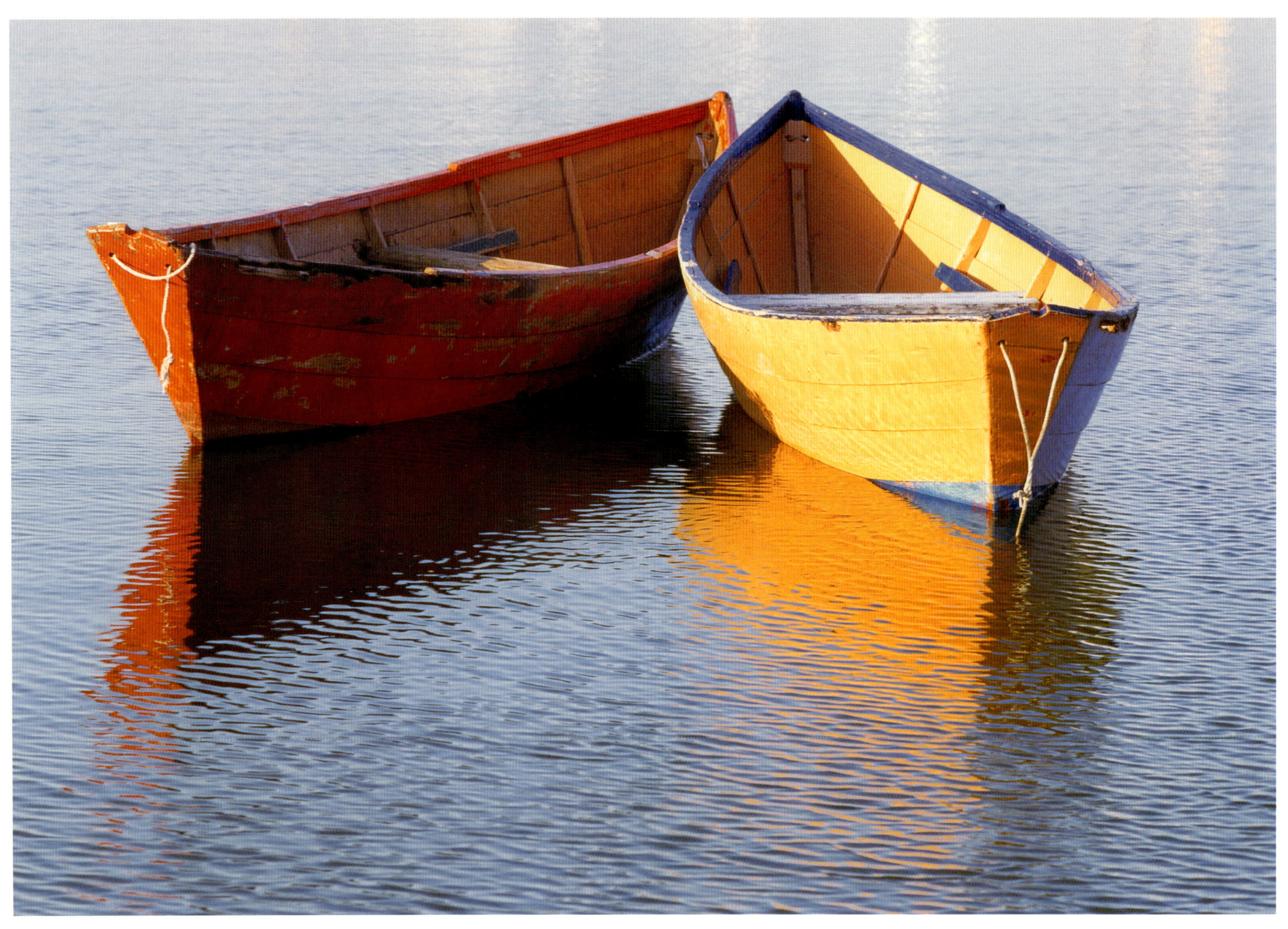

Two old dories

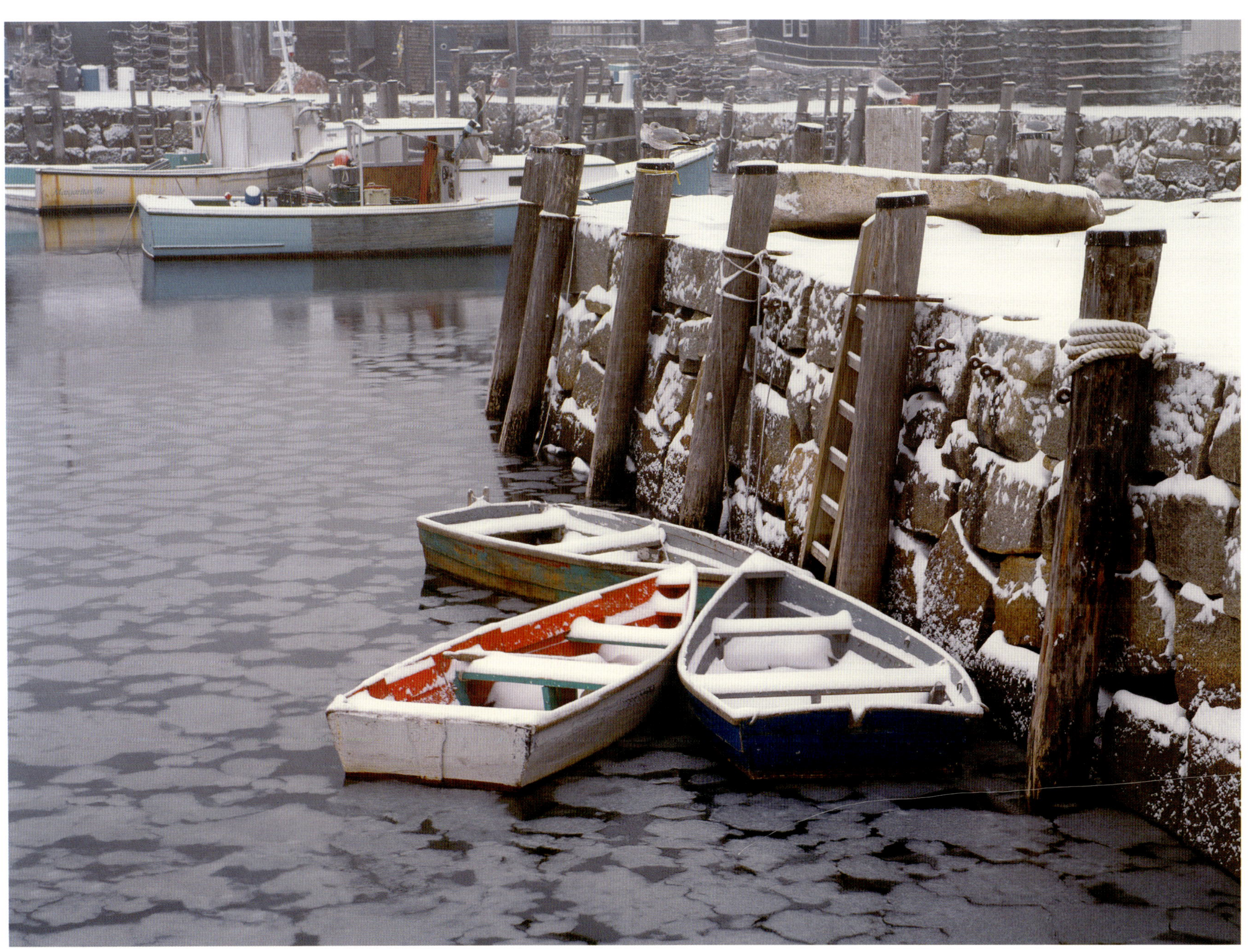

Rockport's inner harbor, where it is a tradition to row small dinks to boats in all seasons and weather

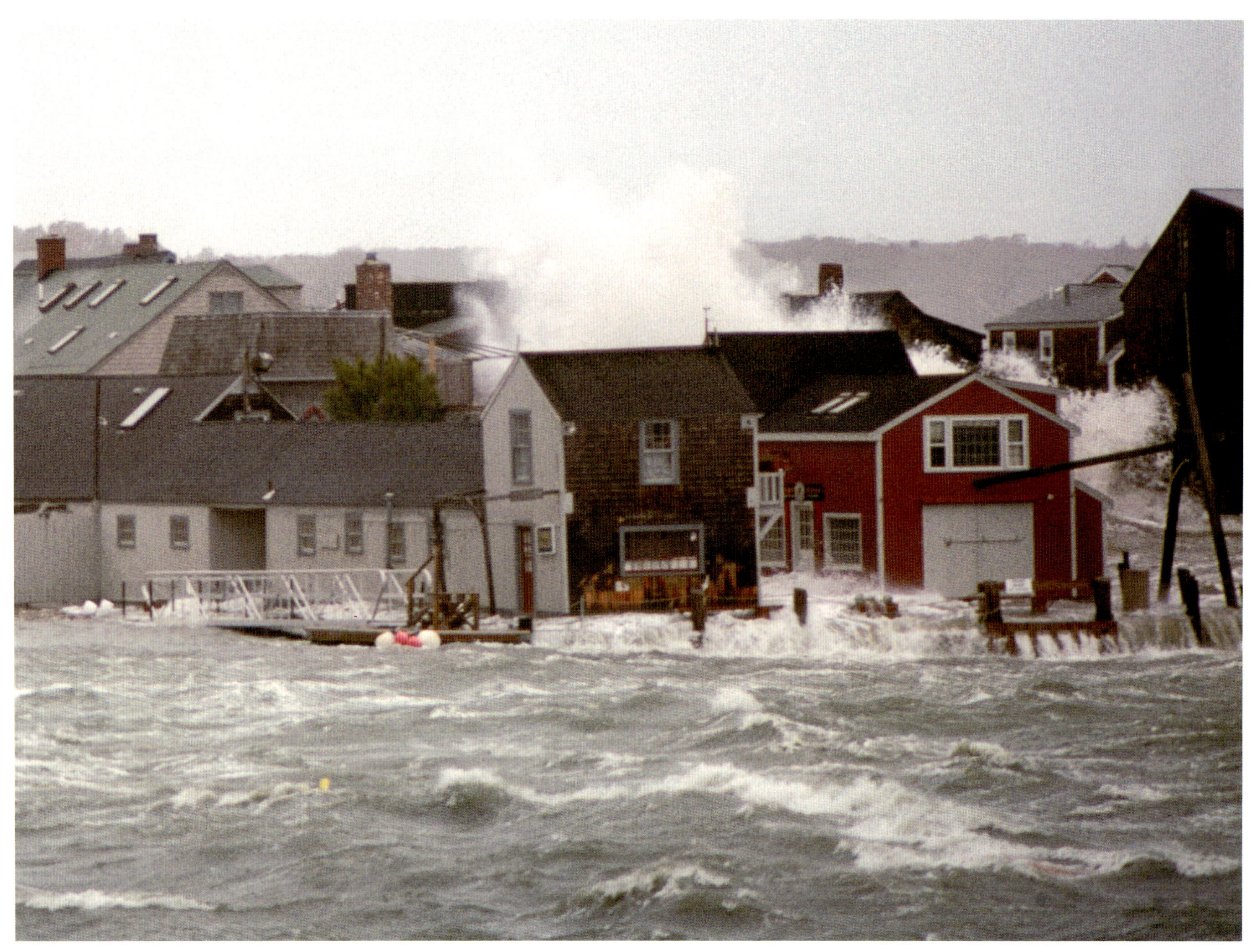

The "Perfect Storm," October 30, 1991, 3:30 p.m. Slamming into Tuna Wharf, the storm blew at its full fury three hours later, at dusk.

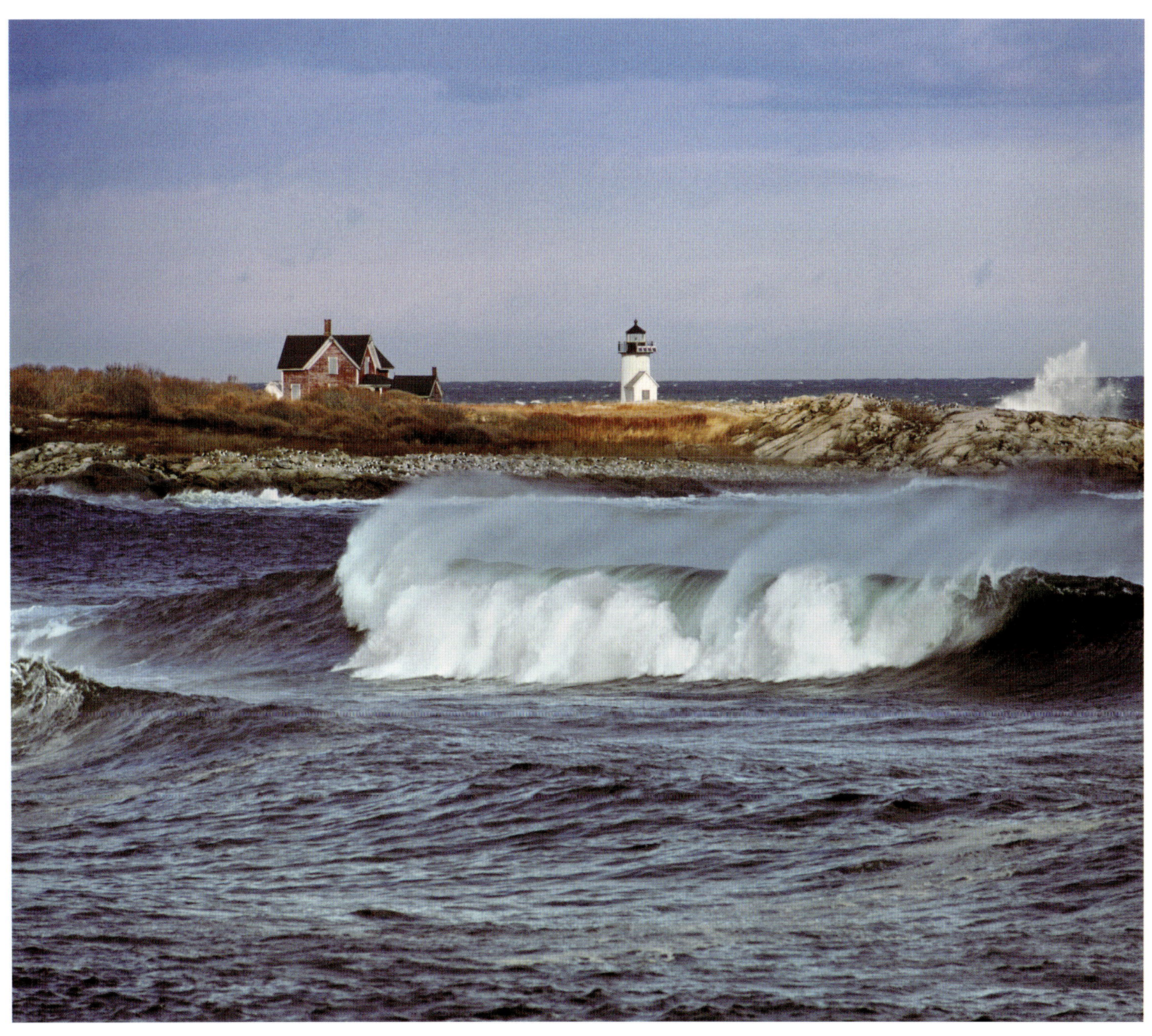

Straitsmouth Island Light from Whale Cove

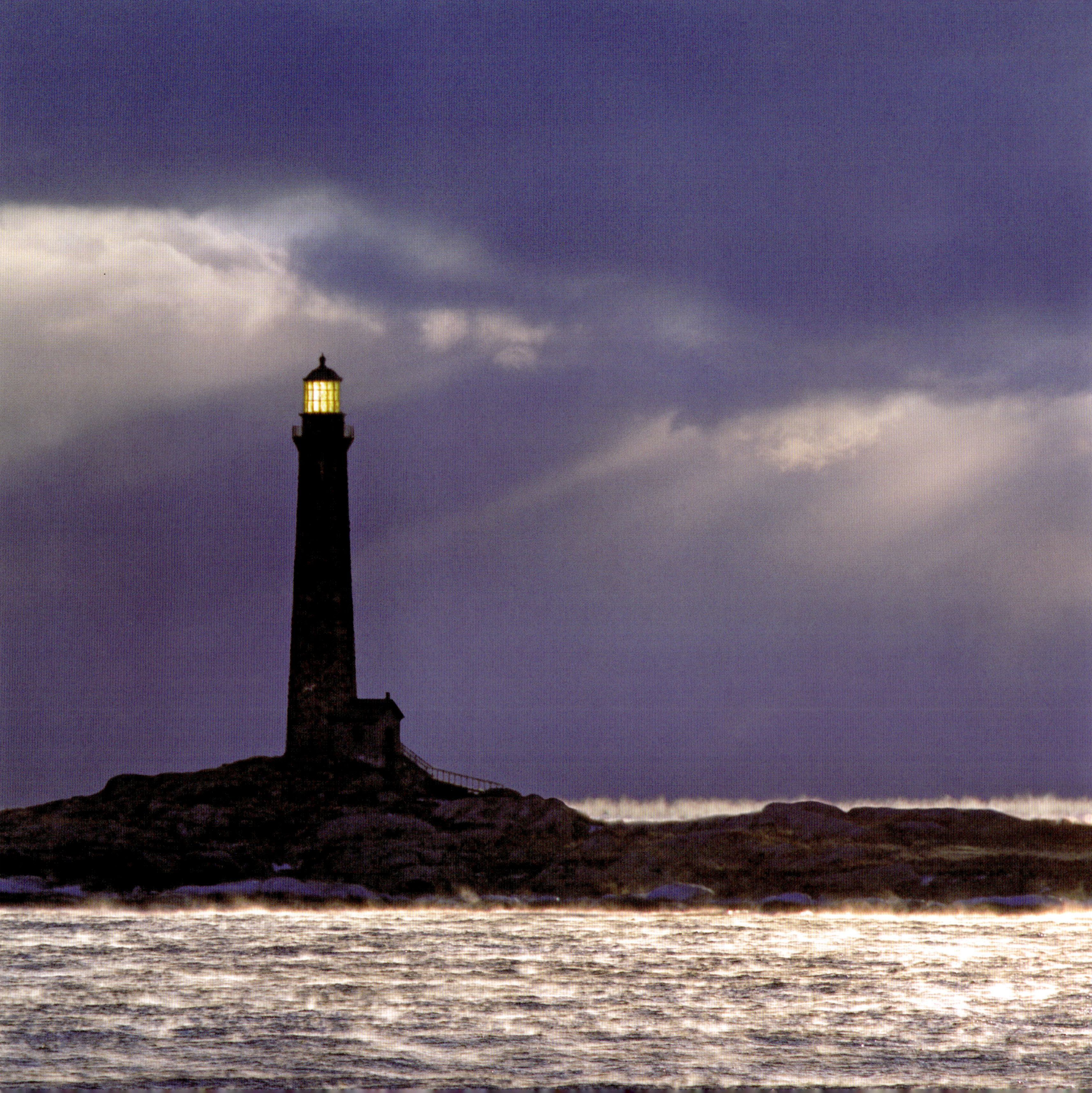

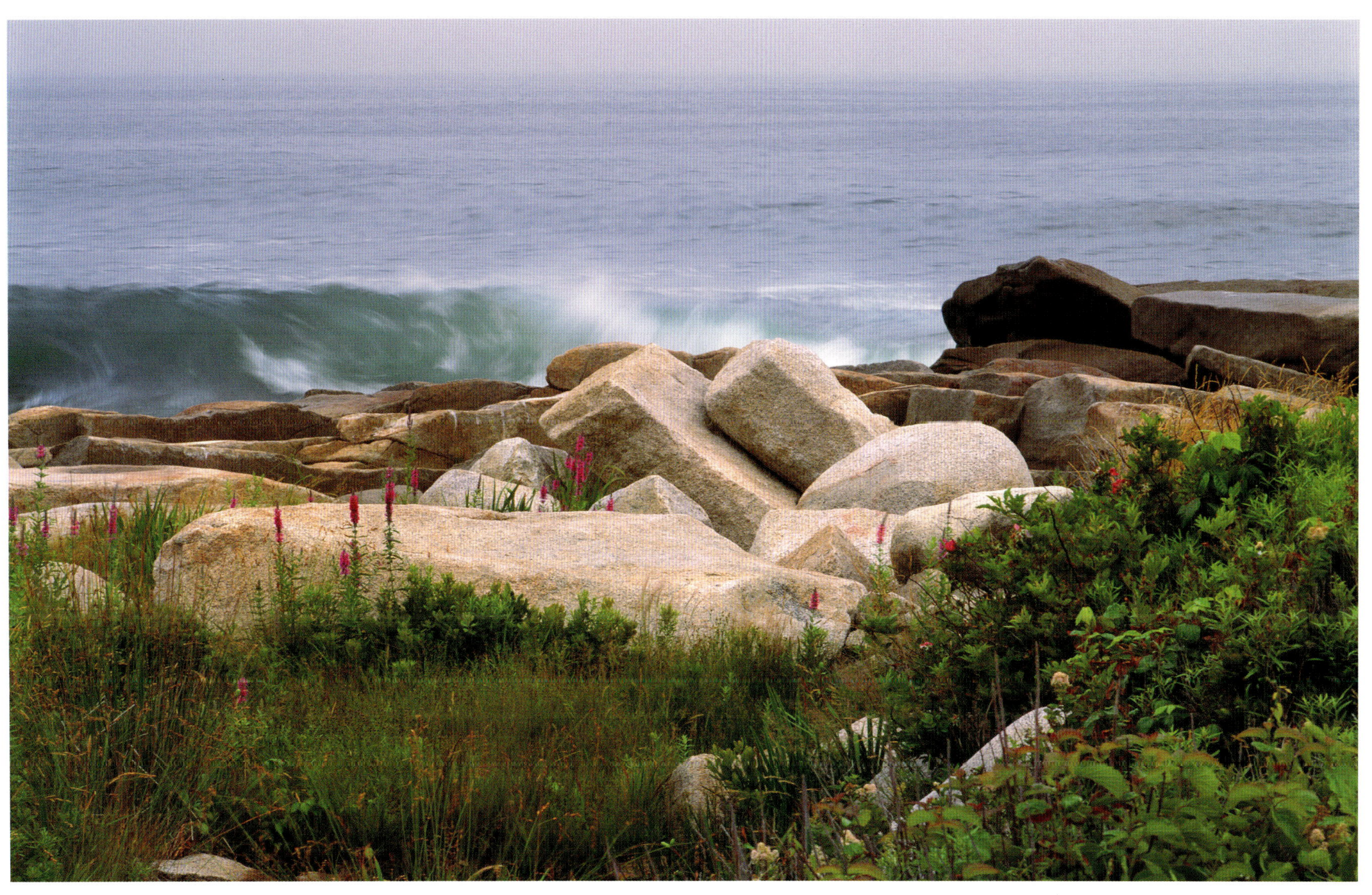

*Above:* Loosestrife, Halibut Point
*Opposite:* My favorite subject, Old North Light, the northern beacon of Thacher Island. I am drawn to it like no other.

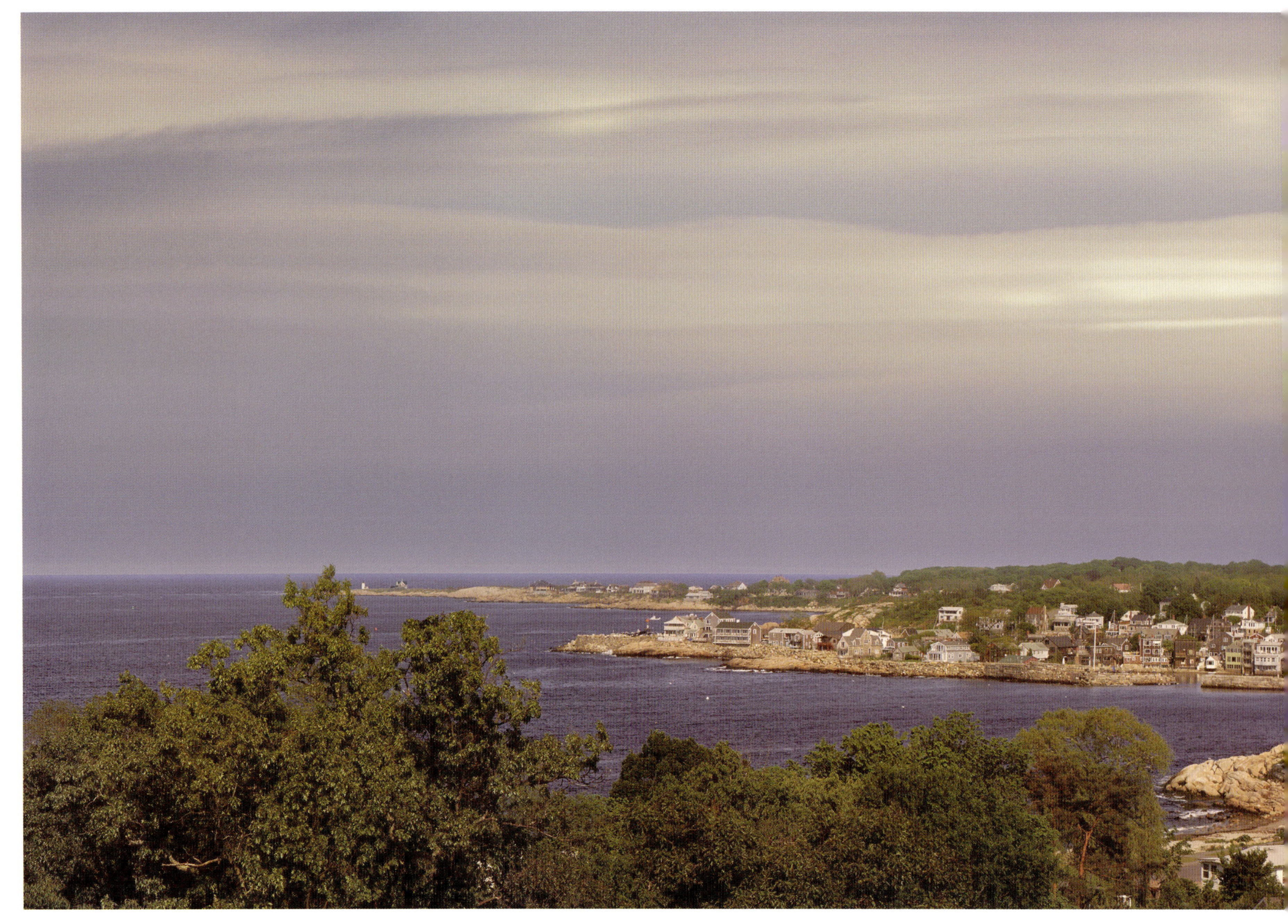

Sandy Bay

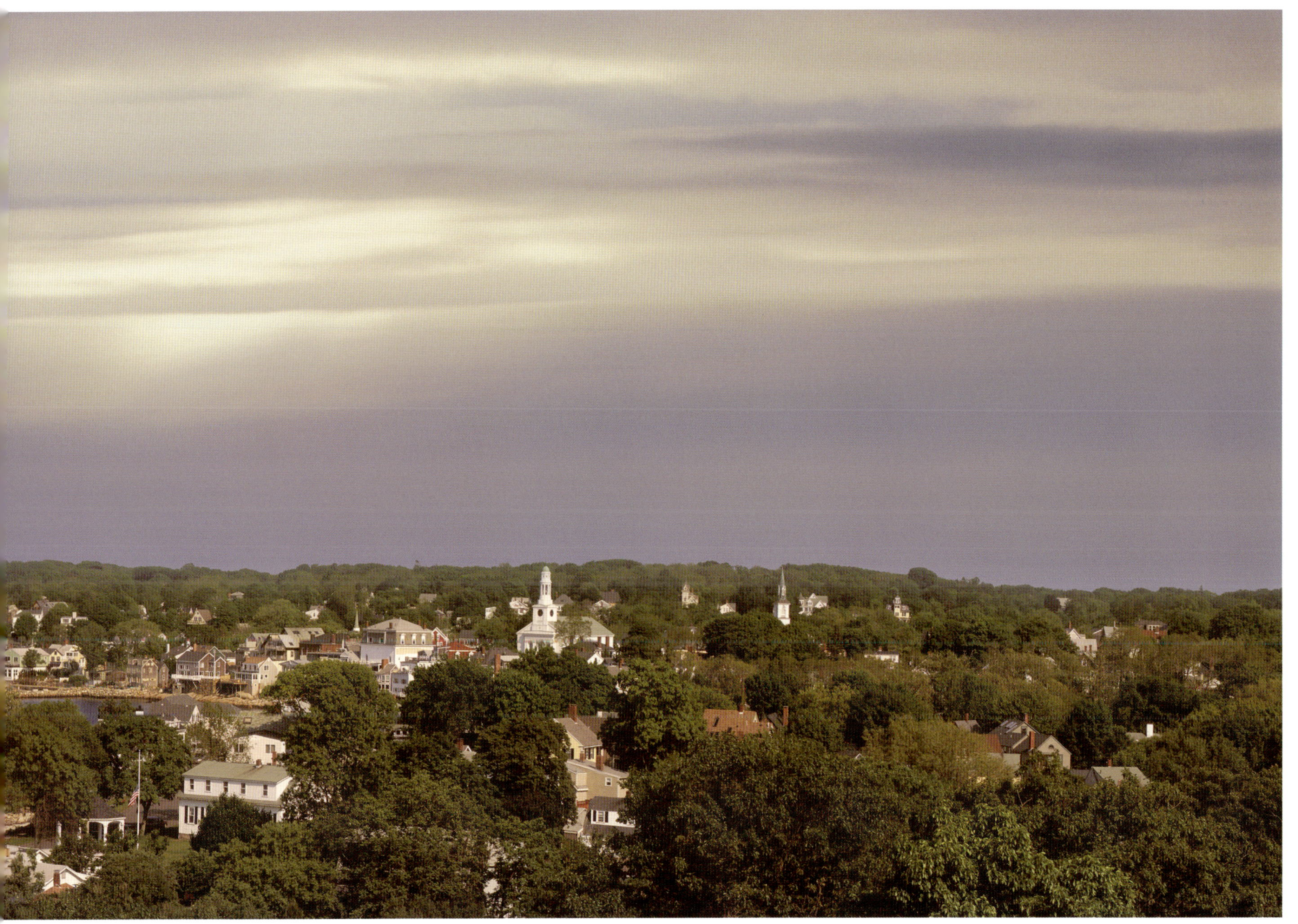

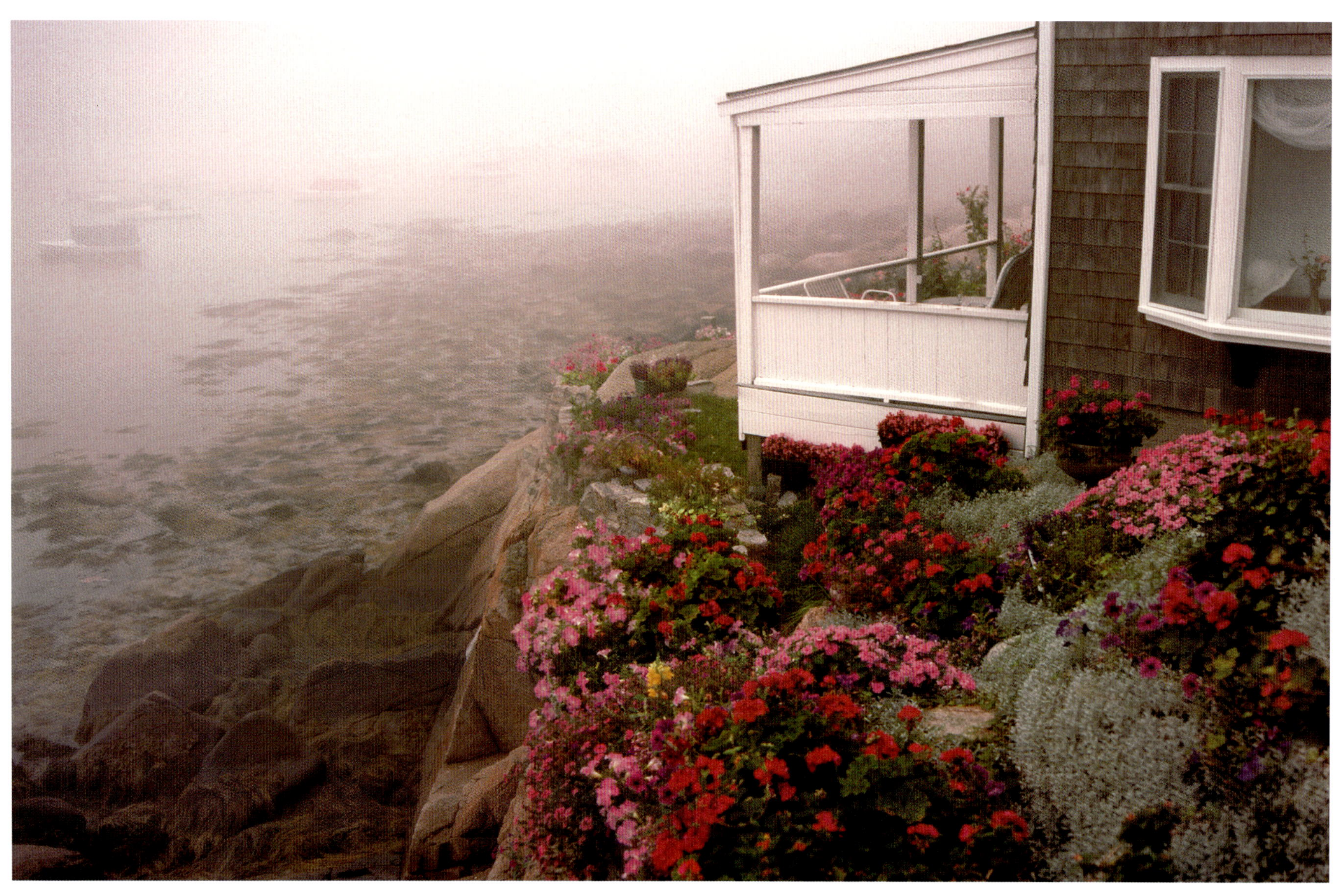

Rockport garden, Bearskin Neck

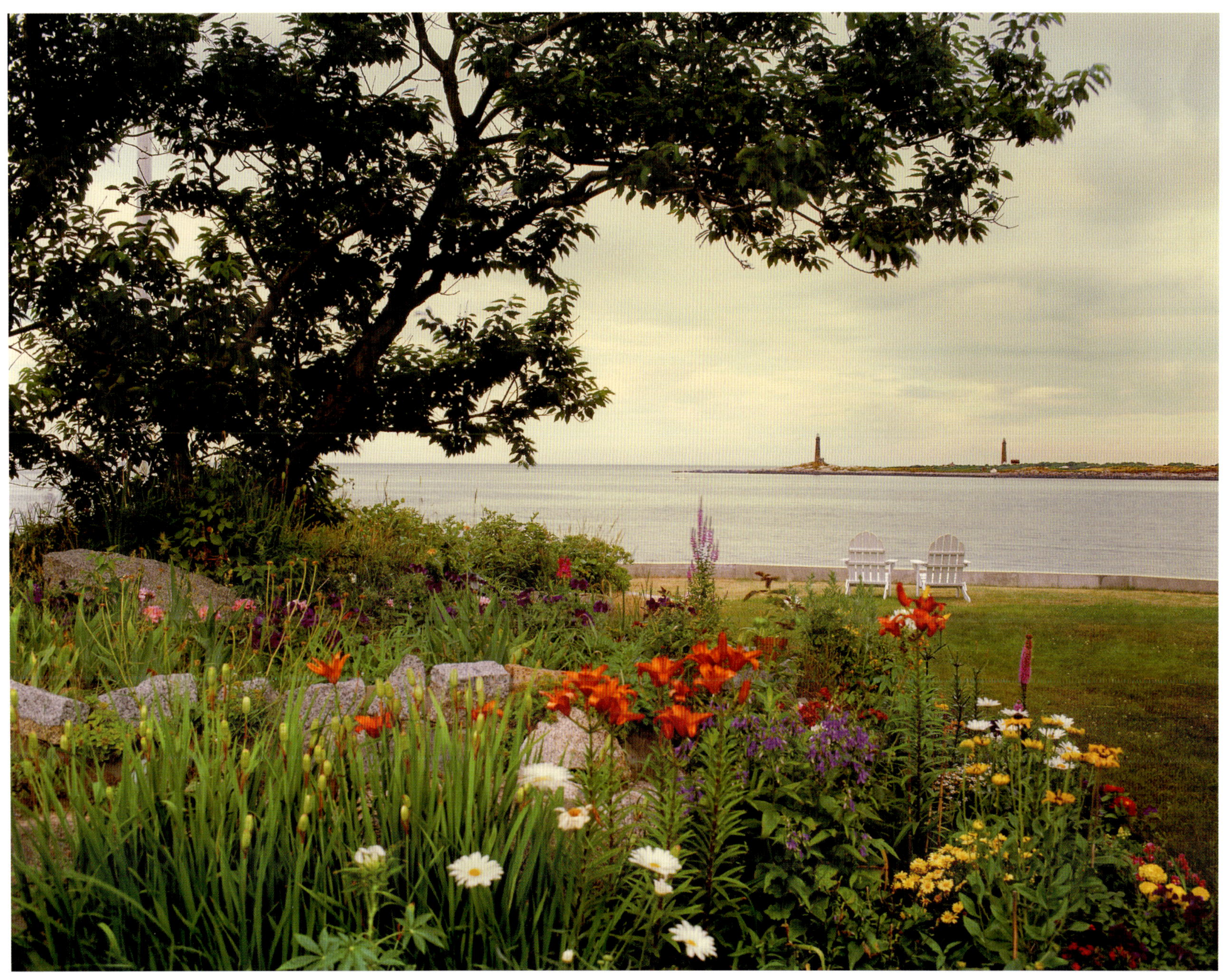

Eden Road

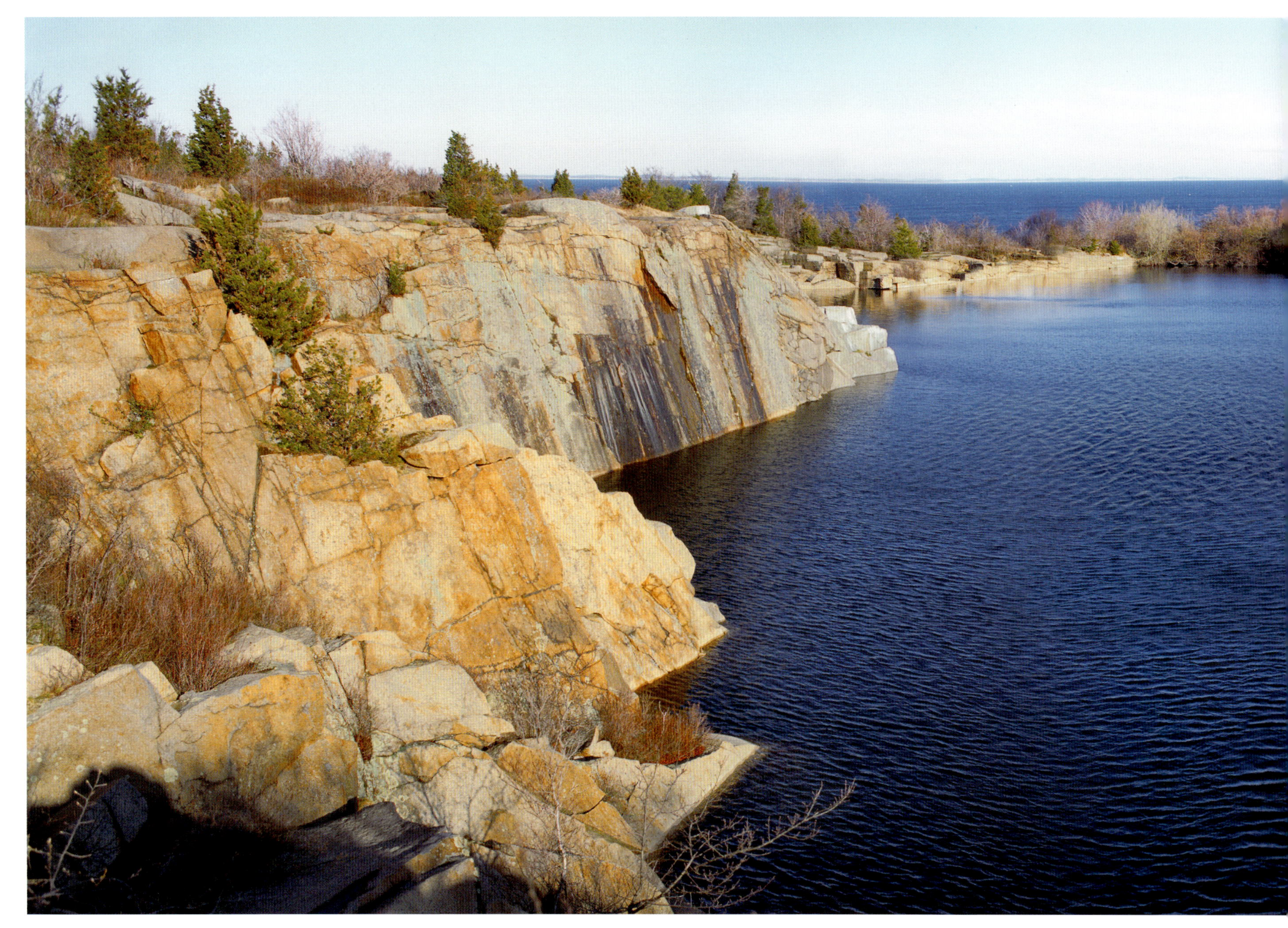

The largest and most beautiful quarry on Cape Ann, Halibut Point

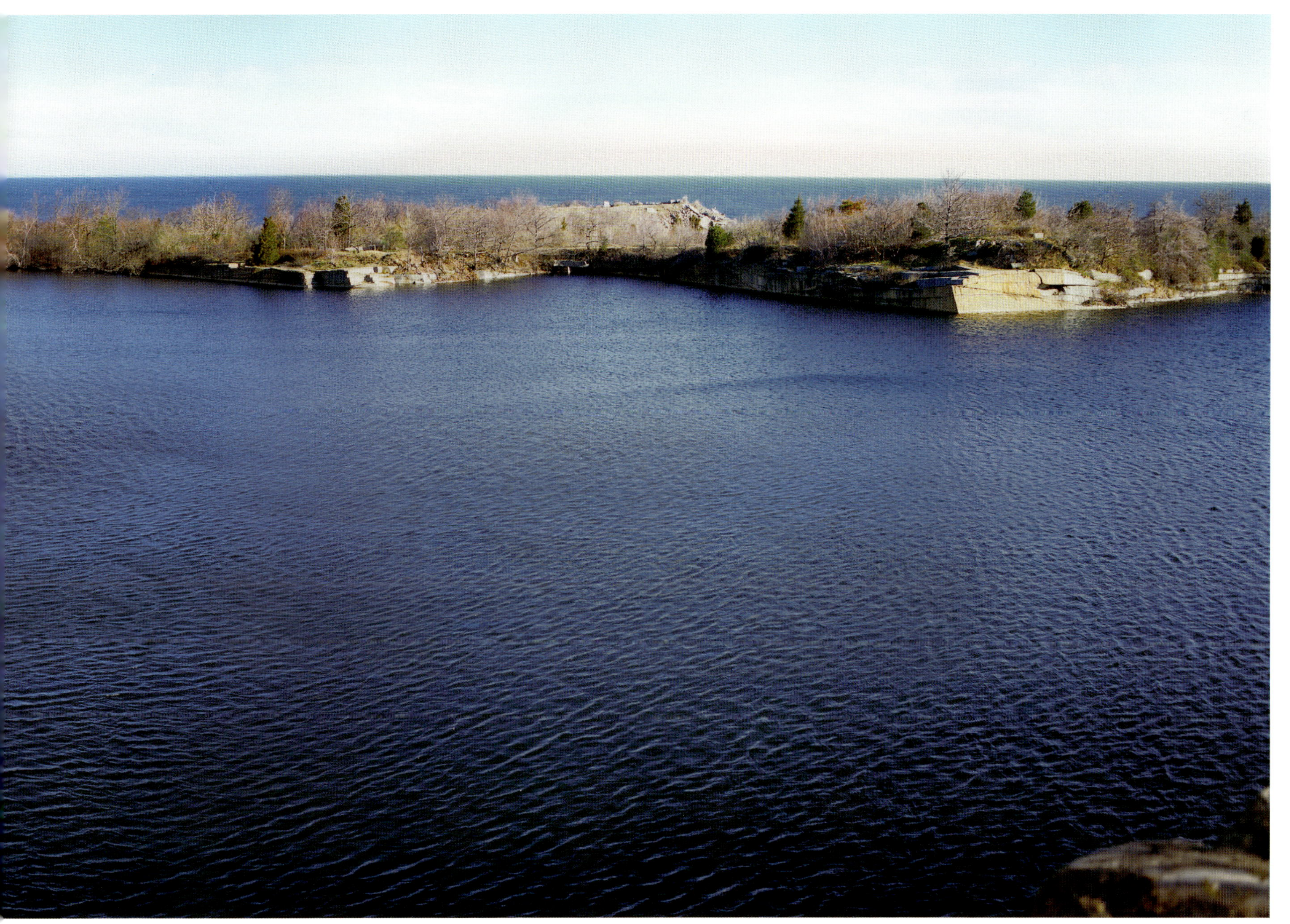

# ESSEX

The smallest town on Cape Ann has as much to offer as any—especially if you have a hankering for fried clams, antiques, or salt marsh hay.

Once a part of Ipswich and called Chebacco Parish as recently as 1911, Essex was first and foremost a shipbuilding town. Puritans from the Plymouth Colony developed the Chebacco boat in 1668, but schooners are the story here. By the twentieth century, more two-masted vessels had been launched from Essex than from anywhere in the world. Burnham's yard carries on the tradition, and the Essex Shipbuilding Museum honors it.

The rocky coast of Gloucester and Rockport gives up this side of the Annisquam River, and Essex is girdled with salt marshes and ravishing vistas. You can rent a kayak or charter a boat and wind your way out the Essex River to the sea. Downtown, the big draws on a summer afternoon are fried fish and faded furniture. Woodman's has said they're the birthplace of the fried clam, and some would argue the point. But everyone needs a legend, and Essex certainly has its share.

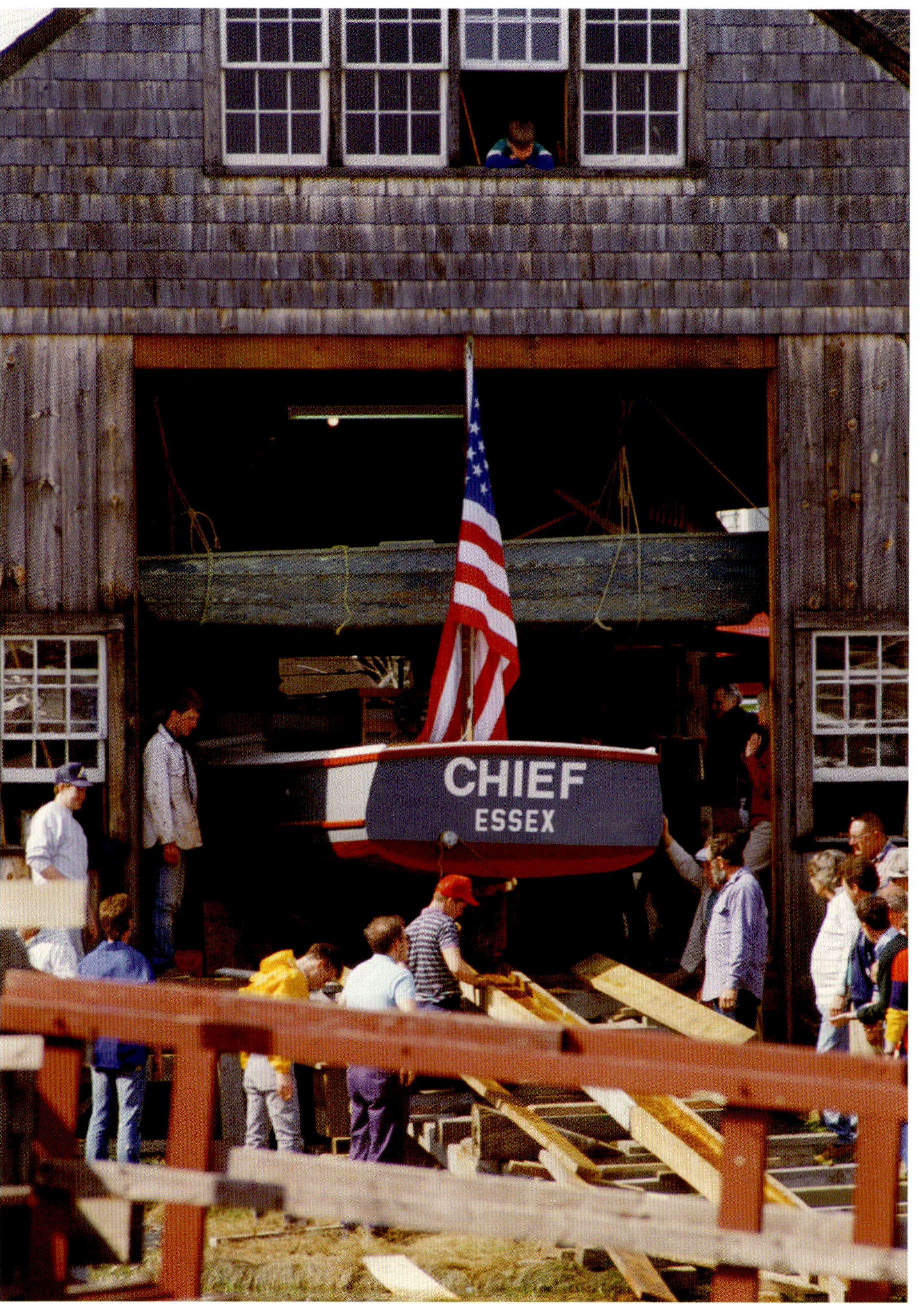


*Above:* Greasing the ways for the launching of *Chief,* H.A. Burnham's historic yard
*Opposite:* House on the salt marsh

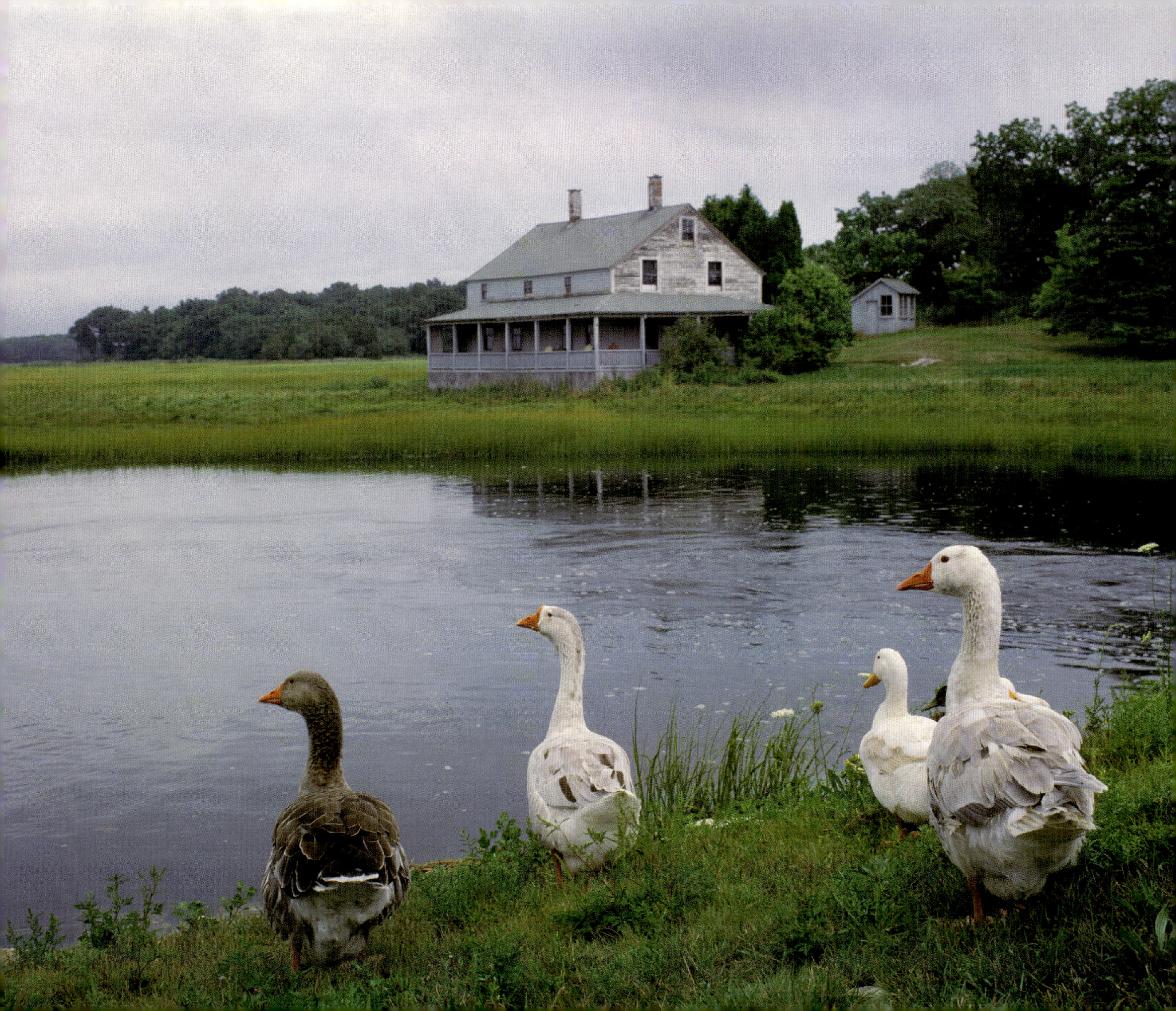

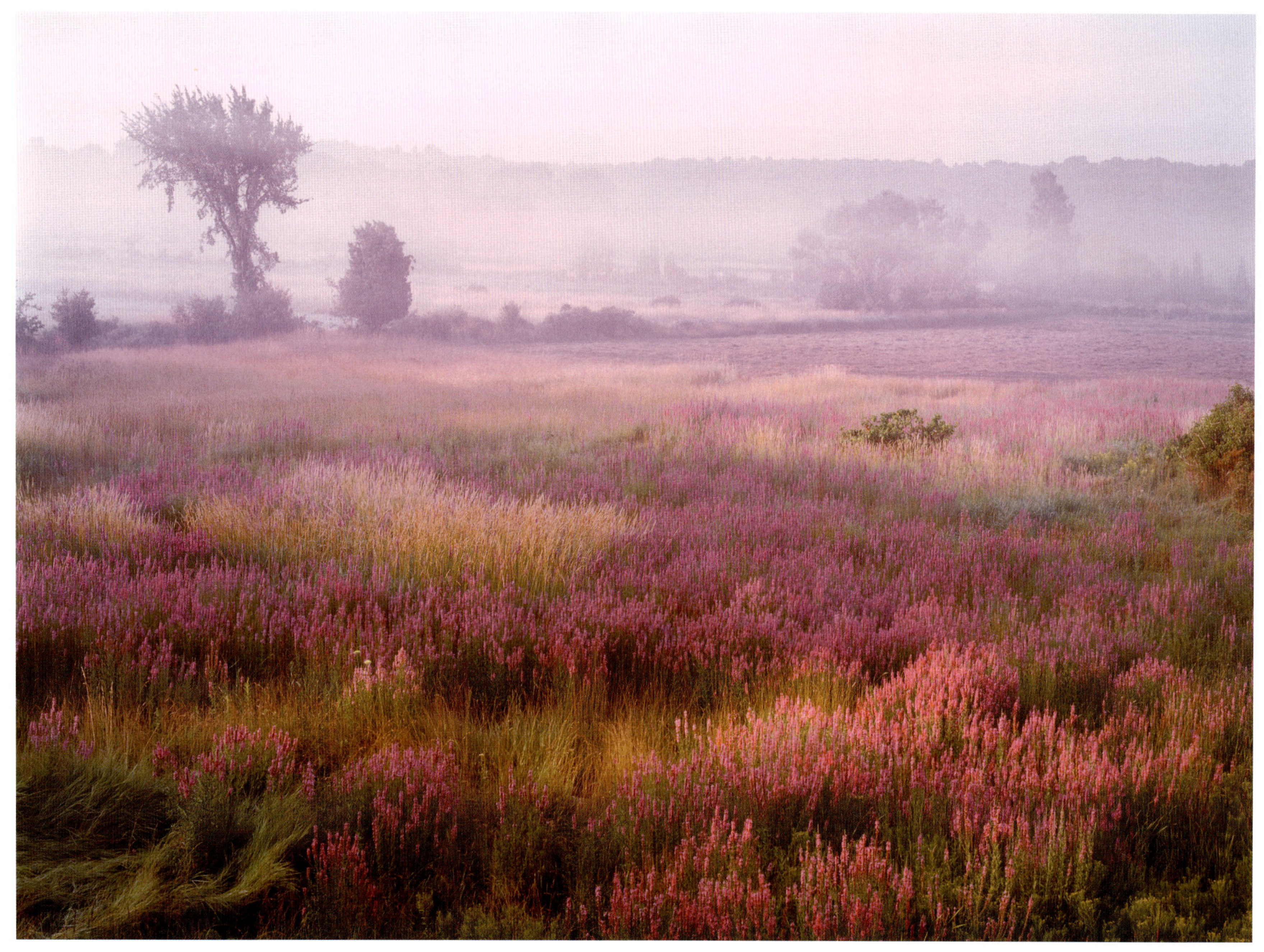

Essex meadow

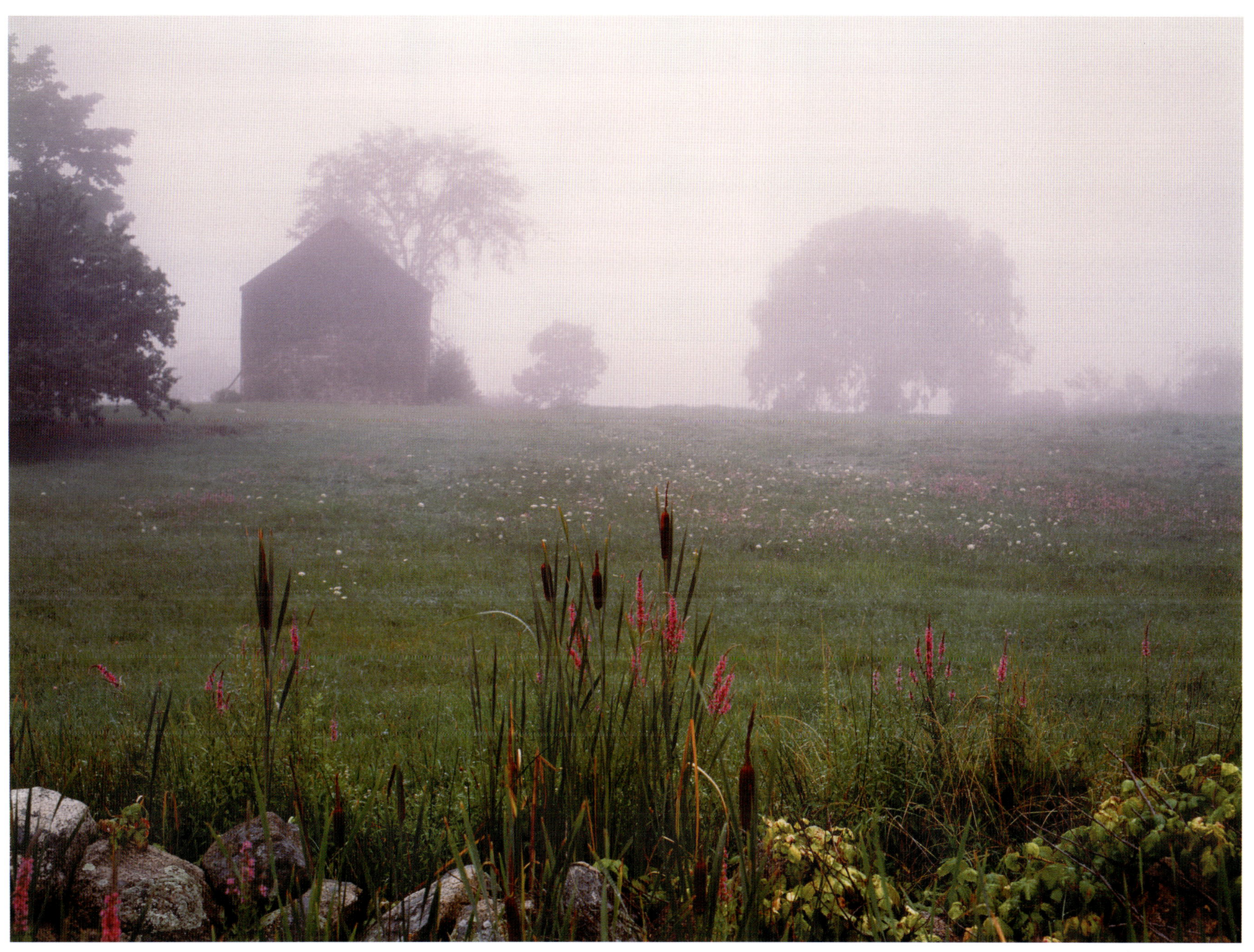

Flower barn, Island Road

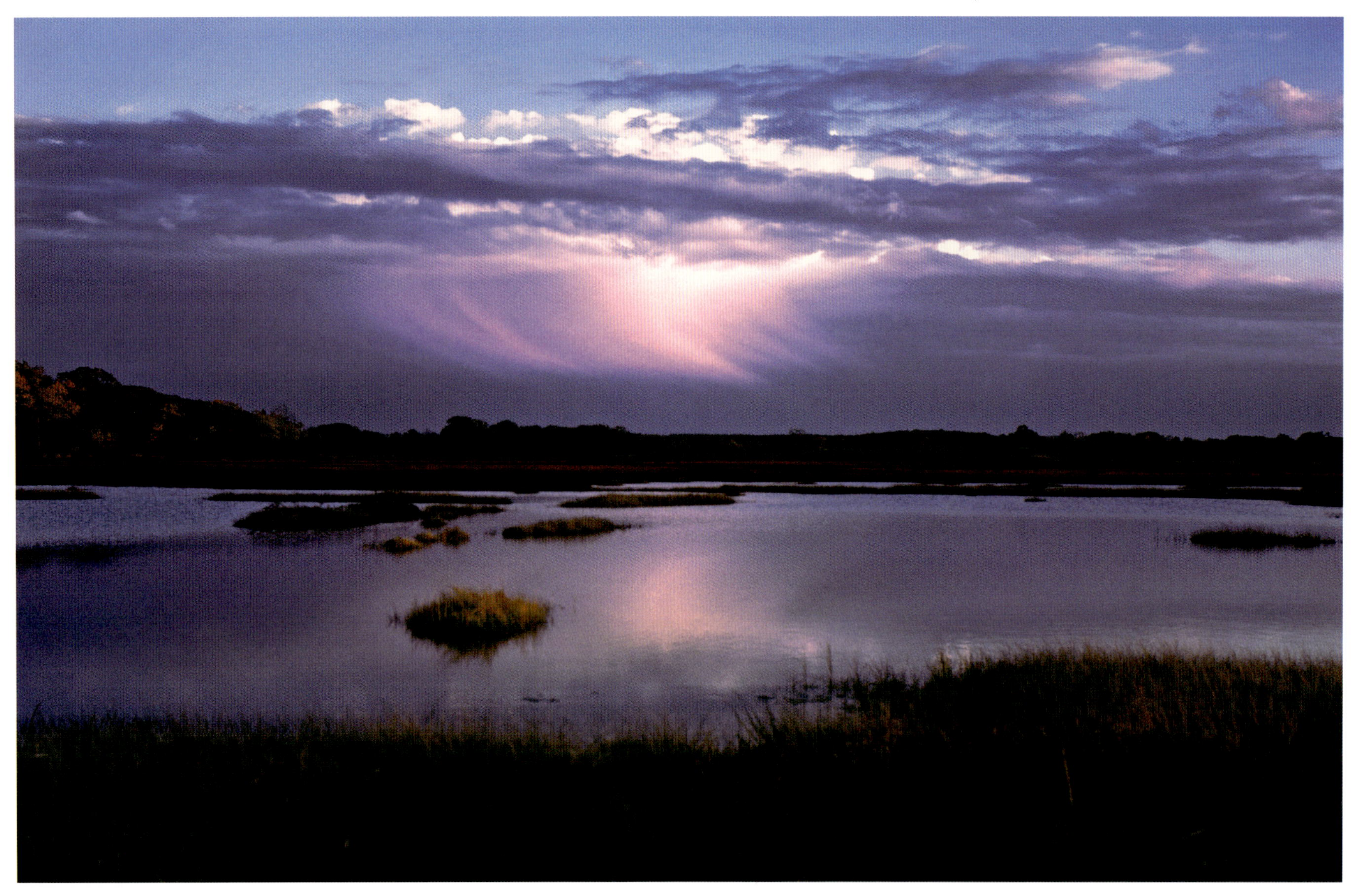

*Above:* Flying cloud twilight, Essex Salt Marsh
*Opposite:* Burning tree, Cape Ann Golf Course

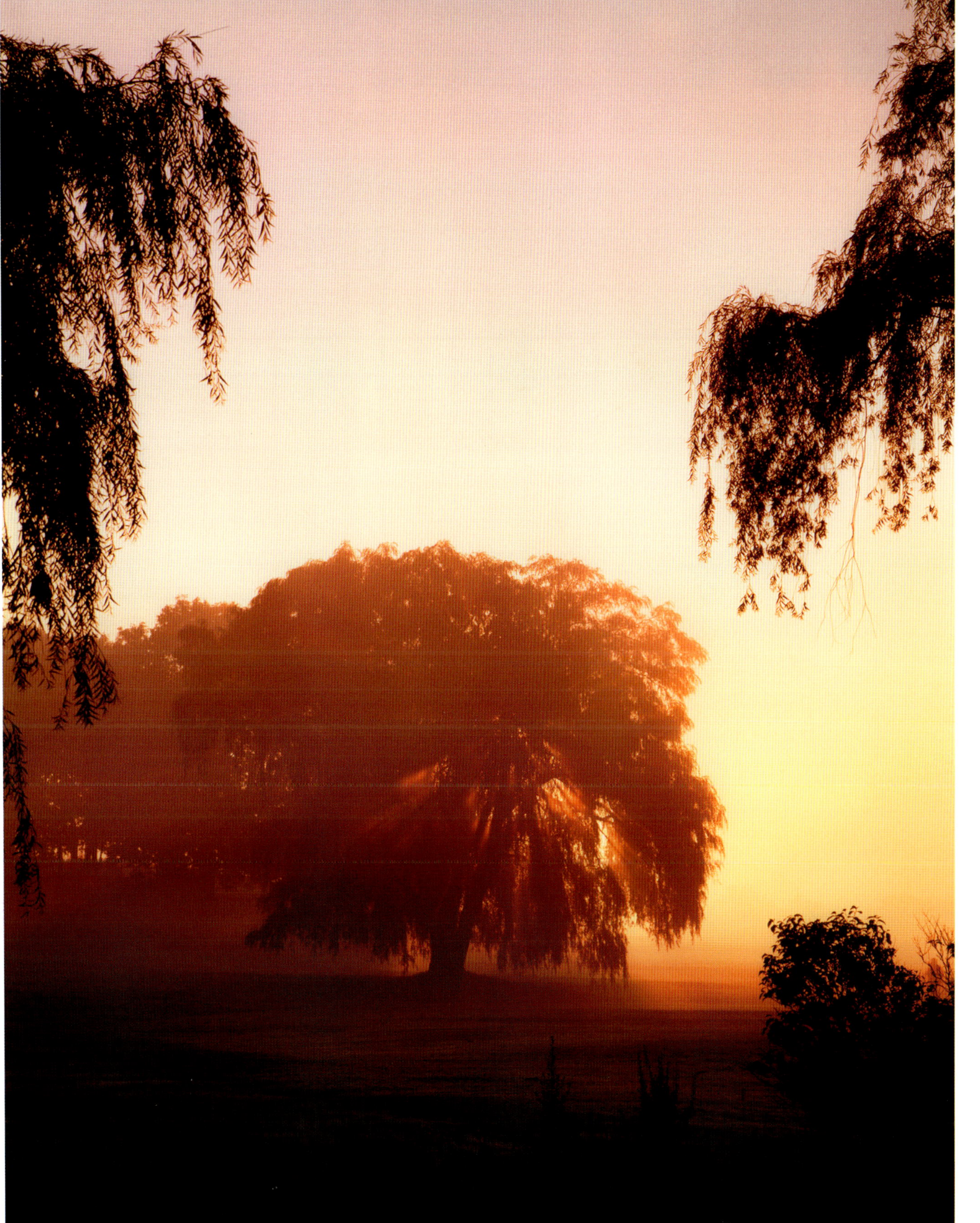

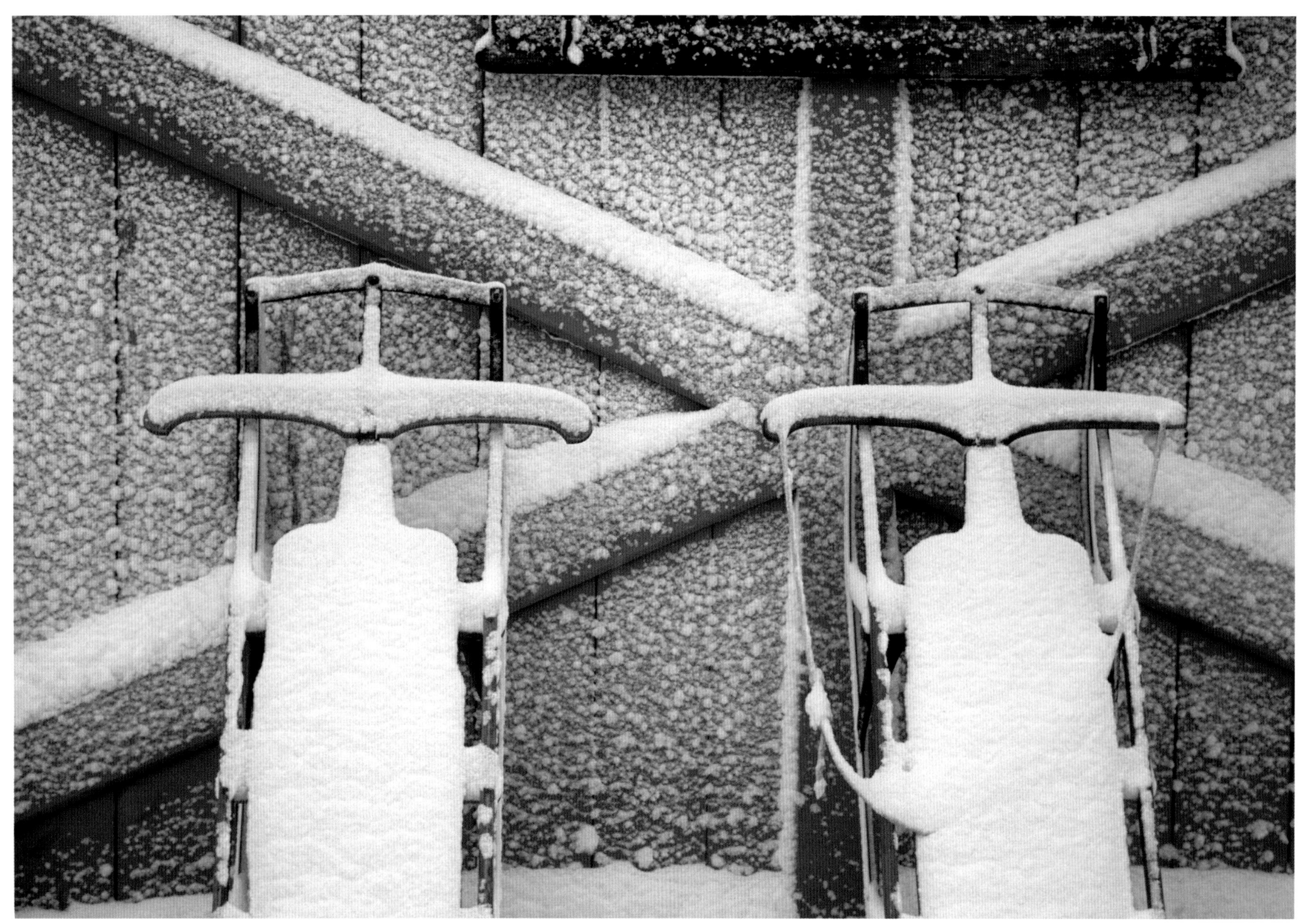

Flexible Flyers suspended in time outside an antique shop

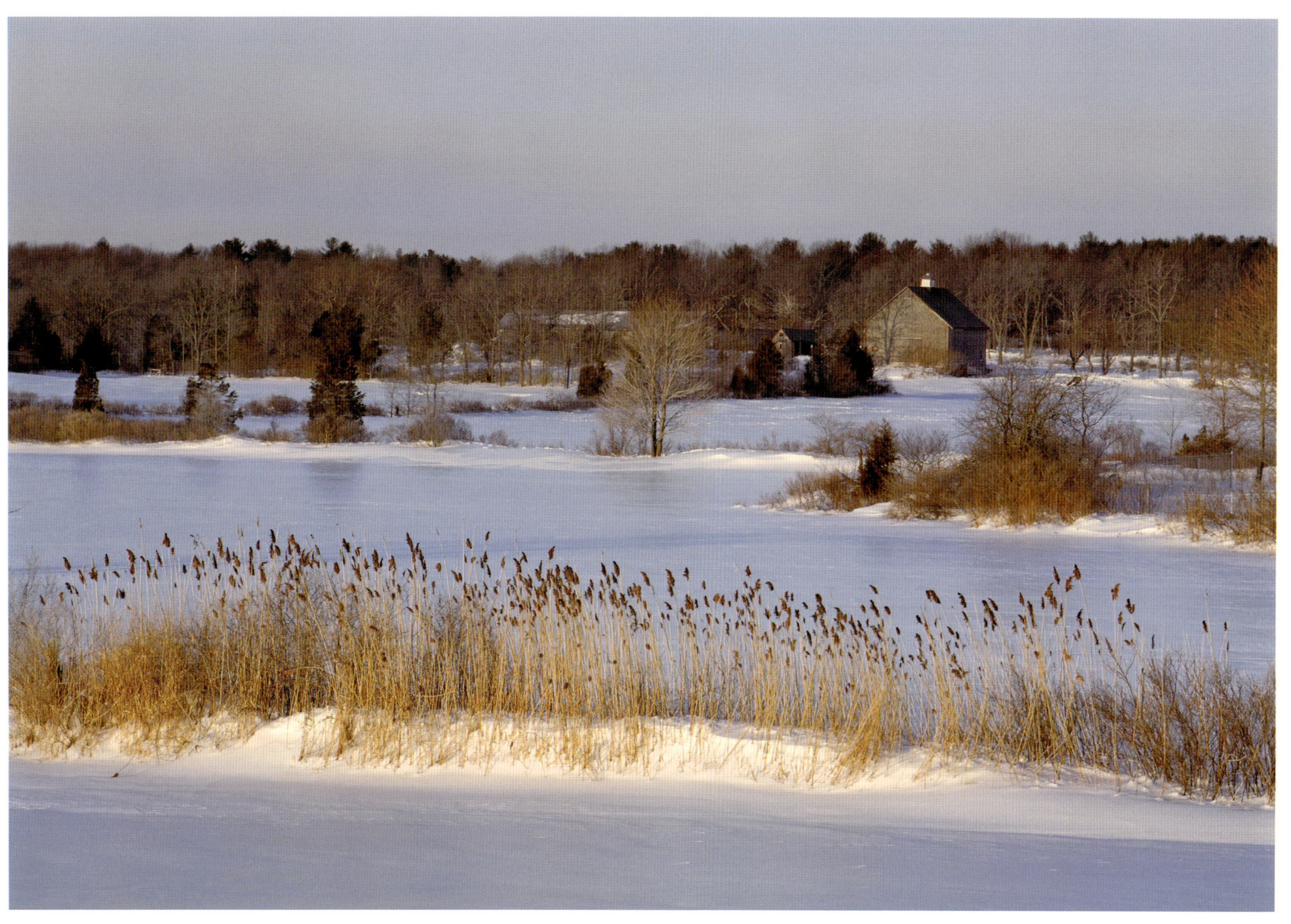

Giddings Farm

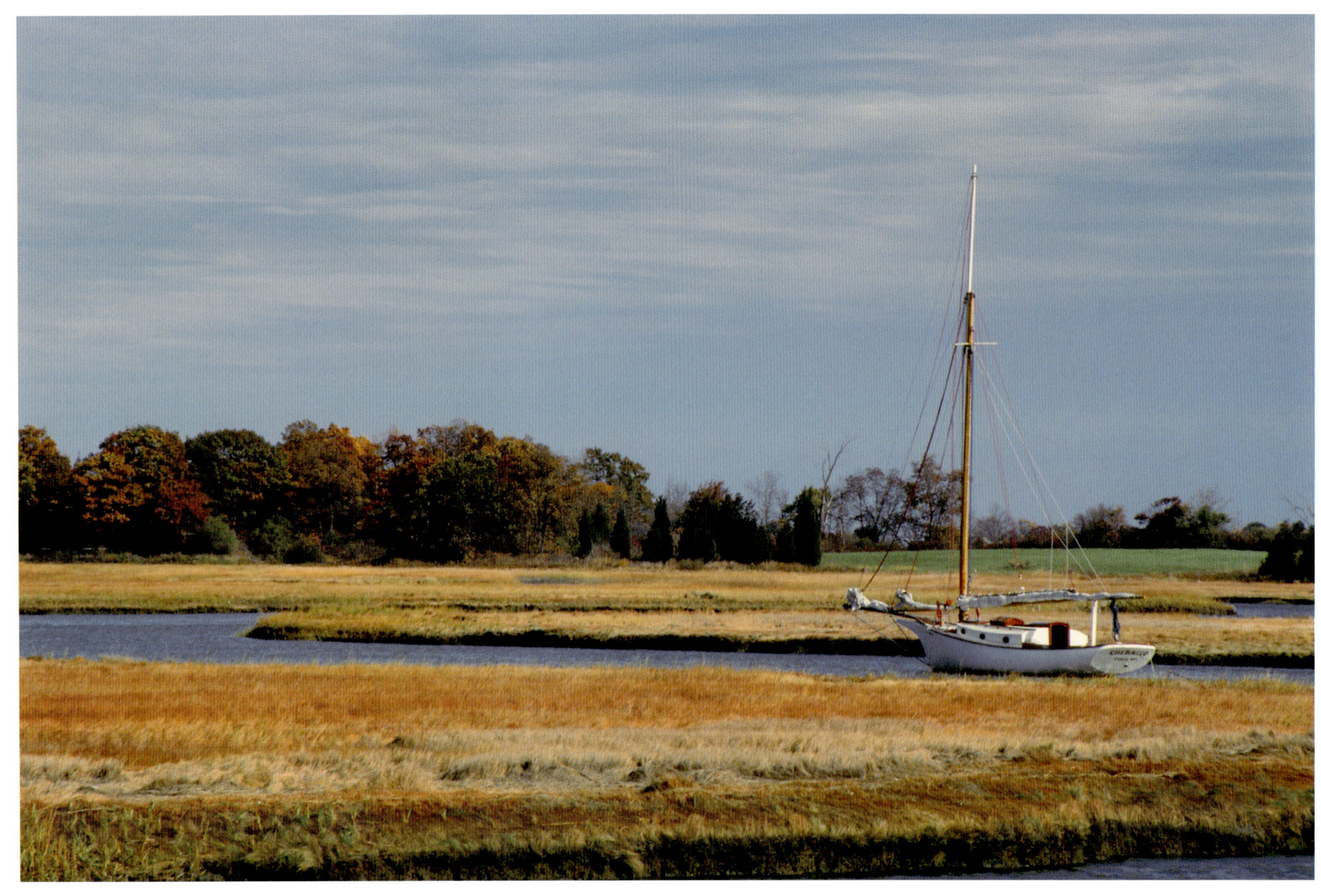

Friendship sloop, on the salt marsh

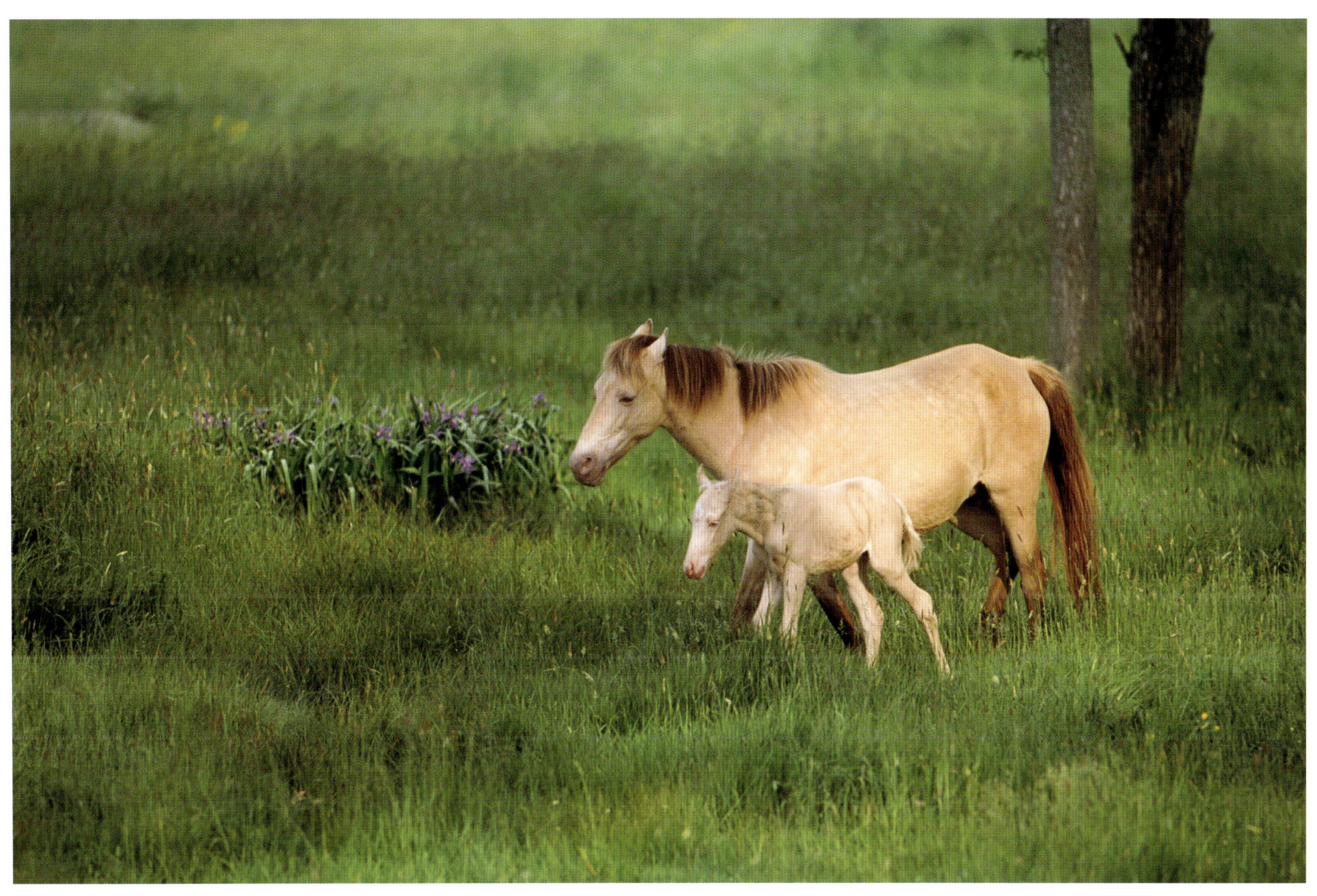

First walk, off Eastern Avenue

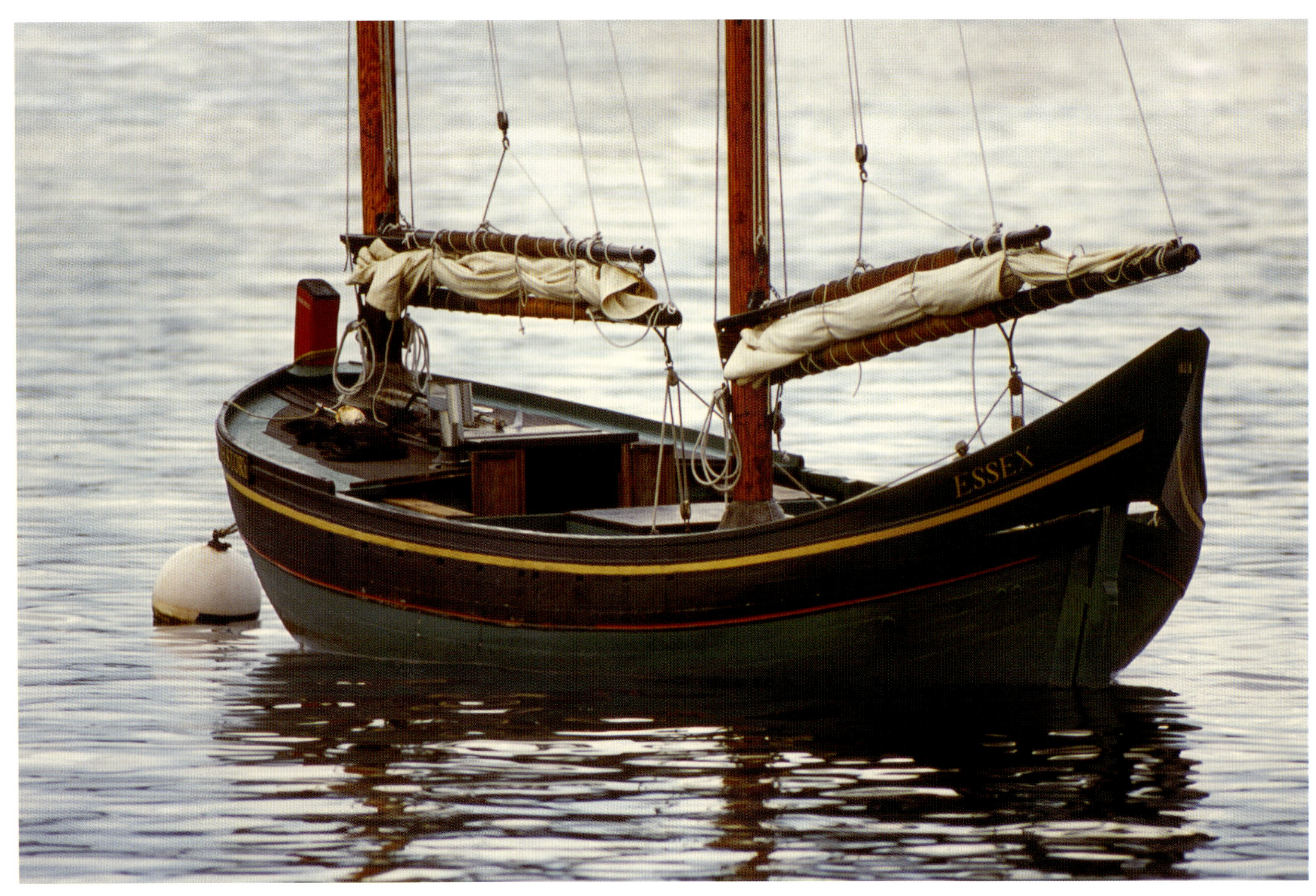


*Lewis H. Story*, replica of an eighteenth-century Chebacco fishing boat, Essex Shipbuilding Museum

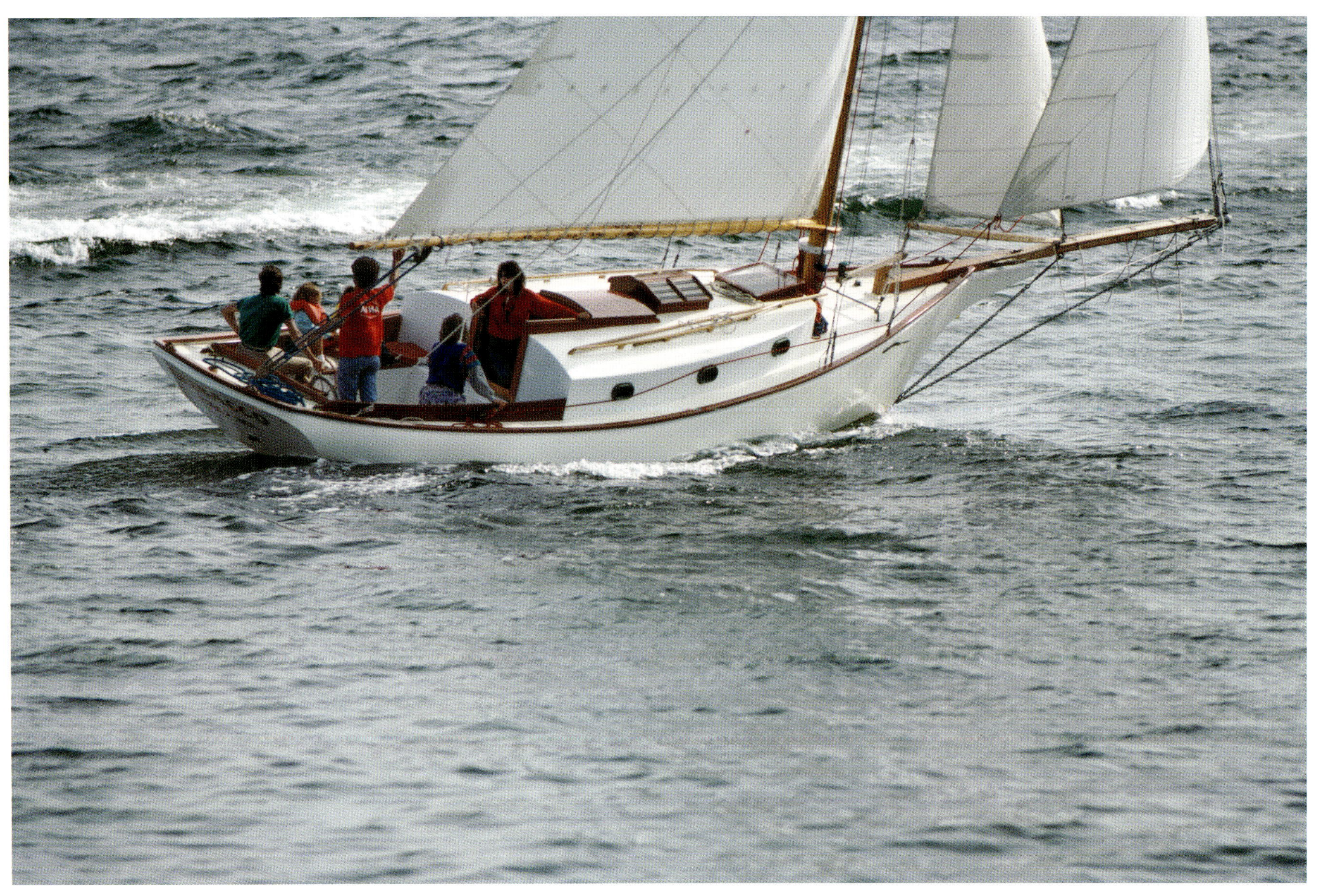

Friendship sloop *Chebacco*, Essex Bay

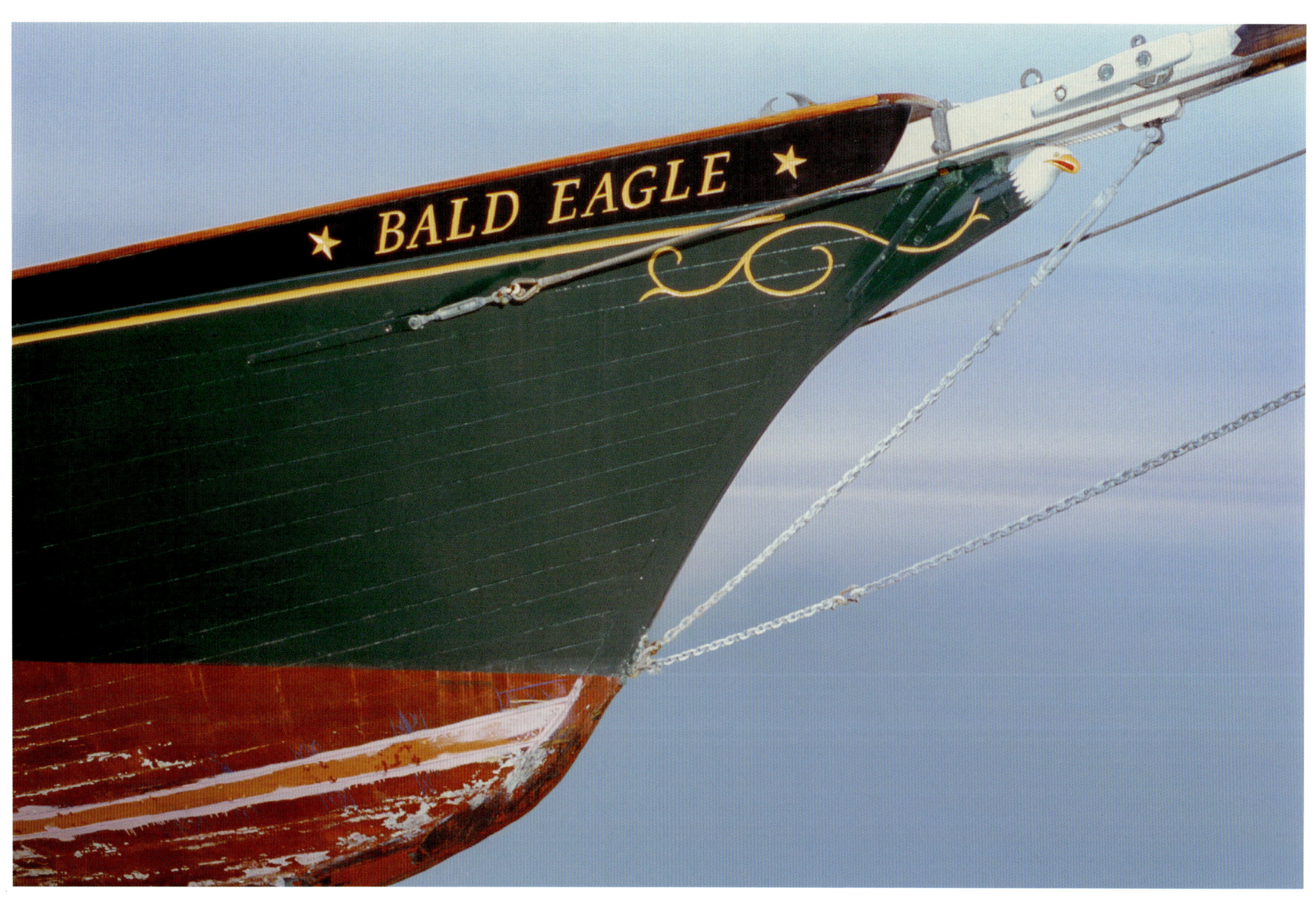


The schooner *Bald Eagle,* after receiving a new plank at the Essex Shipbuilding Museum

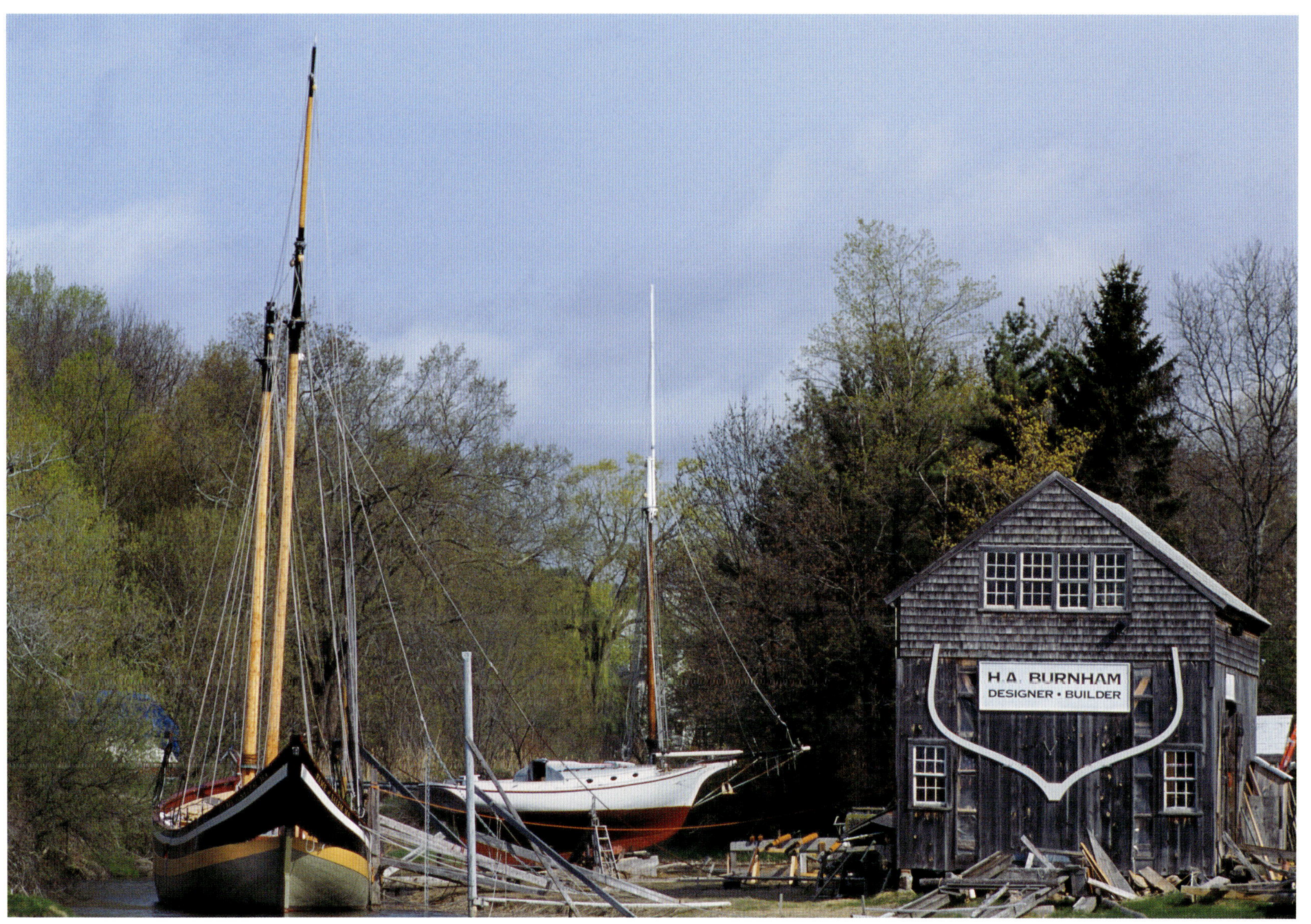


H. A. Burnham Boat Building & Design, with the two-masted *Fame* (at left), one of many historical boats constructed in recent years. Burnham continues a long family legacy of shipbuilding in Essex, a town that claims it has built more two-masted schooners than any town its size in the world.

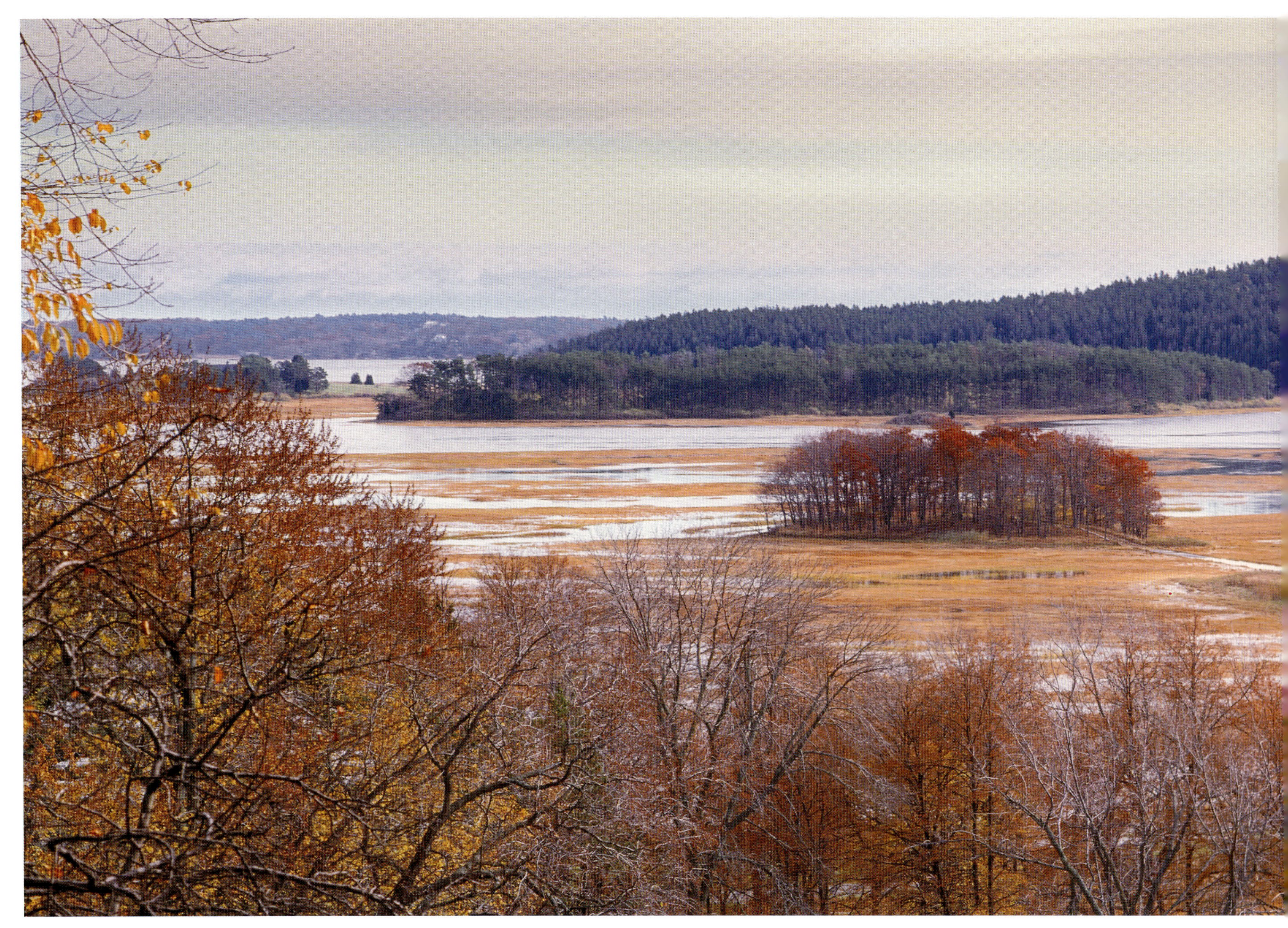

Choate Island on the Essex Salt Marsh. On a clear day ten miles out in the Gulf of Maine, the little dip at the crown of the island can be seen on the coastline, often guiding boats home to Ipswich Bay.

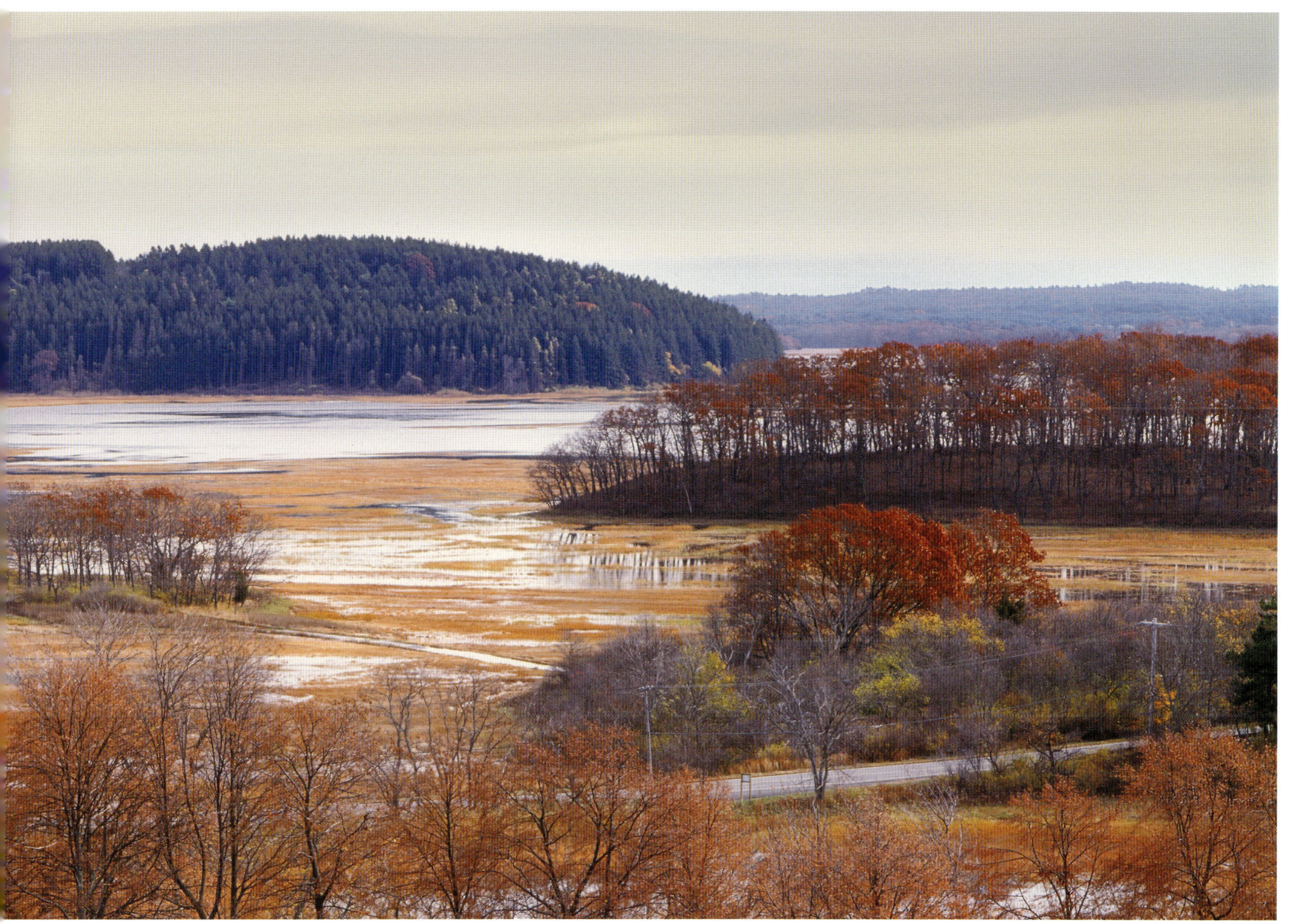

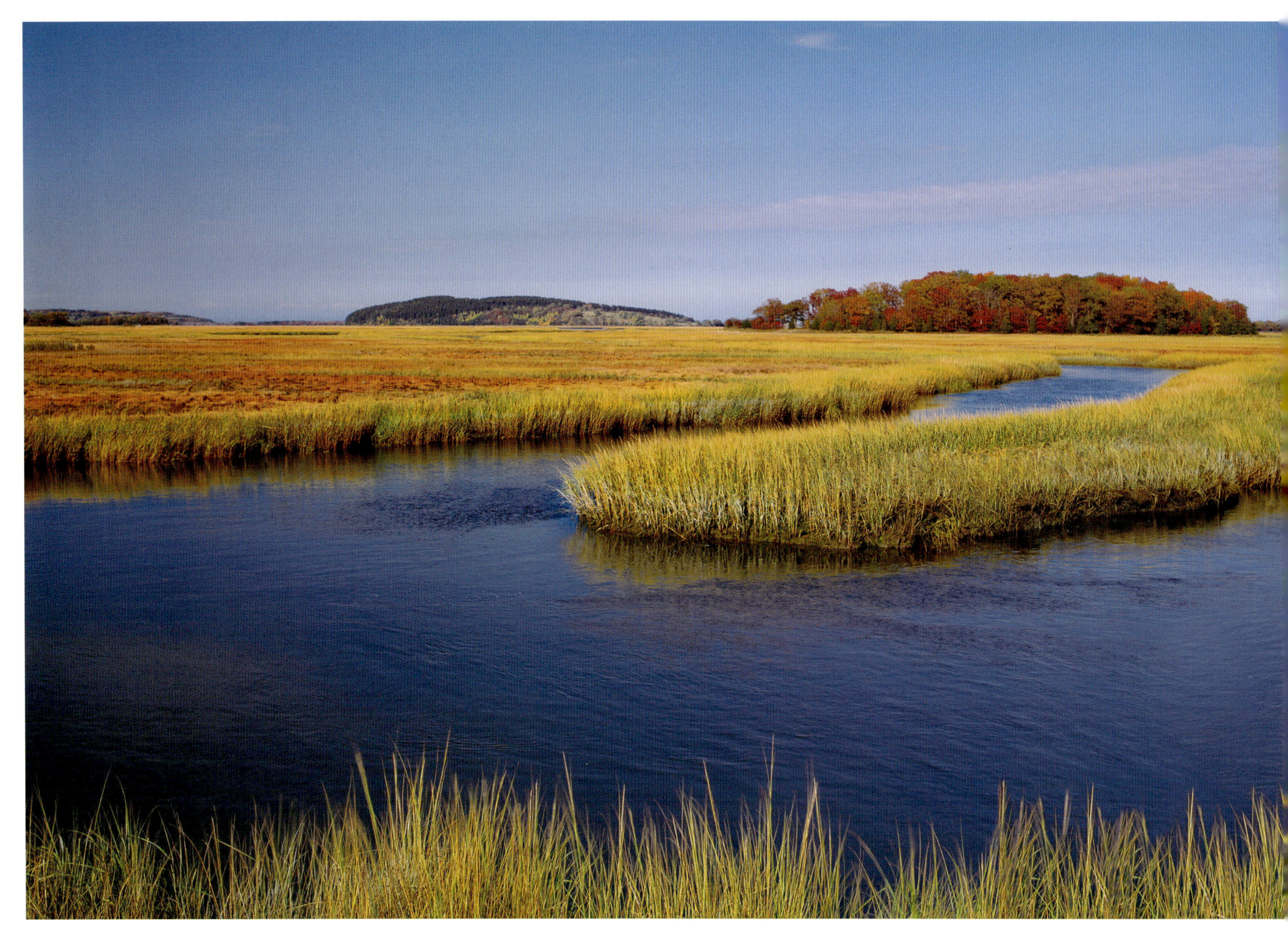

Mabel Burnham house on the salt marsh: Essex's equivalent of Rockport's Motif No. 1

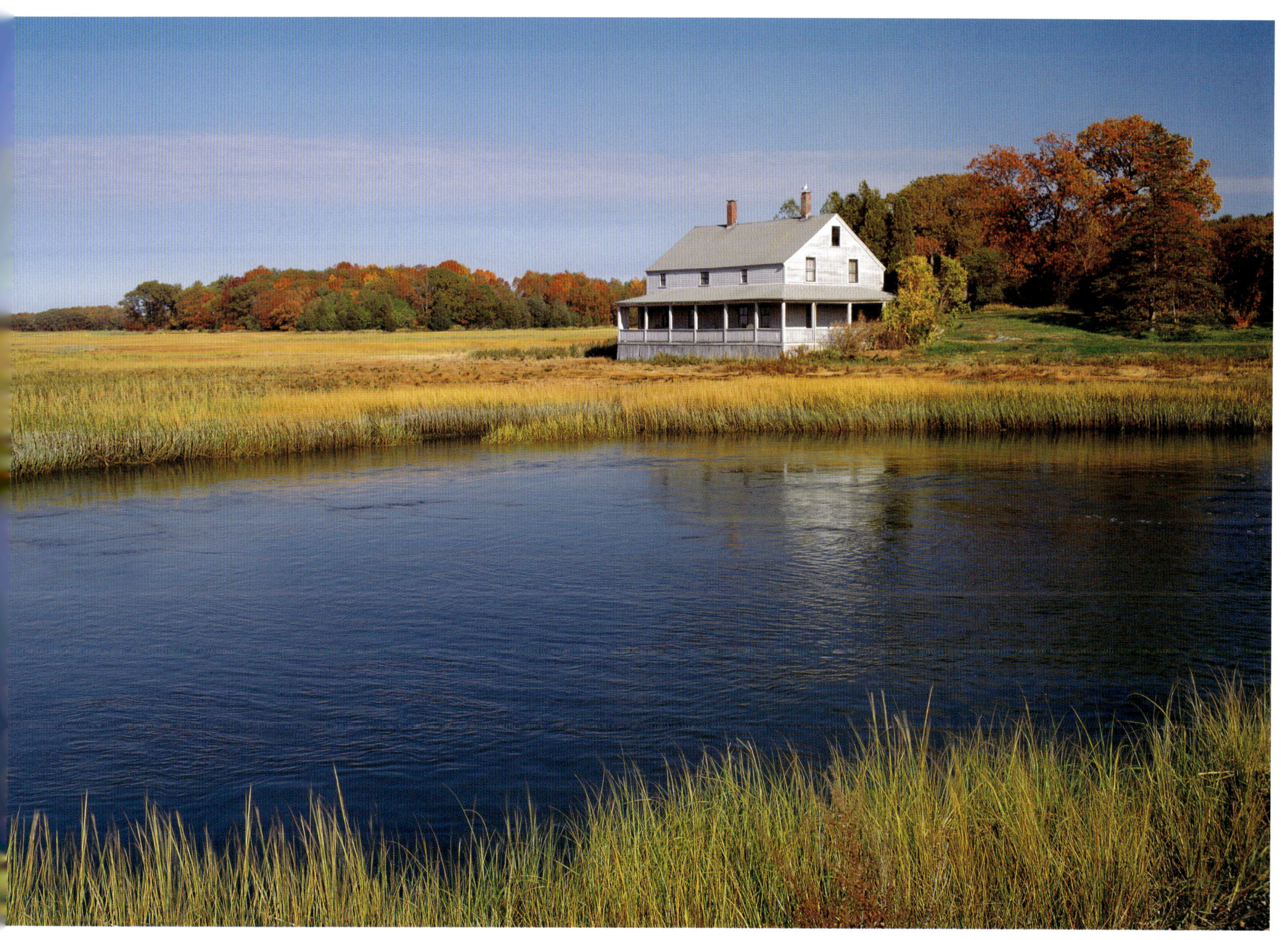

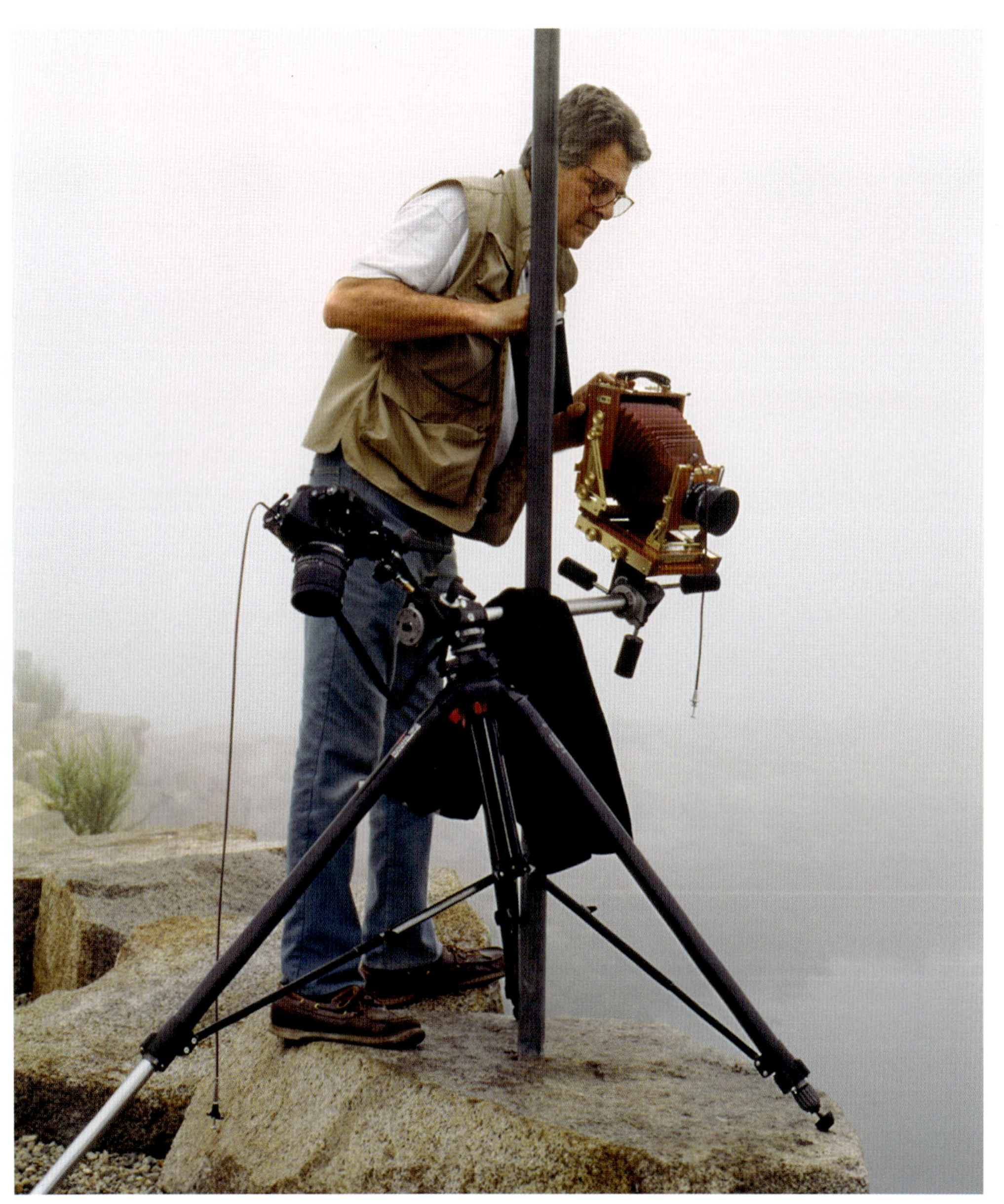

ANDREW BORSARI is a native New Englander and has been actively involved in photography for over forty years. From his gallery in Rockport, his images have gone out to corporate and private collectors in over thirty countries. He is the author of three other books for Commonwealth Editions, *Rockport: A Village by the Sea*, *Ipswich: A Celebration of Light, Land, and Sea*, and *Cape Cod National Seashore*. Andy and his wife, Elvira, reside on Great Neck in Ipswich. Their studio home overlooks Plum Island Sound, Ipswich Bay, and the rim of Cape Ann. This backdrop is the inspiration for much of his photography.